Mandragora s.r.l.
Piazza del Duomo 9, 50122 Firenze
www.mandragora.it

Texts
Giovanni Fanelli (Part One), Michele Fanelli (Part Two)

Editing, design and typesetting
Monica Fintoni, Andrea Paoletti, Michèle Fantoli

English translation
Jeremy Carden, Michele Fanelli, Andrea Paoletti, Mark Roberts

Photographic credits
Accademia delle Arti del Disegno, Florence
Archivio di Stato di Firenze
Archivio Liberto Perugi, Florence
Archivio Scala, Florence (Mauro Sarri)
Bartolini Salimbeni Collection, Florence
Andrea Bazzechi, Florence
Raffaello Bencini, Florence
Biblioteca Nazionale Centrale di Firenze
British Library, London
Casa Buonarroti, Florence
Centre de Recherche sur les Monuments Historiques, Paris
Piero Dini Collection, Montecatini
Giovanni Fanelli
Fogg Art Museum, Harvard University Art Museums (Gift of The Friends of the Fogg Museum of Art Fund), Cambridge, Mass. (Rick Stafford)
Gemäldegalerie, Staatliche Museen zu Berlin, Preußischer Kulturbesitz (Jörg P. Anders)
Kunsthistorisches Institut, Florence
Nicolò Orsi Battaglini, Florence
Luciano Pedicini, Naples
Antonio Quattrone, Florence
Soprintendenza per i Beni Architettonici ed il Paesaggio e per il Patrimonio Storico, Artistico e Demoetnoantropologico per le province di Firenze, Pistoia e Prato
Mandragora Archives, Florence

The authors and the publisher wish to thank Elena Bartolini Salimbeni, Maria Brunori, Niccolò Capponi, Ute Creutz, Piero Dini, Giuliano Matteucci, Raffaele Monti and Franco Vestri.

Printed in Italy

isbn 88–85957–91–9

9 8 7 6 5 4 3 2 1

This book is printed on TCF (totally chlorine free) paper.

Giovanni Fanelli and Michele Fanelli

BRUNELLESCHI'S CUPOLA

Past and Present of an Architectural Masterpiece

Mandragora

Preface

This book, which the publisher has generously decided should be a detailed and comprehensive study worthy of its subject, offers a complete and up-to-date treatment (albeit, of course, not an exhaustive one) of a highly complex question: the history—together with a formal and structural analysis—of one of the greatest architectural monuments of all time, which is also the symbol of a great city.

The arduous sequence of events in the planning and building of Brunelleschi's Cupola, and its troubled existence over the centuries, constitute a sort of imaginary thread linking the thoughts, preoccupations and actions of many scholars and thinkers—a lively debate marked by uncertainties (or by quite unjustified certainties), by gaps in the historical and theoretical knowledge available to past generations of scholars and finally, now that new critical tools have been tested and honed, by the lack of sufficient data. These events and debates have always been of immense interest to Florentines, and the *Cupolone* ('the Big Dome'), as it is familiarly and affectionately called (the nickname suggesting deep emotional involvement behind the inevitable mask of Tuscan irony), has become—together with Palazzo della Signoria, the 'Palazzo Vecchio'—the city's most immediately recognisable symbol. Centuries have passed, cultural perspectives have changed, yet the Cupola has retained an aura of at least partial impenetrability, to which the popular (and not only the popular) imagination has lavishly contributed legendary and even mythical accretions.

Thus there has often been talk of one or more 'secrets' concerning the anatomy and physiology of the Cupola: secrets of construction, form and vault tracing, but especially secrets of conception, which Brunelleschi is supposed to have taken with him to the grave. Distinguished scholars have been perplexed by apparently inexplicable or contradictory aspects of the structural problems which the monument has developed with age; there has been heated debate about the gravity of its condition, about the need for intervention and about what to do and how.

Evidence and surveys, documents and physical objects of vital importance have frequently been mislaid and lost with the dispersal of ancient archives and collections, or have simply not been passed on—through carelessness or through circumstances beyond anyone's control—from one generation to the next. Objective data that can be 'read' in the fabric of the monument itself had to be collected all over again through long, diligent research, and no doubt much information still lies concealed within the brickwork.

Public opinion, whether qualified or not, has periodically become alarmed about the danger of irreversible damage to the Cupola, and even of its total collapse; the response from the authorities has been lethargic and has usually taken the form of appointing a committee to study the matter—a classic, stop-gap solution. These committees have frequently included competent experts with interesting things to say, but they have never been able to achieve any concrete, long-lasting result because of a lack of decision-making and executive powers.

Modern methods of theoretical analysis and experimental research make it possible (or rather would make it possible, if funds were available) to dispel the doubts that still surround the past, present and future of the Cupola, and to set up an efficient, permanent information system capable of preserving and updating the body of acquired knowledge which alone can constitute both the nervous and the immune system of this great organism. The first steps in this direction have already been taken, and the path to take, while neither easy nor short, is now sufficiently clear; the same route has been successfully followed for many other large structures. Modern materials and techniques can supply the necessary means and procedures to define, and if necessary to put into effect, a non-traumatic 'safety-first' intervention that is respectful both of the monument's form and of its conception. It is greatly to be hoped that public awareness will develop to the point where a definitive diagnosis is seen as a pressing need, to be followed by any protective measures that may be required; it is also to be hoped that those responsible will be apprised of the problems to be solved and that politicians will act to procure the necessary funding.

Florence, January 2001

PART ONE

FROM THE PLAN FOR THE NEW CATHEDRAL TO BRUNELLESCHI'S PLAN FOR THE CUPOLA

1.1. The New Cathedral

The construction of the Cupola (1420–36) represents the final act in the long drama of the building of Florence's new cathedral, founded in 1296 (or, according to some, in 1298) to a design by Arnolfo di Cambio, to replace the earlier and much smaller cathedral of Santa Reparata. The new cathedral, dedicated to *Santa Maria del Fiore* ('Our Lady of the Flower', combining the name of the Mother of God with the symbol of Florence), was intended to accommodate the growing number of worshippers and to reflect the new demographic, political and economic dimension of the city. Indeed, the undertaking involved not only the clergy, but the entire citizenry and public administration of one of the most important city-states of 14th-century Europe; in the documents the completion of the work is often referred to as bringing "honour to the Comune and embellishment to the city".[1] For its construction, architects were able to draw on the tradition developed in Florence especially during the building of the Baptistery and the great churches of the mendicant orders, the Dominican Santa Maria Novella and the Franciscan Santa Croce. To appreciate the full significance of the size of the new building designed by Arnolfo, we have to remember that on the one hand it stood at the edge of the old Matildine city walls, that is to say within the compact and crowded medieval centre consisting of low houses alternating with towers and threaded by narrow winding streets; and on the other hand it related to the much wider area enclosed by the new city walls. Like the Palazzo dei Priori, the seat of civic power, the new cathedral was designed, physically as well as conceptually, on a scale with the entire city, so as to bring together all the scattered elements of the old urban structure within a unified whole. The new cathedral was to be capable of containing 30,000 people; it is now the fourth largest in the world, after St Peter's in Rome, St Paul's in London and the Cathedral of Milan.

The city government was involved, also financially, in the undertaking, and a portion of the Comune's income was set aside for the building of the new cathedral. Contributions from private individuals were insignificant, compared to other cathedrals such as those of Orvieto and Milan.[2]

* * *

In 1321 control over the cathedral works was assigned to the Consuls of five of the seven major Florentine guilds—*Calimala* or Merchants Guild, *Cambio* or Bankers Guild, *Lana* or Wool Guild, *Seta* or Silk Guild, *Medici e Speziali* or Guild of Physicians and Apothecaries. Initially, each guild had a one-year spell in charge, but from 1331 onwards representatives of the Wool Guild took sole responsibility. The *Constitutum universitatis Lanificum* of 1333 contained the first statute of the Opera di Santa Reparata—later Opera di Santa Maria del Fiore—, initially consisting of four *operai*, a *camarlingo* (to act as treasurer) and a notary, officially with the mandate to administer the public funds and to monitor the day-to-day progress of the work, though in fact with much wider powers.[3] So the

D · S ·
QVANTVM · PHILIPPVS · ARCHITECTVS · ARTE · DAE
DALAEA · VALVERIT · CVM · HVIVS · CELEBERRIMI
TEMPLI · MIRA · TESTVDO · TVM · PLVRES · MACHINAE
DIVINO · INGENIO · ABEO · ADINVENTAE · DOCVMEN
TO · ESSE · POSSVNT · QVAPROPTER · OB · EXIMIAS · SVI
ANIMI · DOTES · SINGVLARES · QVE · VIRTVTES · XV · K
MAIAS · ANNO · M · CCCC · XLVI · EIVS · B · M · CORPVS · INHAC
HVMO · SVPPOSITA · GRATA · PATRIA · SEPELLIRI · IVSSIT

I.

2.

3.

4.

1. Opposite, top, bust of Filippo
Brunelleschi on the wall of the right
aisle of Florence Cathedral.
Brunelleschi died on 15 April 1446;
he was temporarily buried in the
Campanile until 30 December, when
the Consuls ordered his burial in the
Cathedral. After the site had been
chosen, Carlo Marsuppini, Chancellor
of the Republic, composed the text
for a memorial tablet in marble.
The realistic bust (probably based on
Brunelleschi's funeral mask: → Fig. 2)
was carved by the sculptor and
architect Andrea di Lazzaro
Cavalcanti known as Buggiano
(1412–62), Brunelleschi's adoptive
son, assistant and sole heir.

2. Opposite, bottom left, Filippo
Brunelleschi's funeral mask, based on
a cast taken directly from the corpse,
perhaps by Andrea Cavalcanti himself
(Florence, Opera di Santa Maria del
Fiore Museum). His features display
great vivacity and a vein of dry irony.

Filippo was not an easy man to
deal with. Vasari defines him as an
"immensely daunting" personality,
and has Brunelleschi himself describe
the Cupola as "daunting". Obstinate,
uncompromising, throughout his life
he fought to uphold his ideas, which
he often had to keep secret. Antonio
Manetti recounts that Paolo dal
Pozzo Toscanelli, a scientist friend
of Brunelleschi, was amazed by his
prodigious capacity to solve complex
abstract problems in an intuitive
fashion. Manetti himself testifies to
another aspect of his character,
his sharp irony, relating in minute
detail the celebrated prank he devised
at the expense of a carpenter, Manetto
Ammannatini known as il Grasso
(the 'Fat Man'), which he carried
through with a shrewd ability and
determination that bordered on
cruelty. With the help of Donatello,
Giovanni Rucellai and Tommaso
Pecori, he made Manetto believe that
he had become another person.

Making reality resemble illusion
(and vice versa) was also a crucial
objective of the science of perspective,
in which Brunelleschi played such
a revolutionary part.

3. Opposite, bottom right, Filippo
Brunelleschi in a detail of a portrait
of artists attributed to Paolo Uccello
(Paris, Louvre).

4. Above, Florence Cathedral in
The Militant and Triumphant Church,
frescoed by Andrea di Bonaiuto
between 1366 and 1369 in the old
chapter room of the convent of Santa
Maria Novella, known as "Cappellone
degli Spagnoli" ('Chapel of the
Spaniards'). The Cupola is depicted
here without the raised drum
and without buttresses, which have
however been inserted along
the body of the nave.

Opera di Santa Maria del Fiore, that is the institution in charge of the cathedral works, was not a religious body but a secular one, even though it displayed the *Agnus Dei* (the Lamb of God) on its emblem.

The posts of *operaio* and *camarlingo* of the Opera were supposed to be assigned by lot, but in practice they regularly fell to the members of a small number of families, such as the Ridolfi, the Capponi, the Rondinelli, the Corbinelli and the Barbadori, who held important positions in the Guild itself and in other institutions involved in the construction of public buildings.[4]

Extraordinary matters were dealt with by the eight Consuls of the Guild and by the *operai* appointed by them, whereas the daily running of the building site was entrusted to the *operai*, with periodic checks by the Consuls. Since the construction of the Cupola was an exceptional undertaking, the Opera sought the widest possible approval among the citizens, bringing in experts and promoting architectural competitions, the results of which were presented to the public in the form of models.

In 1390 it was decided to enlarge and reorganise the headquarters of the Opera in a *palazzo* overlooking the north side of the Cathedral, near the entrance to the Duomo that later came to be known as Porta della Mandorla (the 'Almond Door'), where the administration remained until 1420. The coats of arms of the city were placed above the windows on the upper floor; at the two ends of the façade are large roundels with the emblem of the Wool Guild, the *Agnus Dei*.

*   *   *

In the first half of the 14th century work on the new cathedral proceeded very slowly. New impetus was provided by the appointment of Francesco Talenti as *capomaestro*, or master builder (*c.* 1350). A resolution of 1357 determined that the building was to have a nave and aisles, a total length of 164 *braccia* (→ Glossary) and a dome 62 *braccia* wide (corrected to 72 *braccia* in 1367[5]). It is likely that Arnolfo himself had planned a dome, but historians differ on this.[6] In Italy, earlier examples of the integration of a centrally planned structure into a longitudinal one are those of Santa Maria Maggiore at Lanciano (begun in 1226) and Siena Cathedral (begun around 1230).

In 1367 a board of experts—the so-called *otto maestri e dipintori*, 'the eight masters and painters' (Neri di Fioravante, Andrea di Cione known as Orcagna, Benci di Cione, Francesco Salvetti, Taddeo Gaddi, Andrea di Bonaiuto, Niccolò di Tommaso and Neri di Mone), appointed by the Silk Guild and the Guild of Physicians and Apothecaries at the request of the *operai*—prepared a plan for the church and octagonal dome. The plan contained specifications of the dome's height (144 *braccia*), width (72 *braccia*) and curvature, and was demonstrated to the public by means of a large brick model built next to the Campanile. This new measure of 144 *braccia* (it seems that in the original project, the height of the dome had been fixed at 97 *braccia*) is twice the overall width of the nave and aisles, and equal to the internal height of the space to be covered by the dome. The measure of 72 *braccia* is the same as the overall width of the nave and aisles, the internal width of the octagon (measured at right angles to its sides), the height from ground level to the gallery at the base of the drum and the height from the gallery to the vault key. This modular and proportional scheme is immediately noticeable in the church as built. There are two dominant geometrical figures: the square and the octagon. It should be noted, however, that

1. The *Arti* in Medieval Florence

In medieval Florence, as well as in many other urban centres throughout Europe at that time, the *Arti* or guilds represented an integral part of the city's political and economic life. The various groups that made up civic society (merchants, craftsmen, great families, political factions) organised themselves in a corporate fashion for two main reasons: as a defensive reaction against feudal or ecclesiastical authority, and in order to promote shared interests and ensure, in accordance with the religious spirit of the age, reciprocal assistance. Requirements for admission into one of the guilds were of a moral, technical and economic nature (the payment of a special tax). Only those who met these conditions could become *maestri* ('masters'); the others were simply *compagni*, who lived in the master's house and worked in his workshop.

Guilds and political power were closely connected. In making important appointments, the city government would often draw on the experience and administrative skills of the guilds, whose executive officers were called consuls. The *Arti* also played a fundamental role in shaping the layout of the city, setting up and controlling the quarters of the craftsmen and the merchants. In Florence, the prestige of the *Arti* manifested itself most evidently in the control exercised over the construction, maintenance and daily running of public buildings, whether religious or civic—including the most important and conspicuous ones within the urban framework. The guilds' involvement in realising and administering major public works is documented from the 12th century, and increased over the next 300 years. For instance, they spared no expense in decorating the walled-in arcades of the Loggia di Orsanmichele, located halfway along Via de' Calzaiuoli (the axis linking the political and religious poles of the city), in an evident attempt to affirm their role in Florentine political, economic and social life.

The *Arte di Calimala* (Merchants Guild) had charge of the Baptistery of San Giovanni and of the Basilica of San Miniato; the *Arte della Seta* (Silk Guild) had charge of three *spedali* ('hospitals')—the Spedale degli Innocenti (Foundling Hospital), San Matteo and San Gallo (in turns with the other *Arti*)—and of the church and convent of San Marco; the *Arte dei Giudici e Notai* (Guild of Judges and Notaries) had charge of the hospital of San Paolo, of the *palazzo* of the Tribunale di Mercatanzia (the headquarters of the Trade Tribunal which supervised internal and external dealings) and of the Basilica of Santa Croce.

Florence, however, was the only city in which the construction of a cathedral was supervised (after an initial stage in which the task was shared by the more important guilds in rotation) by a single guild, the *Arte della Lana* (Wool Guild). This powerful guild—whose emblem, the *Agnus Dei* (the lamb bearing the banner with the cross) is found countless times all over the cathedral—assumed *de facto* the role of 'public works office' for the Comune; in fact, the city government entrusted it with many other building projects, such as the new city walls, the Loggia dei Priori, the restoration and maintenance of Palazzo della Signoria, the jail of the Stinche (in the area of the present-day Teatro Verdi), a number of fortresses, and even new settlements founded in the countryside around Florence.

in the church as built the height of the drum is about 3 *braccia* higher than was envisaged in the original scheme (21 *braccia* instead of 18): this modification was agreed upon in 1414 in order to provide the exterior with a gallery on two levels and to pierce the drum with great round windows.

In late 1367 the board's model was sanctioned by a referendum, organised by the Consuls and the *operai*, of 500 qualified citizens—a unique event in European history.

A resolution of 1368 bound the *operai*, the *capomaestro*, the counsellors and their successors to adhere to this model. Scholars believe that this resolution remained in force until the approval of Brunelleschi's model in 1420.[7] This document shows that the authorities wanted to put an end to the controversy between two opposing stylistic approaches: the 'gothicising' approach, which favoured the construction of a system of buttresses for the aisles, the apses and the dome; and the 'classicising' one, which rejected buttresses altogether. Valuable iconographical evidence of this controversy is provided by the representation of the Cathedral painted between 1366 and 1369 by one of the "eight masters and painters", Andrea di Bonaiuto, in the chapter room of the Dominican convent of Santa Maria Novella: the dome is shown without the raised drum and without buttresses, whereas there are buttresses along the body of the nave.[8]

A significant earlier example of a dome covering an octagonal structure was the Florence Baptistery, whose double vault consists of an inner shell (with the same curvature as the Cupola's) and an outer pyramidal roof. From an engineering point of view, however, the vast size of the Cathedral's dome posed problems of an altogether different order. The fact that around 1400 the Baptistery had shown signs of weakening and had needed reinforcing strongly suggests that structures of this type may have been regarded with suspicion at the time.

After the resolution of 1367, work proceeded on the connection between the nave and the presbytery, on the piers for supporting the dome and on the apsidal chapels (c. 1382–1421). The Opera frequently sought the opinion of experts. In 1404 Brunelleschi and Ghiberti, already, it seems, publicly acknowledged as skilled in construction techniques, were members of a commission consisting of nineteen masters and eminent citizens, who, on the basis of the 1367 model, decided that the apsidal buttresses built by Giovanni di Lapo Ghini were too high and ordered their reduction.[9] Vasari writes that in 1407 Brunelleschi proposed building the drum with large round windows, "since this would take the weight off the supports of the tribunes [i.e. the apses] and also make it easier to raise the dome",[10] but his statement finds no documentary support.

1.2. The Plans for the Dome (1417–20)

From a technical point of view, the 1367 scheme offered no indication about how such an exceptionally large dome should actually be built. Once the drum was finished and while the third apse was being completed, the Opera—from 1417—began to finance studies, plans and models for the dome. On 19 May 1417 Brunelleschi was paid the not inconsiderable sum of 10 florins "for his efforts in making drawings and for applying himself to matters concerning the great Dome on account of the Opera".[11] Two days later, the carpenter Manno di Benincasa was commissioned to make a model of the dome "secundum ordinem Cupole maioris fiende" ('reproducing the structure of the great Dome to be built'),[12] probably on the basis of Brunelleschi's drawings, perhaps to a scale of 1:16.[13] On 30 June the sum of 5 florins was paid to master Giovanni dell'Abbaco, a mathematician, for counsel and studies—clear evidence that the geometrical and proportional aspects of the work were being discussed.[14]

On 19 August 1418 the Opera announced a competition, still based on the 1367 model, open to whoever "vellet facere aliquem modellum sive disegnum pro volta maioris Cupole [...], tam pro armadura quam pro pontibus quam in aliqua alia re, sive aliquo ordigno pertinente ad constructionem conductionem et perfectionem dicte Cupole" ('would like to make models or drawings for the vaulting of the great Dome ... whether regarding the vault centring and its supporting structure or the work platforms, or whatever device or machine might be required for the construction, execution and completion of the said Dome'),[15] offering a prize of 200 gold florins for the winner and the reimbursement of expenses for labour and materials for the other participants.

On this occasion both Brunelleschi and Ghiberti made models for the dome, not restricting themselves to wood, but also making use of brick. Ghiberti, who was assisted by the carpenter Bartolomeo dallo Studio, used "little unbaked bricks",[16] whereas Brunelleschi, working with the sculptors Donatello and Nanni di Banco, used traditional bricks—*mattoni di quarto* (or *quadroni*, square bricks) and *mezzani* (half the size of square bricks)—and wire and rope "pro mensura" ('to guide the tracing').[17] According to Howard Saalman, this model would have been "at a scale of perhaps 1:8".[18] The Opera then delegated three masters to study and evaluate the model, so as to determine whether it would be possible to construct the dome according to it;[19] the proposal to build "sanza armadura", i.e. to vault the dome without a temporary supporting structure (centring), presented earlier by Brunelleschi, had in fact been viewed with suspicion by the authorities; according to his biographer Antonio Manetti, Brunelleschi had twice been physically expelled from the assembly "as though he were talking nonsense".[20] It was indeed a highly innovative proposal, which eliminated at a stroke the age-old difficulties connected with centring: problems regarding size, weight (both of the centring itself and of the structure being built upon it), availability and cost of wood—not to mention the cluttering-up of the presbytery area and the resulting difficulty of operating the machinery.

The Opera showed interest in the models presented by the teams led by Brunelleschi and Ghiberti, yet no winner was declared. On 27 March 1420 a second competition was announced. It seems that no new models were requested; instead, the Opera called for drawings and advice regarding a single model produced "according to the wishes of the four citizens", that is to say the four Officials of the Cupola.[21] Whereas many unknown woodworkers, goldsmiths and painters had taken part in the earlier competition, this time the number of participants—most of whom had an on-going working relation with the Opera—was limited. On 24 April Brunelleschi and Ghiberti received ten florins for "efforts made and time spent in making one model according to the wishes of the four citizens" and for the advice they had given since 20 November 1419.[22]

*   *   *

Between 1419 and 1420 steps were taken to define the posts of the administrative and executive directors of the work on the Cupola: the *ufficiali della cupola* ('Officials of the Cupola') and the *provveditori della cupola* ('Superintendents of the Cupola').

2. The Models for the Project

The use of architectural models had been common in Italy since the Middle Ages. These models permitted a more realistic and immediate assessment of the spatial and formal characteristics of the building, and also enabled patrons to understand and evaluate the projects they were paying for. Moreover, according to the scientific theory prevailing throughout the Renaissance period (eventually disproved by Galileo), there was an absolute correspondence between the statics of the model and the statics of the building itself (provided, of course, that they were both made of the same materials).

The models made for the construction of the Cupola, which are mentioned several times by Manetti and Vasari, have for the most part been lost. It was in fact common practice to dismantle the model after it had served its purpose, so that the materials could be reused. Thus there is now no trace of the large brick model of the Cathedral which was built at the base of the Campanile and served to check the construction until 1431, when—at an advanced stage in the building programme—the Opera decided to dismantle it; a new wooden model of the whole Cathedral had been commissioned from Brunelleschi and Ghiberti in 1429, but was possibly never completed. In February 1432 the Opera decided to dismantle Brunelleschi's model of the Cupola as well.*

Only two wooden models have survived, now housed in the Opera di Santa Maria del Fiore Museum: one of the Cupola with the drum and apsidal chapels and one of the lantern. Both have been attributed by some scholars to Brunelleschi.

* See C. Guasti, *La Cupola di Santa Maria del Fiore, illustrata con i documenti dell'Archivio dell'Opera secolare* (Florence: Barbera Bianchi e Comp., 1857), 33–4 (docs. 61–8); H. Saalman, *Filippo Brunelleschi. The Cupola of Santa Maria del Fiore* (London: Zwemmer, 1980), 128.

5.

6.

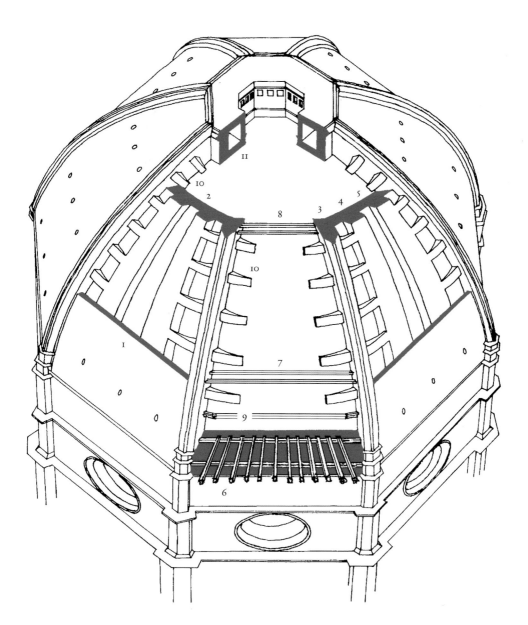

7.

5. Opposite, left, the wooden model of the Cupola and of the apsidal chapels, attributed by some scholars to Brunelleschi (Florence, Opera di Santa Maria del Fiore Museum).

6. Opposite, right, the wooden model of the lantern (Florence, Opera di Santa Maria del Fiore Museum); in recent times, the attribution of this model to Brunelleschi himself has been challenged by many scholars.

7. The structure of the Cupola:
  1. outer shell;
  2. inner shell;
  3. corner spur;
  4–5. intermediate spur;
  6. first, non-elastic stone chain;
  7. second stone chain;
  8. third stone chain;
  9. elastic wooden chain;
  10. horizontal arches;
  11. oculus ring (*serraglio*) and springing line of the lantern.

As Auguste Choisy observed in his *Histoire de l'architecture* (Paris, 1899), "as a result of its many empty spaces the Cupola is relatively light, and due to the interconnection of the two shells it almost possesses the density of a solid mass: solid matter is accumulated […] where it is needed" (→ Part Two, Fig. 1.1.6).

The regular staff of the Wool Guild could not possibly cope with the exceptional nature of the undertaking: more personnel were needed. On 15 November 1419 the position of Official of the Cupola was established, reserved for four members of the Guild, who each served for six months and were paid in kind; their job was to supervise the work of the *provveditori* (with whom they sometimes collaborated), to assist the consultants and experts on the building site and to draw up periodic reports on the progress of the work. Although they had no decision-making powers, the Officials had voting rights in the assemblies convened by the Opera to discuss and decide upon crucial matters relating to the building programme.

The position of Superintendent of the Cupola (*provisor operis Cupole construendi*) was a higher one than the traditional position of *capomaestro*. The new title was awarded on 16 April 1420 to Filippo Brunelleschi, Lorenzo Ghiberti and Battista d'Antonio. The resolution established for them a monthly salary of 3 gold florins and laid down their duties in general terms: "eligerunt [...] Filippum ser Brunelleschi, Laurentium Bartoluccii, et Batistam Antonii, in provisores dicti operis Cupole construendi, et ad providendum, ordinandum, et construi, ordinari, fieri et hedificari faciendum, a principio usque ad finem, ipsam maiorem Cupolam et hedifitium, illis hedifitiis magisteriis muramentis modis formis et condictionibus, et illis sunptibus, et aliis quibuscunque, de quibus et prout et sicut eisdem videbitur convenire, et expedire iudicabunt" ('they appointed ... Filippo di ser Brunellesco, Lorenzo di Bartoluccio and Battista d'Antonio as *provveditori* for the building of the said Cupola, that they should provide, dispose and do what is necessary to construct, dispose, make and build, from beginning to end, the same great Dome and edifice, with those structures, instructions, building works, and in the manners, forms and conditions, and with those expenses and whatever else, which shall seem most expedient to them and which they shall judge most suitable').[23]

At the same assembly, eight master masons—one for each side of the octagon—were appointed to carry out, as was the traditional practice, the actual building work.

The appointment of both Filippo and Lorenzo may have been dictated by residual resistance to Brunelleschi's proposals. According to the biographer Antonio Manetti, the appointment as *provveditori* of the two leading competitors of the planning stage was in line with the traditional political stance of the Opera, which sought to reconcile differences and to affirm the significance of the building as the end result of a combined effort on the part of the entire community. Furthermore, the appointment reveals the Opera's desire to ensure the greatest possible continuity between the planning and the construction stage, so as not to repeat the mistake of 1367. On that occasion the task of carrying out the plan of the 'eight masters and painters' had been entrusted not to them, but to the two *capomaestri*, Lapo Ghini and Francesco Talenti.

Compared to his rival Ghiberti, Brunelleschi certainly played a much more active part in running the building site. Ghiberti was in fact suspended as *provveditore* from July 1425 until February 1426, when his salary was confirmed as 3 florins per month; Brunelleschi's was raised to 100 florins per year and he was obliged to attend the site daily. It was no great obligation. Brunelleschi's presence on the site was continuous, and his versatile genius made itself felt in a number of ways: he not only produced the overall plan, making complete and partial models of the structure—as well as templates for the cutting of the stone and marble—in order to check the results against the original design and to highlight structural and ornamental details; he also directed the work, devised ingenious site machinery, procured and checked building materials, organised and oversaw the workmen. From 1433 onwards, Brunelleschi had sole responsibility for the project: "the patrons seem to have renounced collegial direction of the building work, probably in consideration of Filippo's merits and of the approaching end of the project. The role played by Filippo seems to mark a complete break with the corporate organisation of work which had characterised the medieval building site. The break with 14th-century practice is emphasised by Brunelleschi's non-payment of the registration fee due to the *Arte dei Maestri di Pietra e Legname* (Guild of Stonemasons and Woodworkers): in 1434 his refusal to pay led to his imprisonment, though he was immediately released at the request of the Opera. In Filippo we see the emergence of a new professional figure, the architect, who is recognised for his knowledge and resourcefulness and for his technical and practical skills, as well as for his theoretical and planning ability".[24]

Battista d'Antonio, although promoted to *provveditore*, retained his daily wage of 20 *soldi* as stonemason (*pro magistro seu scarpellatore*). His appointment was apparently justified by the need to complement the two great architects with a trustworthy technician, who had extensive experience at the Cathedral building site and was familiar to the workforce.[25] Battista also saw to the procuring of materials: there is documentation of his journeys to Campiglia and Pisa, in company with Brunelleschi, to procure marble for the lantern. He supervised the work of stonecutters in the walkways of the apsidioles and he replaced some of the iron chains in the nave with new ones designed by Brunelleschi; in 1422 he was consulted, together with Brunelleschi, about the furnishings for the Mass Sacristy and about the stained-glass windows for the drum of the Cupola.

The appointment of the three *provveditori* marks the conclusion of the planning phase. After lengthy deliberation and a number of competitions, the Officials of the Cupola had finally reached the decision to adopt the model produced by Brunelleschi.

*   *   *   ⁓

The decision to proceed on the basis of this model was taken at a meeting of the Opera on 30 July 1420 at the headquarters of the Arte della Lana. On this occasion, an additional document was drawn up describing the essential components of the project and including the features, arrangement and shape of the Cupola. It is an exceptional document, unprecedented in the history of the plans for the Cupola and, for that matter, in the history of the construction of the other great Italian cathedrals built from the end of the 13th century onwards (Orvieto, Milan, Siena).

Focusing on the vertical section of the Cupola along the midline of one of the eight faces or segments of the vault, the document illustrates the structural elements first, indicating their dimensions and vertical development and introducing functional considerations. Two vault shells are described, an inner and an outer one, as well as the (accessible) space between them, with walkways at various levels connected by stairs, "so that all things between one shell and the other may be sought out", i.e. reached; it is specified that the outer shell should protect the inner one "from humidity" and improve the overall shape of the structure, so that it might prove to be "more magnificent and swollen [*gonfiante*]". The solution of the two concentric vault shells has a typological precedent (albeit with some differences) in the Florentine Baptistery; in Brunelleschi's project, how-

3. The Cupola Building Programme (30 July 1420)

This document* is of great interest not only because of the light it casts on the history of the construction of the Cupola, but also because it is one of the first known examples—if not the very first**—of a 'specification' as it is understood today, that is to say a written undertaking whereby the *maître d'oeuvre* assumes responsibility in relation to his client (in this case the Opera). The programme, which lays down the essential elements of Brunelleschi's plan for the Cupola, would undergo partial modification in 1422 and 1426 in the light of the progress of the work.

* Archivio di Stato di Firenze (ASF), Arte della Lana 149, fols. 59v–60r. A slightly different version of this document is found in the MS Magliabechiano XIII 72 of the Biblioteca Nazionale di Firenze, attributed to Antonio Manetti, who quotes it in his biography of Brunelleschi. The latter is also the source of the corresponding passage in Vasari.
** See Saalman, *Filippo Brunelleschi. The Cupola*, 77.

Die trigesima mensis Julij | Antedicti domini consules, una cum operarijs Sancte Marie del Fiore et quactuor offitialibus per dictam Artem electis super constructionem maioris cupule operis Sancte Marie del Fiore predicti cathedralis Ecclesie florentine in sufficientibus numerijs in palatio dicte Artis collegialiter congregati, attendentes ad constructionem dicte maioris cupule Ecclesie prelibate | Et considerantes legem in consilio dicte Artis firmatam sub die vigesima mensis novembris MCCCCXVIIII disponentem in effectum de electione dictorum iiij offitialium et de balia auctoritate et potestate eisdem consulibus una cum operarijs et dictis quactuor offitialibus concessis circa constructionem et hedificationem ipsius maioris cupule | Et considerantes auctoritatem, potestatem et baliam eis per dictam legem et reformationem concessam | Cupientes itaque pro honore ipsius Artis iuxta posse et quo citius fieri potest ad perfectionem constructionis ipsius hedifitij devenire | Et considerantes modellum de quo infra fit mentio | Credentes secundum formam et tenorem ipsius modelli suo recto ordine procedere ut convenit ad honorem communis et dicte Artis, habitoque super predictis et in dicto modello contentis conloquio et consilio cum delibe-

ratione matura inter eosdem dominos consules, operarios et offitiales predictos et cumque pluribus de huiusmodi materia praticis et expertis premisso facto et celebrato inter eosdem solemni et secreto scruptineo | Et obtento partito secundum formam ordinamentorum dicte Artis vigore ipsorum offitij etc omnique modo etc providerunt, ordinaverunt et deliberaverunt | Quod per dictos offitiales ad constructionem cupule antedicte procedatur et procedi possit et debeat modis ordine et formis infrascriptis et prout et sic et quemadmodum construj et fit mentio in modello infrascripto | Et providentes quod quidquid per dictos offitiales secundum tenorem dicti modelli factum fuerit valeat et teneatur et executioni mandetur | Ac si factum foret per totam dictam Artem | Cuius quidem modelli vulgari sermone scripti tenor talis est:

('On the thirtieth of July the aforesaid Consuls, assembling officially and reaching the quorum in the palace of the said Guild with the *operai* of Santa Maria del Fiore and the four Officials elected by the said Guild to supervise the construction of the great dome of the said edifice of Santa Maria del Fiore, cathedral church of Florence; concerning themselves with the construction of the said great dome of the aforesaid Cathedral; and considering the decree ratified on the twentieth day of November 1419 by the council of the said Guild, which makes provision for the election of the said four Officials and for the power, authority and prerogative conferred on the same Consuls together with the *operai* and the said four Officials with regard to the construction and building of this same great dome; and considering the power, authority and prerogative conferred on them by virtue of the said decree and statute; desiring therefore, for the honour of the same Guild, to complete the construction of this edifice by whatever means possible and as quickly as possible; and considering the plan which is to be mentioned shortly; judging that work should proceed according to the approach and content of that plan, adhering to it as befits the honour of the Comune and of the said Guild; and having the aforesaid Consuls, *operai* and Officials debated among themselves and given due consideration to these matters and the content of the said plan; having consulted many specialists and experts; and having held a solemn and secret ballot; and having reached a decision in accordance with the statutes of the said Guild, by virtue of their office &c., and in an entirely appropriate way &c., they provided, disposed and deliberated: that work should commence; and that the said officials could and should proceed to the construction of the aforesaid dome in the fashion, order and forms written below and closely following the instructions laid out in the plan described below; and establishing that whatever shall be done by the said officials according to the content of the said plan shall avail and be regarded and be executed as though it had been done by the whole Guild itself. Of which written text the content in the vernacular is as follows:')

Here we shall give a detailed account of all the parts contained in this model exemplifying the great dome.

First the dome on its inner side is vaulted following the measure of the pointed fifth in the angles; and at the springing line it is 3 ¾ br. thick, and proceeds pyramidally so that where it ends in the oculus at the top it remains 2 ½ br thick.

Another dome [i.e. shell] is made on the outside over this one to protect it from humidity and so that it turns out more magnificent and swollen; and this is 1 ¼ br. thick at its springing line, continuing pyramidally up to the oculus at the top where it remains ⅔ br. thick.

The space remaining between one dome and the other is to be 2 br. wide at the springing line; in this space are placed the stairs so that everything between one dome and the other may be sought out, and at the oculus at the top this space is 2 ⅓ br. wide.

24 spurs are made, that is 8 at the corners and 16 in the sides; each corner spur is 7 br. thick on its outer end at the foot; and between the said corners of each side are to be two spurs, each 4 br. thick at the foot; these bind the said two vaults together; and [are] built pyramidally up to the height of the oculus with equal proportion.

The said 24 spurs with the said domes are encircled by 6 rings of strong and long sandstone beams, well tied together with cramps of leaded iron; and over these stones there are iron chains that encircle the said vaults with their spurs. It is to be built solid from the bottom to a height of 5 ¼ br.; and then follow the spurs.

The first and second ring is 2 br. high; the third and fourth ring is to be 1 ⅓ br. high; the fifth and sixth ring 1 br. high; but the first ring at the foot is to be further reinforced with long sandstone beams placed transversally, so that both domes rest upon said sandstone beams.

And every 12 br. or so along the height of these vaults there are small barrel vaults between one spur and the next for passage around said domes; and under the said small vaults are chains of great oak beams binding the said spurs together and over said wooden beams an iron chain.

The spurs are built entirely of *macigno* and *pietra forte*; the mantles or faces of the domes entirely of *pietra forte* bound to the spurs up to a height of 24 br.; and from there upwards the masonry is to be built of bricks or porous stone, as shall be decided by whoever will at that time have to do it, but of a material lighter than stone.

An outer walkway is to be made above the 8 round windows below [i.e. the drum], supported by consoles, with openwork parapets about 2 br. high, like those of the apsidioles below; or rather two walkways, one above the other, over a finely decorated cornice; and the upper walkway is to be uncovered.

Rainwater running off the dome will end up in a marble gutter ⅓ br. wide, the water running off into *pietra forte* spouts built under the gutter.

There are to be 8 marble ribs over the corners on the surface of the outer dome, as thick as necessary and rising 1 br. above the dome, profiled and sloping, 2 br. wide overall so that 1 br. will extend from the ridge to the gutter in all directions; and it is to be built pyramidally from the springing line up to the top.

The two domes are to be built in the manner described, without any scaffold-supported centring, up to a height of 30 br., but with platforms, as shall be considered and decided by those masters who will build it; and from 30 br. upwards according to what shall be deemed advisable, because as building proceeds only practical experience will teach that which is to be followed.

ever, it takes on multiple structural, distributive and formal values. The principle of 'continuous diminution'—the progressive thinning of the various elements with increasing height, so as to ensure the gradual lightening of the structure—affected not only the two shells themselves, but also the spurs, the stone chains and the marble ribs. To ensure this gradual lightening it was also decided that above a certain level the *pietra forte* (a fine-grained limy sandstone) should be replaced with brick, *spugna* (porous volcanic stone), or other lighter material. The document then considers the plan of the structure, illustrating the distribution of twenty-four spurs which vary in size according to their position and are indicated as elements of structural and constructional connection between the two shells, also due to the use of the same building materials up to a height of 24 *braccia*. A description is then given of the elements that ensure structural interconnection between the various parts: a complex system of annular chains at various heights, supplemented by a series of little barrel vaults placed at regular intervals so as to link the spurs and the inner shell and to form a platform for the internal walkways. Whereas the use of linear wooden or iron chains was fairly common in late Gothic architecture, the adoption of chains composed of blocks of stone placed one next to the other and connected by metal tie rods had no significant precedent in Gothic architecture. In fact, it derives from ancient Roman models observed and studied at first hand by Brunelleschi.[26]

Having described the elements forming the Cupola's skeleton, the document moves on to consider some features of the exterior: a gallery on two levels (with two ambulatories) supported below by consoles and with "openwork parapets", a gutter of white marble (*racta*) for rainwater runoff, eight marble crests or ribs, "profiled and sloping", and "built pyramidally from the springing line to the top" along the ridges where the segments intersect. Finally some practical construction matters are considered: the structure was to be raised "without any scaffold-supported centring", except for the service platforms. This directive stands only up to a height of 30 *braccia*, probably because the innovative nature of this solution (already considered by Brunelleschi in 1418) suggested a degree of caution, leaving the way open for other possible solutions as building progressed.

*   *   *

Construction of the Cupola thus relied on a special building technique that avoided any dangerous discontinuity in the masonry (approximately 29,000 tons) and also did away with the enormous problems involved in the use of traditional wooden centring on such a huge scale. Brunelleschi managed to solve the problem by building each successive layer of bricks as a closed ring, linked—through lines of vertically slanted bricks placed at regular intervals within the masonry (the so-called herringbone brickwork)—to the consecutive lower and upper rings, and as such capable of supporting itself until completion of the work.[27] The Cupola thus rose as a self-supporting structure (→ Part Two).

The Building Site:
Organisation, Materials, Schedule

2.1. The Workforce

In the spring of 1420 preparations were made for the great undertaking. The Opera had acquired a great deal of experience while building the Cathedral, and had become very efficient in organising the workforce. Without it—and without the skill of the master builders, above all of Brunelleschi himself—such a vast and complicated project could never have been carried out in such a comparatively short time, nor to the standard that has allowed it to stand up to centuries of wear. And we may be sure, even though no precise figures are available to us, that the expenses incurred were much lower than they would have been if the organisation had not been so efficient and tightly controlled.

The construction of the Cupola was made possible by the presence of expert and reliable teams of builders, by a tried and tested system for organising and controlling the building work, and by efficient and economically advantageous arrangements for obtaining materials, especially timber and marble—materials which the *operai* even supplied to other builders in the public and private sectors,[1] since the Signoria had granted them the rights to the forests of the Casentino (from 1378) and the quarries of Campiglia (after 1459).[2]

Workers were chosen by lot from amongst the names enrolled in special lists—the *ruoli*—compiled at the beginning of the summer (1 April to 30 September) and winter (1 October to 31 March) working semesters. Wages varied according to the number of working hours. Unlike the situation at other large building sites, such as that of Milan Cathedral, in Florence there was a core of workers who enjoyed a rare degree of job security, highly unusual at the time. There was of course some degree of turnover in the labour force, but also consistent rehiring from one year to the next of the workmen permanently included in the lists as able-bodied; a certain continuity in the presence of expert personnel was thereby ensured. The workmen's pay was adjusted on the basis of the quality of work they had turned in during the previous semesters. Anyone who did not comply with precise rules of conduct was excluded from the lists.

2.2. Main and Subsidiary Building Sites

The building site was organised at the foot of the Cupola in the large presbytery area (separated from the nave and the aisles, which were reserved for liturgical functions[3]) where materials and machinery were situated. Other parts of the site were organised in the four areas at the base of the drum where the apsidioles (the so-called *tribune morte*, which today house building materials, and ancient tools and machinery; → Glossary) would be built in 1439, and especially on the great work platform set up at the level of the Cupola's springing line, supported by great beams (probably of fir or chestnut) inserted into a series of putlog holes (*buche pontaie*). These holes, at the level of the exterior gallery, are still visible today.

4. Documentary Evidence About the Workforce

The loss of a considerable portion of the relevant documents prevents us from precisely quantifying the workforce employed in the construction of the Cupola and from identifying the various professional categories which composed it over the years.

The lists themselves (*ruoli*) do not allow us to determine the actual numbers of workers hired; such numbers result from the ledgers, which however have survived only from 1434 onwards.

In 1418–9 the lists include over 80 names; numbers then vary between 61 for the summer season and 55 for the winter. The number of bricklayers and hodmen increased in April 1422 after the approval of modifications to the building programme, which reduced the height at which the stonework was to be replaced by the brickwork. In April 1426 a reduction of the workforce was requested, in an attempt to keep down the rising costs which were threatening the feasibility of the enterprise. The number of stonecutters also varied; it increased in 1421 "pro fulciendo et complendo cornicem marmoris cupole maioris et raguaglios lapidum" ('to sustain and complete the marble cornice of the great Cupola and to finish the stones'),* and again in 1424–5 when twelve stone beams were acquired for the round windows and work was begun on the blocks of the second chain.

The lists mention specialised professional skills such as those of the bricklayers (referred to as *magistri ad murandum* or *maestri di cazuola*), of the stonecutters (*scarpellatores, magistri de scarpello*), and occasionally of the sawyers, carpenters and blacksmiths. Only in a few cases are there lists of hodmen and lads (*pueri*). In general, the non-specialised workers are not included in the lists because their recruitment was delegated to the *capomaestro*, who also fixed their wages. Nor do the lists mention the carters (*carradori*) who transported the building materials.**

* Saalman, *Filippo Brunelleschi. The Cupola*, 256 (doc. 138).
** On these topics, see M. Haines, "The Builders of Santa Maria del Fiore: an Episode of 1475 and an Essay towards its Context", in A. Morrogh et al. (eds.), *Renaissance Studies in Honor of Craig Hugh Smyth*, 2 vols. (Florence: Giunti Barbera, 1985), 1.89–115.

Around the Cathedral a number of subsidiary building sites were set up. The most important of these was located in the large area to the north-east of Piazza del Duomo, between Via dell'Oriuolo and Via de' Servi, where in 1398 the Opera had acquired Palazzo Falconieri (which was immediately demolished, its remains dumped into the river) and in 1418 had rented some properties from the Alessandri and the Tedaldi, properties which would be definitively acquired in 1434.[4] Here deposits for marble and timber were set up, protected by makeshift roofs which even covered the courtyard of the Opera's headquarters, as well as several covered spaces reserved for the artists, including Brunelleschi, who used these premises to build his brick model of the Cupola. In a "shed" there was a smithy, used for forging the metal implements needed by the builders (especially the chains) and for mending the various working tools. In Via Ghibellina there was a kiln, acquired by the Opera in 1415, where some of the bricks used for Brunelleschi's model of the Cupola were made.[5]

According to Manetti, who is supported by Vasari, Brunelleschi also designed new types of platforms as required.[6] In the absence of contemporary written or visual documentation, scholars have advanced differing and often opposing theories concerning the nature of the temporary platforms devised for the construction of the Cupola.[7] Apart from the large work platform at the springing line of the Cupola, it is difficult to figure out exactly what kind of solution was employed for the upper platforms as work proceeded. These may have been attached to the many metal rings, placed at regular intervals on the intrados of the inner shell, which are mentioned by Vasari and are still in place today.

2.3. The Organisation of the Work

Most of the workmen—stonecutters, bricklayers, hodmen—worked on the platforms, while on the ground others operated the machinery and officials weighed, checked and paid for the materials as they arrived. Up on the platforms, the workmen were organised into teams directed by a master mason, one team for each of the eight segments, so that building proceeded evenly along the entire perimeter of the Cupola. One of the eight masters "ad murandum" appointed by the resolution of 16 April 1420 was Filippo di Giovanni, active from the first decade of the 15th century, whose presence is documented in 1427 on another important building site directed by Brunelleschi, that of the church of San Lorenzo.

As building work proceeded, increasingly tight measures were taken to ensure the safety of the workmen. Protective parapets were added to the platforms (a resolution of 1426, for example, speaks of "boards set up to block the view of the void for the safety of the masters") and it was forbidden to drink unmixed wine while working high up.[8] Workmen were allowed to choose tasks of greater or lesser risk, but their choice had a bearing on their wages—those who chose to work on the lower platforms were paid less.[9]

An official of the Opera, the special pay clerk (*scrivano delle giornate*), was appointed to check the daily production of each workman and to record overtime and periods of leave (*scioperi*), which were to be granted only by special permission from the *operai*; workmen taking unauthorised leave lost their jobs. On the basis of the register kept by the *scrivano*, at the end of each working week one of the *provveditori* issued orders of payment, which were paid and transcribed into the ledgers by the *camarlingo*. An hour-glass was kept "up on the wall of the greater apse" to measure the breaks in the working day; there was also a chalk board on which the *scioperi* were recorded.[10]

In order to eliminate dead time and to keep a better check on the workmen, they were forbidden to descend from the work platforms more than once a day. Nor were they allowed to take their tools to the blacksmith for repair; the blacksmith himself was responsible for collecting and returning the tools directly to the site. According to Manetti, Brunelleschi ordered that on the platforms there should be "those who sold wine, and others who sold bread, and cooks".[11] When the weather was bad, however, only four or five stonecutters, chosen by lot, were allowed to work on the ground, attending to the limewash, the plaster or the bricking; the rest of the workmen did not receive their daily wage.[12]

In accordance with ancient custom, the Opera celebrated with the workmen each important stage of the construction: in addition to the inaugural banquet, there are documentary references to the workmen being offered wine when the brickwork was begun (1426) and when the second stone chain was put in place; and there was of course a great celebration on 30 August 1436 to mark the closing of the Cupola.

2.4. The Materials

Rigorous checking of the quality of materials was carried out by the *capomaestro* and by Brunelleschi personally, who paid particular attention to the bricks and the lime, from the firing of the limestone in kilns to the mixing of the slaked lime with sand. Manetti, exalting the great architect, asserts that "not a single little stone, not a brick… was set into position without his checking to see that it was good and well baked and well cleaned".[13]

The timber came mainly from the forests of the Casentino (donated by the Signoria to the Opera del Duomo in 1378 as a contribution towards the costs of the Cathedral), where it was possible to find an uncommonly tall variety of white fir. The sawing of the wood, which generally took place from January to March, was authorised by the Consuls and the *operai*. It appears that the selection and cutting of the wood was supervised by Battista d'Antonio, *provveditore della cupola* (1420), who also journeyed to Pistoia to obtain oak for the first wooden chain (1421).[14] From the uplands of Campigna the tree trunks were dragged by teams of oxen down to Pratovecchio, where they were sawn and stamped with the Opera's mark before being floated down the Arno as *foderi* (rafts formed by trunks lashed together, steered by *foderatori*) to Florence. There they were unloaded at the wharf known as the Porticciola d'Arno, or delle Travi ('of the Beams'), which was demolished in 1862 (only the steps and ramp remain). Timber of lower quality came from the countryside immediately surrounding the city; batches of beech and chestnut were generally purchased from Florentine woodworkers; oak came from the Apennines above Pistoia.

The sandstone (*arenaria macigno*) came for the most part from the quarry of Trassinaia, in the hills to the north-east of Florence, between Maiano and Vincigliata, for which the Opera had a concession from 1421. At Trassinaia blocks of sandstone were extracted and worked, under the supervision of a *provveditore* who resided in a house nearby; the quarrymen and stonecutters used another building, where they could find shelter and if necessary continue to work inside in bad weather. One of the stonecutters was deputed to act as blacksmith, to keep the working tools in order.[15]

After the completion of the Cupola, the quarries of Trassinaia supplied *macigno* for the church of San Lorenzo in 1441.[16] Stone was also obtained in smaller quantities from the quarries of San Gaggio (outside Porta Romana), of Monte Oliveto, of the Carmelite friars and others.

Bricks came mainly from the kiln in Via Ghibellina and also from one belonging to the Abbot of San Salvatore a Settimo, rented for five years and then handed over to the brickmaker Pardo d'Antonio, the major supplier of building bricks, to run. Subsequently supplies also came from other producers at Campi Bisenzio and Lastra a Signa. In 1418 the Opera stipulated a contract with Pardo d'Antonio for the supply of 200,000 bricks over a two-year period; they placed this order well in advance, probably on account of the limited capacity of this sector of the Florentine economy.

White marble came from the quarries of Carrara and Campiglia, where contracts were stipulated with local quarrymen for the supply of unblemished blocks of marble, rough-hewn according to measurements and templates supplied by the Opera. Inspections of the quarries were carried out by the master stonecutters and by the *provveditori*, in particular by Battista d'Antonio and Brunelleschi. The blocks were transported in carts drawn by oxen from the quarry to the beach, where they were loaded (with the help of rollers) into ships which took them to Pisa. They were then transferred into flat-bottomed river craft (*scafi*) capable of navigating up the Arno as far as Signa. There they were again loaded into carts for the final stage of the journey to Florence. Brunelleschi tried to deal with the many problems created by this system of transport—the damage caused to the marble by constant loading and unloading, the modest proportions of individual loads, the impossibility of river transport during the summer and winter months—by designing a new kind of vessel, the *badalone*, or barge, propelled neither by the wind nor by oars nor by hauling, but by a system of paddles combined with a pair of wheels, which when necessary would transform the boat into a vehicle that could travel on land.[17]

The most often-used metal was iron—for the chains, bars, nails, *occhi con rampo* (→ Glossary), brackets, templates for specific marble parts and so on. This mineral, extracted mainly from rich deposits on Elba, was worked in the foundries of the Tuscan Apennines, where wood fuel was readily available, and then transported to Florence for final transformation into finished products; although the Opera had its own smithy, it nevertheless stipulated numerous contracts with blacksmiths, most of whom came from the Apennines.

Most of the rope was imported from Pisa, where for a long time there had been a flourishing rope industry.

The mortar used by the bricklayers was prepared from quicklime mixed with sand; possibly the lime was also mixed with brickdust (*cocciopesto*), which has the same properties as pozzolana, and would have made the mortar to some extent 'hydraulic' (i.e. capable of binding even in the presence of water), making it resistant to leaching and chemically aggressive agents, as well as ensuring a slow but steady development of its mechanical properties, long after the initial drying and hardening. Indeed, the mortar seems to be of excellent quality and contributes in a decisive fashion (except possibly along the herringbone layers: → Part Two, Chapter Two) to the continuity and resistance of the masonry, instead of being a weak point, as is often the case with less carefully composed mortars. Recent chemical analysis has identified the presence of sodium carbonate in the mortar,[18] a substance which speeds up setting. This would have had a favourable effect on the sloping mortar bed joints, as it would have permitted more rapid consolidation of the successive octagonal rings, thereby assisting their self-supporting capacity; however, it is not known whether the presence of sodium carbonate was deliberate or accidental.

'Fresh' brickwork would have been soaked in hot weather and covered up during the winter cold; in this way the builders managed to attenuate the strains caused by changes in temperature—frost would also have interrupted the setting process—and hygrometric variations; these might both have created problems, causing premature fissures.[19]

2.5. Quantity of Materials and Pace of Construction

The weight that had to be raised, in the twelve years required to erect the structural portion, from ground level to the springing line of the vault right above the drum, may be estimated—on the basis of the dimensions of the shells and spurs, and of a specific mass of the masonry of about 1.8 t/m^3—at about 29,000 tons. Thus an average of over 2,000 tons had to be raised each year, and since there were about 270 working days in a year, the daily average was of the order of 8 tons. Piero Sanpaolesi estimated that the Cupola grew about 2.5 metres per year on average, measured according to the progress of the meridians.[20] The construction proceeded according to the schedule to ensure perfect settling.

As for the amount of labour involved, if we suppose an average presence of sixty men for the 270 working days in the year, that makes a total, over twelve years, of about 200,000 man-days; supposing an average working day of ten hours, we arrive at about two million working hours.

Several million bricks were laid,[21] delivered at a rate of perhaps 400,000 a year, and so on average only a few bricks would be laid in one man-hour (about twenty a day per workman and therefore a little over a thousand as a daily total); these figures underline the importance of other aspects of the work such as the curvature control and careful preparation of the mortar bed joints and the herringbone brickwork, as well as the placing of the temporary supports intended to hold the first rows of bricks in the intrados of the inner shell above the point where the slope began, where the freshly laid bricks would have tended to slither inwards on their bed of mortar.

THE STAGES OF CONSTRUCTION

3.1. The Cupola (1420–36)

Work started in April 1420 to prepare the blocks of *macigno*; these were to be joined together by metal rods to form the first chain—at the height of the springing line of the Cupola, above the drum—which like the successive ones was intended to ensure that every individual section contributed to the overall structural equilibrium.[1] In June a committee was sent to the Casentino to select the timber needed for the templates, platforms and machinery;[2] on 7 August 1420 work was officially inaugurated with a banquet ("cholezione") for the teams of workmen.

The construction of the Cupola according to Brunelleschi's programme began at the level of the internal gallery at the top of the drum (53.85 m above the ground), where the building site was laid out—a circular platform running around the drum, which permitted the movement of machinery and workmen, the temporary storage of materials and perhaps also the support for the higher work platforms as work proceeded. Traces of this provisional structure can be seen at the base of the Cupola in the square putlog holes (one *braccio* wide) which were left open at the end of the work.

During the month of June 1420 the first eight fir-wood templates (*centine*) were made, to be installed at the beginning of construction to guide the profiling of the first section of the vault following "the measure of the pointed fifth in the angles on its inner side". The templates were progressively fixed to the masonry by pairs of metal clamps placed at height intervals varying from 30 to 60 cm. Eight more templates are documented as having been finished by June 1424, probably to guide the curvature at a higher level, following the profile established by the ones already installed. In the mid 16th century Giovan Battista Gelli wrote that Brunelleschi, having levelled the sand and gravel on the bank of the Arno over an area of half a mile, drew the Cupola at full scale, "and, after establishing a point in the middle, made drawings of all the stones". Some scholars have linked this episode with the designing and moulding of the templates.[3]

*   *   *

During construction it emerged that changes would have to be made to the original programme of 1420, as regards both dimensions and building methods. These changes were discussed and decided at meetings of the Consuls, the *operai* and the Officials of the Cupola. A short time after work began, at a meeting on 13 March 1422, it was noted that it had become necessary to reduce the weight of the Cupola, and it was therefore decided to cut down the thickness of the intermediate spurs and to replace the stonework with brickwork at a height of 12 *braccia*, instead of the 24 *braccia* originally envisaged.

In June 1425, with the construction of the second stone chain, the inclination of the brickwork towards the centre of the octagon reached a critical point; work was suspended and lengthy discussions took place with the help of models, drawings and reports written by the three *provveditori* and by others.

At meetings on 24 January and 4 February 1426 the plan devised by Brunelleschi, Ghiberti and Battista d'Antonio in collaboration with the Official of the Cupola, Giuliano di Tommaso Gucci, was discussed and approved, and a month later work was resumed according to the new scheme,[4] but only to a height of half a *braccio*, because the formal and constructional modifications to the original programme were considerable, and it was therefore decided to test them on a limited portion. These modifications involved: the substitution of the small barrel vaults initially envisaged with horizontal arches traced between the corner and the intermediate spurs in order to support the outer shell (these arches are called *vivi*, 'alive', in the text of the amendment, probably because they were free and projecting rather than incorporated into the masonry—once the vault was closed over, they could be eliminated in case they hindered movement around the inside or turned out to be formally unpleasing); the creation of circular apertures in the inner shell (to facilitate the construction of the scaffolding which would be necessary for decorating the vault with mosaic and for a "view of the church" from the walkways—for safety reasons it was decided to brick them up temporarily); the introduction of superimposed chains of stone and iron; and the use of special bricks for the herringbone pattern so as to correct the problems posed by the increasing inclination of the mortar bed joints towards the centre of the octagon. Howard Saalman has observed that from the level of the herringbone pattern upwards the layers of bricks on the sides of the octagon are laid radially,[5] demonstrating the architects' intention to ensure the continuity of the brickwork right round the perimeter of each layer. For the first time mention is made of the lantern. It was also decided not to modify the curvature of the Cupola towards a perfect circle, which might well have been stronger and more beautiful, but, as construction had already begun, it would have proved extremely laborious and would have required the introduction of scaffold-supported centring, an option that had been excluded right from the beginning.[6]

In March 1426, after the enforced pause, work was resumed at the level of the second walkway. Between July and November 1432 a new crane was built for raising materials.

In 1435 work began on the construction of the *serraglio*, the vault's oculus ring. The oculus ring is the key to the whole structural system—it provides the junction between the two shells and also constitutes the linking element between the Cupola and the lantern. Its elements, unified in shape and size, were prepared on the ground and then assembled in position, particularly the pieces of *macigno* for the jambs and architraves of the passages through the corner spurs. From September to November 1435 there are records of payments made for "square bricks [...] to pave the floor of the great cupola", i.e. for the pavement of the octagon.[7]

On 25 March (the first day of the Florentine year until the reform of the calendar in the mid 18th century) 1436, in the presence of over 20,000 people from the city and the surroundings, Pope Eugenius IV processed from Santa Maria Novella "on a raised walkway about two *braccia* from the ground, adorned with carpets, cloths, drapes, myrtle and other adornments, which was ordered so as to avoid the crush of the crowds", to consecrate "the magnificent cathedral church of Florence", according to Feo Belcari, the clerk of the Chapter of San Lorenzo.[8] The completion of the Cupola was celebrated by the singing of a motet for four voices, *Nuper rosarum flores*, by Guillaume Dufay.

On 30 August the Bishop of Fiesole consecrated the laying of the final stone of the Cupola. The event was celebrated with music and banquets.

3.2. The Lantern (1437–71)

We have already seen that the amendment of 1426 mentions the lantern. As the construction of the Cupola neared completion, different designs—circular and polygonal—were studied and evaluated, and a full-scale model of the oculus ring was installed "pro vano lanterne … in aere in medio cupole".[9] On 30 October 1432 the Opera commissioned from Brunelleschi a model of the *serraglio* and a model of the lantern ("modellum clausure magne cupole et modellum lanterne dicte opere").[10] By a resolution issued on 25 June 1433 the diameter of the lantern was determined at 9 and ⅔ *braccia* (5.65 m).[11] The model of the lantern prepared by Brunelleschi for the competition of 1436 was approved at the meeting on 31 December of that year for its "superior form" and because it was more resistant, lighter, better lit and more waterproof.[12]

The lantern designed by Brunelleschi echoes the polygonal plan of the Cupola. It is articulated in eight buttresses in line with the spurs of the Cupola, which thus support the weight of the lantern. Brunelleschi died in April 1446, probably shortly after the laying of the first stone for the lantern. Because of the difficulty of finding suitable marble and of the complexity of the delicate carving and mounting, the structure was not finished until 1471, substantially according to Brunelleschi's design, with the positioning of the ball and cross.

On 30 May 1471 the gilded cross was set on top of the ball "at about the twentieth hour and a half, with much rejoicing: and the *Te Deum* was sung". The ball, made to a design by Andrea del Verrocchio, had a diameter of about 4 *braccia* (2.35 m) and weighed 4,368 *libbre*; it was of brass, cast "in eight pieces […] and silver-soldered",[13] gilded on the outside and fixed to the *pergamena* (i.e. the upper, spire-like portion of the lantern) by means of a copper bracket running through the underlying knob.

3.3. Interior and Exterior Decorations after 1471

The facing of the drum with black and white marble was executed, slowly, in the later 15th century by—according to Vasari—Giuliano da Maiano, following a model left by Antonio di Manetto Ciaccheri; the two-dimensional pattern of rectangular panels is part of a Florentine tradition going back to the Romanesque. All that was now lacking to complete the Cupola was the exterior gallery at the top of the drum and the mosaic decoration on the intrados of the vault's inner shell.

For the gallery Brunelleschi had prepared drawings which were lost, according to Vasari, because of the "negligence" of the Opera's officials.[14] Some aspects of his design can be gleaned from the building programme agreed upon in 1420: "An outer walkway is to be made above the eight round windows [i.e. above the drum], supported by consoles [*imbecchatellato*], with openwork parapets about 2 br. high, like those of the apsidioles below; or rather two walkways, one above the other, over a finely decorated cornice; and the upper walkway is to be uncovered". After holding a competition in 1507 the Opera commissioned the construction of the gallery—to be made "secundum modum et ritum veteris architecturae et modellorum antiquorum" ('according to the practices and customs of ancient architecture and the models of the ancients')[15]—from Simone del Pollaiolo known as Cronaca, Baccio d'Agnolo and Giuliano da Sangallo. Cronaca died in September 1508 and Sangallo abandoned the enterprise; the work, begun in 1512, was

8. The 15th-century wooden model of the facing of the drum: traditionally attributed to Giuliano da Maiano, Sanpaolesi assigned it to Brunelleschi and Ghiberti (Florence, Opera di Santa Maria del Fiore Museum).

9. Below, Simone del Pollaiolo known as Cronaca, Baccio d'Agnolo, Giuliano and Antonio da Sangallo, wooden model of the facing of the drum and of the exterior gallery at the springing line of the Cupola (Florence, Opera di Santa Maria del Fiore Museum).

8.

9.

10.

10. Aristotile da Sangallo, design for
the exterior gallery and the drum,
c. 1510 (Florence, Gabinetto Disegni e
Stampe degli Uffizi, GDSU, 6714 A).
Sangallo envisaged removing
the existent facing of the drum and
the great round window, while his
design for the gallery follows
Brunelleschi's original plan for two
walkways one on top of the other.

11.

11. Michelangelo Buonarroti, sketch for the drum, cornice and exterior gallery, *c.* 1516–7 (Florence, Casa Buonarroti, 50 Ar). The artist planned to accentuate the shape of the cornerpieces with twin pilasters (extension of the marble ribs) topped by a substantial entablature.

12. Opposite, Michelangelo Buonarroti, sketch for the drum, *c.* 1516–7 (Florence, Casa Buonarroti, 66 Av). Michelangelo wanted to replace the four rectangular panels to the right and left of the great round window with two large panels framed by a relief cornice rather than by a two-dimensional chromatic pattern.

12.

therefore directed by Baccio d'Agnolo, who completed the section of the gallery at the base of the south-east segment in 1515 with the help of Antonio da Sangallo the Elder. The Florentines were highly critical of the gallery—Michelangelo famously dismissed it as "a cricket cage" (*gabbia da grilli*). The Opera suspended the work, which was never resumed despite various later projects. Michelangelo produced a number of drawings and a model (preserved, together with the competition models, in the Opera di Santa Maria del Fiore Museum), envisaging different solutions for the gallery and the facing of the drum: one drawing shows how he planned to reinforce the cornerpieces with twin pilasters (along the axis of Brunelleschi's marble ribs) supporting a substantial entablature; another shows a suggestion for replacing the four rectangular panels to the right and left of each round window with a single gigantic panel outlined by a cornice in relief instead of the two-dimensional marble pattern.

As for the interior of the vault, it had been decided back in 1426 that it should be covered in mosaic, like the interior of the Baptistery. Between 1434 and 1436 the glazier Francesco di Domenico Livi da Gambassi, who lived in Lubeck, was asked to make coloured glass for the round windows and tesserae for the mosaic.[16] In 1436, when the Cupola was closed over, the inner shell was covered with a plaster made of lime and sand, suitable as a bed for mosaic, which made the interior look very bright. The idea of the mosaic was later revived by Lorenzo the Magnificent. But on 11 June 1572 Giorgio Vasari, at the request of Grand Duke Cosimo I, began the great fresco cycle of the *Last Judgement*, starting at the top, just below the lantern. The frescoes were completed in 1579 by Federico Zuccari, who took over after Vasari's death in 1574.[17] Alessandro Parronchi has suggested that Brunelleschi wanted Heaven and Hell to be represented as in the *Divine Comedy*, and that the illustrations of Dante's poem which Botticelli made from the early 1470s onwards were in fact intended for the mosaics.[18]

THE FORM OF THE CUPOLA

4.1. The Exterior

Looking at the Cupola from the outside, one notices an evident departure from the traditional solutions of Gothic architecture, both in the refusal to multiply upward-pushing forces (free-standing pinnacles, spires, buttresses and so on), and also in the rigorous, controlled convergence of these vertical forces, the formal solution consisting of a formidable synthesis of continuous lines and surfaces. Multiplicity is sought in unity, and the Cupola shrugs off the elaborate and decoratively more minute design of the rest of the Cathedral.

The first powerful expression of a deliberate synthesis of the Greek and the Gothic cultural worlds, the Cupola is in fact a sensitive diaphragm stretched between external and internal space, the boundary between two spatial entities. The thrust and the dynamic form (the pointed fifth and the elliptical section) resolve their internal tensions in a controlled equilibrium, thanks to which the Cupola appears to float tethered above the city, the wondrous result of internal and external forces being held in balance. The Cupola organises and integrates the volumetric masses beneath it into a coherent, proportionally measured whole: within the powerful framework of the marble ribs—an unprecedented feature for a dome—the eight segments converge towards the vanishing point of the lantern, defined in its turn by uniform radial components converging towards the ball supporting the cross.

At the base of the drum the four *tribune morte*, the apsidioles designed by Brunelleschi as the crowning elements of each of the four piers that support the dome, have a series of niches separated by paired Corinthian columns. The rhythmical succession of concave and convex elements in each apsidiole introduces new nuances in the overall apsidal articulation. These apsidioles balance the large apsidal chapels, which on their own would form far too isolated and conspicuous concentrations of mass along the circular apsidal circuit. At first sight, the *tribune morte* add to the interplay of plastic elements, but in fact they contribute to the formal continuity around the base of the Cupola: by dilating the visible surface, they offset the effect of mass, rendering the marvellous soaring of the Cupola even more consistent in formal terms.

In the design of the facing of the drum, carried out in the late 15th century, there is an evident intention to reconcile the horizontal emphasis of the bulk of the Cathedral with the vertical development of the domed apsidal block. The facing is in fact divided into two superimposed strips, separated by the entablature of the lower one, which coincides with the entablature of the main body of the nave. The intention to reaffirm the continuity of the horizontal organisation of mass up to that level evidently led to the decision to diminish the width of the corner pilasters in the upper section of the drum in relation to those in the lower section; according to Manetti, this contradicted the instructions of Brunelleschi, who had envisaged for each corner of the drum "a single member", and not "two members, one above the other".[1]

13.

13. A stylised rendering of the Cupola as it was around 1434, in a detail of one of Giovanni di Paolo's miniatures illustrating the IX Canto of Dante's *Paradiso* (London, British Library, MS Yates Thompson 36, fol. 145r).

14. Opposite, the Cupola in a detail of Domenico di Michelino's tempera painting of Dante and his poem, realised to a drawing by Alessio Baldovinetti and intended for the interior of Florence Cathedral, 1465. This realistic depiction of Santa Maria del Fiore portrays the recently constructed north-east *tribuna morta* and, beside it, a small, faced portion of the drum. The facing of the nave is complete.

The book held in the figure's hand bears an inscription:

PROQUANTA
PER VIVALE
PECOSAD
VRAQVE
STASILVA
SINFOGGI
ASPRALET
FORTE CHE
NELPEN
MARTI

14.

15. A detail of the *Archangels Michael, Raphael and Gabriel with Young Tobias* by Biagio d'Antonio (Florence, Bartolini Salimbeni Collection). Dating to around 1470–1, the painting provides valuable evidence of the scaffolding built around the lantern. The bronze ball, still missing, was realised and positioned in 1471. For the first time the Cupola, which dominates the city, is viewed from the hills to the north. This vantage point was later adopted by Piero del Pollaiolo (→ Fig. 16) and reached its maximum expression in the 18th-century work of Giuseppe Zocchi (→ Fig. 75).

16. Opposite, detail of the view of Florence in Piero del Pollaiolo's panel painting of the *Annunciation, c.* 1472 (Berlin, Staatliche Museen Preußicher Kulturbesitz, Gemäldegalerie). Like Biagio d'Antonio, Piero depicts Florence from the north, artificially raising the viewpoint so as to create a bird's-eye view of the city.

16.

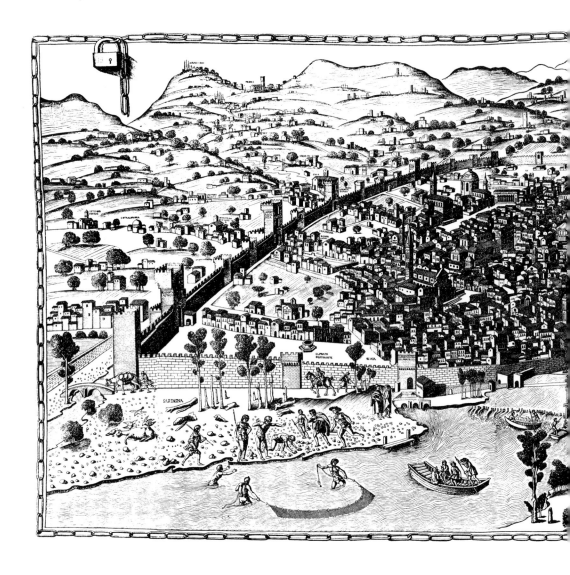

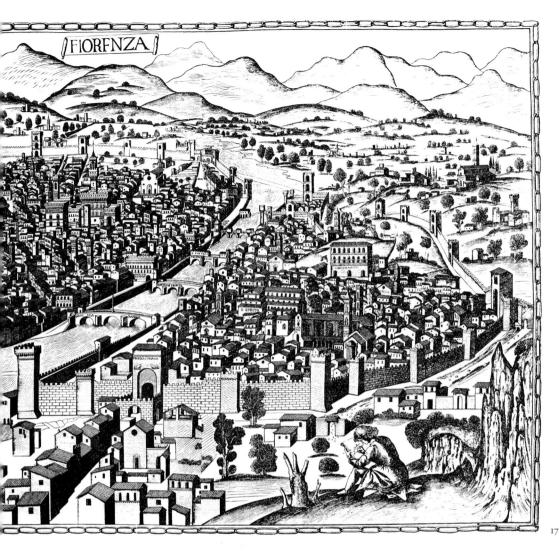

FIORENZA

17. View known as "della Catena"
('of the Chain'), six-sheet woodcut,
58.5 × 131.5 cm, attributable to
Francesco di Lorenzo Rosselli and
dating to the period between 1471 and
1482 (Berlin, Kupferstichkabinett).
This is the first known representation
of an entire city as an independent
work of art. Rather than being
a poetic projection of the imagination,
it fully exploits the possibilities of
perspective to check and correct direct
observation, and of topography
to verify the volumes and layout
of the city. Given the contours of the
area around Florence, the vantage
point from the *campanile* of the
church of Monteoliveto provides
the best combination of appropriate
distance and broad view of the walled
city, the other possible viewing points
being either too distant (Bellosguardo,
Fiesole, Montughi) or too close
(San Miniato). The viewpoint has
been artificially raised to emphasise
the structure of the city.

18.

18. *View of Florence*, tempera painting attributed to the circle of Francesco Rosselli and dating to the period between 1489 and 1495 (London, private collection). Compared to the "Catena" woodcut, this view emphasises the Cupola's position as a fulcrum for the city and its surroundings; this is enhanced by the use of colour.

19. Opposite, view of Florence from the south in a detail of a panel by Filippino Lippi dating to the period between 1483 and 1485 and depicting the *Annunciation with St John the Baptist and St Andrew* (Naples, Museo Nazionale di Capodimonte). The Cupola stands out amidst the city's main monuments.

20. [p. 46] View of the Baptistery, the Cathedral and the Campanile in a detail of a fresco by Domenico del Ghirlandaio depicting *St Zenobius Enthroned*, c. 1483 (Florence, Palazzo Vecchio, Sala dei Gigli). The cathedral complex is viewed from the west. The marble facing of the drum is not yet in place.

21. [p. 47, top] Panoramic view of Florence from the north, woodcut by Lorenzo Morgiani and Giovanni di Pietro illustrating *Le bellezze et chasati di Firenze*, a poem by Bernardino da Firenze, c. 1495.

22. [p. 47, bottom] View of Florence from the south-west (Bellosguardo) in a detail of the *Mystic Crucifixion* by Sandro Botticelli, tempera on canvas, c. 1502 (Cambridge, Mass., Fogg Art Museum). Botticelli was perhaps the first painter to adopt the Bellosguardo vantage point, which became very popular in the 18th and 19th century.

20.

23.

23. Giorgio Vasari, view of Florence besieged by the troops of Emperor Charles V in 1529–30, fresco, 1561–2 (Florence, Palazzo Vecchio, Sala di Clemente VII). In the *Ragionamenti* Vasari explains in detail how he painted this view from the hill of Arcetri, to the south of Florence: "It would have been very difficult to paint this scene from the natural viewpoint and in the manner generally used to draw cities and villages. They are usually drawn freely from life, but all the high structures tend to hide the lower ones from view. [...] This is what happened to me when I wanted to portray Florence in this way. [...]

I went to draw from the highest spot I could find, which turned out to be the roof of a house [...]. I took the compass and placed it on the roof of the house: I pointed a measuring stick straight to the north and from there I began drawing the hills, the houses and the closest places; then I moved the stick until it was aligned with the highest point of each element of the landscape, to achieve a broader view". Painted with meticulous attention to detail and remarkable compositional skill, this view of the city and the hills surrounding it from an artificially raised vantage point is centred on the Cupola.

24.

24. Stefano Bonsignori, *Nova
pulcherrimae civitatis Florentiae
topographia accuratissime delineata*,
nine-sheet etching, 1584 (Florence,
"Firenze com'era" Topographical
Museum), detail of the city centre.
The use of axonometric perspective
is a reflection of the desire for a clearly
established hierarchy, in which
the Cupola is the principal point
of reference.

The uppermost section of the drum, intended to be "encircled" by an "outer walkway", remains without facing. As we have seen, in 1515 Baccio d'Agnolo completed the construction of the gallery at the base of the south-east segment. However, by interpreting this element as a gigantic entablature supported by the projecting cornerpieces of the drum, he betrayed Brunelleschi's original plan to unify the design of the consoles and openwork parapets with that of the lower, existing passageway crowning the apses; this was meant to emphasise the sharp break of the Cupola from the underlying structure by concealing its springing line. Baccio's gallery was criticised by contemporaries for both technical and formal reasons: as mentioned above, Michelangelo called it a "cricket cage".

In the uppermost section of the drum, where the stonework has not been dressed, there are twelve stone consoles on each side; according to Saalman, these are the protruding ends of the cross-beams (perpendicular to the sides of the octagon) supporting the two parallel stone courses, clamped with metal brackets, that compose the first annular stone chain. This undressed section of the drum terminates at the top with the marble cornice and gutter (*ratta*): the cornice, supported by the consoles at the springing line of the outer, brick-covered shell, is shaped to collect the rainwater running off the segments and channel it into the *doccie di macignj*, vertical chutes installed at the corners of the drum between 1421 and 1428.

At the base of the outer shell, in the middle of the north, east, south and west segments immediately above the *ratta*, are four openings with marble surrounds. Corresponding to the first internal walkway, they were intended to provide access to the outer walkway, which was never realised.

The roof tiles are quadrangular (37 cm wide and 50 cm high) with lateral raised ribs— a variety specially designed by Brunelleschi to avoid using additional semicylindrical tiles (*coppi*) over the joins. They are laid side by side on the bed of lime mortar, and overlap along the top and bottom edges. They are prevented from sliding downwards by the ridge between the ribs; at the corners, they are further secured by small terracotta blocks cemented with lime mortar; finally, each tile is fixed with two nails, a Northern European practice. Some of the tiles are stamped with the maker's mark.

The option of using marble for the facing, previously adopted for the Baptistery, was rejected, probably because it was expensive and difficult to maintain; a copper- or lead-sheet covering (as used on the Baptistery in Pisa) would also have been too costly. In any case, the Cupola's red tiling is undoubtedly a unique feature.

The white marble ribs or "crests" envisaged in the initial programme as "profiled and sloping" along the lines where the vault segments intersect contrast strongly with the colour of the tiles, their curved profile emphasised by the red segments. Originally they were supposed to taper pyramidally towards the top, but in fact their width is constant. This change, while diminishing the perspectival effect, nevertheless accentuates the pure geometrical abstraction of the design.

In each of the eight segments there are three orders of circular apertures, one *braccio* in diameter, three in each order; they have a regular vertical and horizontal arrangement, and each one is pierced in a monolithic block of *macigno*. There are also small rectangular openings (50 × 40 cm), cut into the tiling to provide light and ventilation for the walkways between the two shells. The light from the circular apertures falls on the extrados of the inner shell and deliberately does not reach the interior of the church.

As we have seen, the lantern echoes the polygonal plan of the Cupola. It consists of an octagonal *tempietto* reinforced by radial buttresses, aligned with the corner spurs of the Cupola and joined by volutes to the piers of the *tempietto*; these are decorated with twin pilasters and frame eight tall and slender round-arched windows. Surmounting the robust entablature is the *pergamena*, the cone-shaped element with a mixtilinear perimeter that crowns the lantern and supports the ball with its gilded copper cross.

It has been pointed out that "the sumptuous form of the *tempietto* was of classicising inspiration, though adapted to its specific function with the same inventive freedom which had brought together the disparate elements that inspired the Cupola. Of crucial importance in this connection was the adoption of voluted consoles connecting the buttresses to the central structure: these volutes are of the type found on classical cornices, but here they are upside down—used as a crowning rather than a supporting element— and of gigantic proportions. They were to give rise to a host of derived motifs".[2]

The Cupola was often struck by lightning.[3] On one occasion, in 1601, the ball was knocked down,[4] and much of the spire and cornice were destroyed; the ball was remade slightly smaller, and on the advice of Bernardo Buontalenti a window was made in it, to give light and to improve access to the cross. In 1859, more than a century after Benjamin Franklin's invention, lightning conductors were eventually installed.

In 1475 a friend of Brunelleschi's, the Florentine scientist and mathematician Paolo dal Pozzo Toscanelli (1397–1482) installed a bronze tablet pierced with an aperture of about 2 cm in diameter on the inside sill of the southern window of the lantern. From the end of May to the end of July, around noon, rays of sunlight pass through it and fall on the pavement of the chapel of the Cross—in the left (north) apse—where there is a gnomon and two marble slabs indicating the solstices. This gnomon was restored in the 18th century by the Jesuit Leonardo Ximenes.[5]

In the architecture of the lantern the monumental quality of the various elements is determined above all by the need to be seen from a great distance, and is appreciated as such only when seen from close up, from the platform on which the structure rests. In the radial buttresses and in the pyramidal spire the modulations, shaping and hollowing out of the surfaces produce chromatic variations which, when seen in perspective from below or from far away, give the lantern a two-dimensional, almost weightless quality. Brunelleschi's customary preference for dichromatic alternation of marble and brick, *pietra serena* (grey sandstone) and white plaster, would not have been appropriate here; instead, chromatic modulation was obtained by working the marble in undulating shapes. In full daylight the only colour capable of transforming matter into immaterial lightness is the absolute white of marble, which also provides the necessary resistance to the elements.

4.2. The Interior

Inside the Cupola, the internal surface of the drum is delimited by two balustraded walkways. The first is reached by four sets of stairs, and the second gives access, in the southeast segment, to the first flight of steps between the inner and the outer shell.

The presbytery is lit by the lantern and by the eight great round windows in the drum, filled with stained glass. The inner shell is pierced by sixteen round apertures one *braccio* in diameter, two along the midline of each segment, at the level of the second and third walkway; they provide no light. The amendment of 1426 explains that the purpose of these apertures was to support temporary platforms to be used by the mosaic-makers, and to allow "a view of the church" from the internal walkways.

The overall effect of diffused and attenuated light under the vault seems to be in harmony with the mystical criteria later expressed by Leon Battista Alberti in his treatise *De re aedificatoria* ('On the Art of Building').[6] But undoubtedly the effect of Vasari's and Zuccari's frescoes is very different from what had originally been envisaged.

The profile of the Cupola balances with its height the length of the nave and aisles. "Even today, when we enter the Cathedral by the doors in the façade and walk down the nave as far as the apse, we are struck by the difference between the initial and the final sight; from the nave or the aisles, the area under the Cupola appears as a distant background, decidedly further back with respect to the architecture of the piers and the 14th-century vaulting; from beneath the Cupola, on the other hand, the body of the nave and aisles is in turn pushed way back, assuming a subordinate position which is not dissimilar to that of the apses, so that it seems that the enormous octagonal space has the symmetry of a centrally planned structure."[7]

4.3. The Cupola in the Urban Landscape

With the addition of the Cupola the city is no longer a fluid urban mass out of which vertical points of reference (towers and *campanili*) suddenly emerge here and there: the Cupola, by virtue of its size and shape, detaches itself from, and dominates, the whole landscape. The towers and *campanili* (including Giotto's) take on an order and form a set of relationships between each other, but always in relation to the Cupola, which floats between the roofs and the sky at the heart of the urban system.

The role of the Cupola in the urban landscape of Florence is magnificently and concisely expressed in Leon Battista Alberti's dedication to Brunelleschi in his treatise *De pictura* ('On Painting'): "erta sopra e' cieli, ampla da coprire con sua ombra tutti e' popoli toscani" ('rising above the skies, broad enough to cover with its shadow all the peoples of Tuscany').[8] 'Rising above the skies' expresses on the one hand the tension and thrust of the soaring profile of the ribs, and on the other the fact that the Cupola is not dominated by universal space: rather, the Cupola dictates its own space by establishing itself as the focus for all relations and measures. 'Broad' expresses the fundamental qualities of the dimension, extension and circularity of the soaring dome, while immediately ('broad enough to') introducing the notion of the Cupola's relationship with the city and the surrounding countryside. The balanced contrast of 'rising above' and 'broad enough to' expresses with admirable concision the resolution of all the forces, all the structures, all the equilibria, all the proportions in themselves and with respect to the city, in the absolute abstraction of the relationship between ribs and segments, between lines and surfaces. Finally, Alberti's words emphasise that the new dimension and the new order also correspond to the new political dimension of the city.

The Cupola is huge, but its great size is not that of a Gothic cathedral, which from close up 'draws in' and enraptures, and from a distance becomes an atmospheric mass and blends into nature. "Magnificent and swollen", the Cupola is an exact and dynamic form

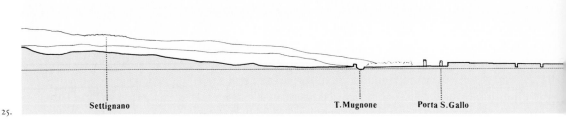

Settignano   T.Mugnone   Porta S.Gallo

25.

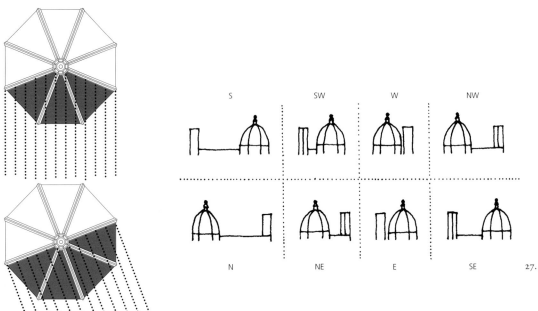

S   SW   W   NW

N   NE   E   SE   27.

26.

25. Top, a north–south section of the city showing the extraordinary size of the Cupola (91 m excluding the lantern, 110 m to the cross) and its carefully calculated relation to the city and the surrounding hills.

26. Above, left, illustration of the two basic positions an observer can adopt in relation to the Cupola:
(1) on an axis perpendicular to one of the sides of the octagon—three segments are visible;
(2) on an axis that is at an angle to any side of the octagon—four segments are visible.

27. Above, right, illustration of the relative positions of the Cupola and the Campanile as seen from various observation points in the city and surrounding area.

28–30. Opposite, photographic views of Florence from Carmignano (*c.* 1870), from the Torre del Gallo (*c.* 1870) and from the south-east (*c.* 1930) that show the extraordinary size of the Cupola and its status as a landmark in the local area.

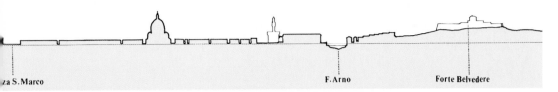

za S.Marco   F.Arno   Forte Belvedere

28.

29.

30.

55

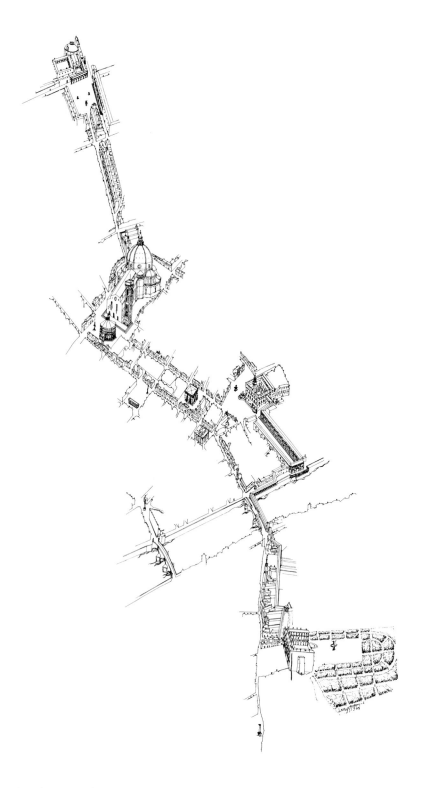

31. The Cupola in the context of the
city's architecture and urban fabric.

which from close up attracts, gathers and coordinates volumes, forces and sight lines, and which from a distance retains—by means of the relation between white ribs and red segments—the qualities of a perfectly defined and verifiable measure and form, establishing a hierarchical and proportional order among the various elements within the visual field. *Irrespective of the distance from which one views it, the geometric figure of the Cupola (defined by lines and surfaces) remains unvaried.*

The impression of extreme clarity gained by the observer who looks at the Cupola from a distance is surely responsible for the not uncommon examples, in the Tuscan countryside, of place names such as "l'Apparita" or "l'Apparenza" ('appearance, emergence'), deriving from the fact that from such localities the city could be recognised thanks to the clearly delineated shape of the Cupola.

Given the structural characteristics of the medieval layout of Florence, the Cupola has never really dominated individual streets. Indeed, it is visible only from a small number of routes leading haphazardly into the Cathedral square (such as Via dello Studio or Via dell'Oriuolo, which was widened in the 19th century in order to "facilitate the flow of traffic" and to "offer admirers a more beautiful view of Giotto's Tower and Brunelleschi's Cupola"), or from specific points in Piazza Santa Croce and Piazza del Mercato Vecchio (today, Piazza della Repubblica). It is significant that the only street from which the Cupola can be seen all along its length is Via de' Servi; its straightness is the result of the 14th-century fascination with order and regularity, and at the northern end of it Brunelleschi himself would lay out Piazza Santissima Annunziata.

The Cupola can be better appreciated when seen from the upper levels of the urban fabric, from the top floors of buildings and towers, or from vantage points outside the city walls. It is only from such points that "the view from afar determines [the Cupola's] unity, its relationship to the profile of the surrounding hills and to the sky";[9] it also sets up new relations between the other rising monuments, by acting as a fulcrum. This abstraction from the immediate context, the achievement of a building's definition from varying observation points from which its unity becomes apparent recur—obviously with different connotations, determined by the different environmental contexts—throughout the work of Brunelleschi (and also that inspired by him), also evidently through a pondered reinterpretation of the stylobate of classical architecture. One might think of the Pitti Palace, set back from Via Romana, raised on top of the sloping piazza, so that when we have passed through the portal and reached the inner courtyard, turning around we see that the houses opposite appear to be suspended without foundations, their roofs at the level of the horizon and, behind them, the *campanile* of Santo Spirito on the main perspectival axis. One might also think of the loggias of the Spedale degli Innocenti, set on the visual horizon when viewed from the piazza; vice versa, the piazza is distanced and objectified when seen from the raised platform of the loggias. The churches of Santo Spirito and San Lorenzo, both of them raised above the level of their respective piazzas, also come to mind.

Rising far above the other buildings of Florence, the Cupola is subject only to the conditions of natural light, unlike the streets and squares of the city, where the lighting is affected by the relations between the buildings. The creeping shadow of the Cupola during the day—influenced by the curvature and texture of the segments and by the projecting profile of the ribs—nevertheless changes in tandem with the lights and shadows of the streets and piazzas, since they are all due to the same natural cause, the movement of the sun. Thus the gradual and regular alternation of light and shadow on the surfaces of the Cupola, stretched between one rib and the next, marks moment by moment the dynamic variation of light and shadow in *every* part of the city, the latter being affected by the orientation and profiles of the lines of buildings along the streets, by the varying width of the space between two facing blocks and by other, more specific environmental factors. It is no accident that it was within the perfect structural mechanism of the Cupola that Brunelleschi's friend Paolo dal Pozzo Toscanelli installed his gnomon for measuring the position of the sun, which uses a ray of sunlight shining through the lantern.

THE LATER HISTORY OF THE CUPOLA:
CRITICAL RECEPTION AND SCIENTIFIC STUDIES

5.1. The Comments of Contemporaries and the Influence of the Cupola on 15th- and 16th-Century Architects

When Brunelleschi died, the Florentines acknowledged not only his greatness—granting him, as Manetti noted, "the great honour of being buried in Santa Maria del Fiore and setting up there his likeness, as it were, sculpted in marble as a perpetual memorial, with a most distinguished epitaph"[1]—but also the lucid clarity and economy invariably displayed in his works. To celebrate his greatness they chose, in fact, just a few, carefully chosen words. On his tomb slab (discovered in the crypt of Santa Reparata in 1972) is the inscription: CORPUS MAGNI INGENII VIRI | PHILIPPI S. BRUNELLESCHI FLORENTINI ("The body of that man of great genius, Filippo di ser Brunellesco, Florentine"). In the funerary inscription put up on the wall of the right aisle, near the entrance to the Cathedral, Carlo Marsuppini, Chancellor of the Republic and one of the great humanist scholars of his age, summarised the architect's exceptional qualities as displayed in the making of the Cupola and in his technical inventiveness: D.S. | QUANTUM PHILIPPUS ARCHITECTUS ARTE DAE|DALEA VALUERIT CUM HUIUS CELEBERRIMI | TEMPLI MIRA TESTUDO TUM PLURES MA-CHINAE | DIVINO INGENIO AB EO ADINVENTAE DOCUMEN|TO ESSE POSSUNT QUAPROPTER OB EXIMIAS SUI | ANIMI DOTES SINGULARESQUE VIRTUTES XV KL | MAIAS ANNO M CCCC XLVI EIUS B M CORPUS IN HAC | HUMO SUPPOSITA GRATA PATRIA SEPELLIRI IUSSIT[2] ('Holy is the Lord. How greatly Filippo the architect excelled in the art of Daedalus [i.e. architecture] may be documented both by the wonderful dome of this most famous church and by the numerous machines he invented with almost superhuman genius. Whence for his exceptional talents and his rare virtues, on 17 April 1446 the grateful fatherland ordered that his well-deserving body should be interred in this earth').

*   *   *

Whether we see it from close by—from the narrow medieval streets or from the comparatively small containing space of Piazza del Duomo, which still closes in on the Cathedral and the Baptistery—or from afar—from the hills or from the ancient routes leading to the city—, the immediate impression produced by the Cupola is that of a unique magnitude and grandeur.

The magnitude and grandeur of the Cupola, in many respects unprecedented even in the architecture of ancient Rome, immediately aroused amazement and stirred the admiration and imagination of both foreign and Florentine contemporaries, giving rise to a body of writings—comments and definitions, studies and research—that has continued down to the present day.

Among the first, if not the very first, to leave written evidence of his admiration for the Cupola was another great figure in the history of 15th-century architecture, Leon Battista Alberti. The prologue to the vernacular edition of his treatise *De pictura* ('On Painting'), written in 1436, just as the great structure was being closed over, contains, in the context of the dedication to Brunelleschi, what still remains the most wonderfully concise, powerful and effective definition of the great masterpiece: "Who could ever be hard or envious enough to fail to praise Pippo the architect on seeing here such a large structure, rising above the skies, broad enough to cover with its shadow all the peoples of Tuscany, built without the aid of centring or wooden scaffolding: an achievement, if I judge rightly, such as in these times it was unbelievable that it could be accomplished, and was perhaps never known or even thought of among the ancients". Alberti not only found apt and noble words with which to express his admiration for the Cupola: he acknowledged in Brunelleschi the technical merit of having built the vault of Florence Cathedral without the aid of centring. In his treatise *De re aedificatoria* ('On the Art of Building'), Alberti suggests that the possibility of building a vault with a polygonal base without centring relies on the inscribing of a circular base within the polygon.

Another great artist who was a contemporary of Brunelleschi's and took part, to an extent which is now difficult to determine, in the great undertaking was Lorenzo Ghiberti. He promised to write about it, but unfortunately never did so. In his *Commentari* he says: "We both worked, Filippo and I, on the building of the Cupola, for eighteen years at the same salary: so long we concerned ourselves with the said Cupola. I will write a treatise on architecture and I will deal with this subject there."

Following Alberti, many other contemporaries stress the greatness of the Cupola and the achievement of overcoming the difficulties involved in building it without centring. Among these are St Antoninus (1389–1459), archbishop of Florence; Flavio Biondo (1392–1463), man of letters; Fra Domenico da Corella (1403–83); Matteo Palmieri (1406–75), statesman and philosopher; and Bartolomeo Scala (1428–97). Fra Domenico writes: "huius enim templi sublatus ad ethera vertex qualibet ingenti celsior arce patet" ('the summit of this temple raised to the skies seems in fact higher than any citadel').[3]

Antonio di Tuccio Manetti (1423–97) was Brunelleschi's first biographer. The manuscript of the *Life of Brunelleschi*, attributed to him by Gaetano Milanesi in 1887, probably dates from the 1480s.[4] It has been pointed out that a profound sympathy seems to have linked the biographer to his subject, "the two of them brought together by a series of 'external' coincidences".[5] Manetti had a humanist education and a good grasp of scientific, philosophical and technical issues. He was a member of the Wool Guild, and held public office: he served as *operaio* of the Foundling Hospital and was a member of the commission appointed to judge the competition for the Cathedral façade (1491).

Manetti's biography is not wholly reliable from the historical point of view, but it is lively and shows remarkable narrative and interpretative powers. His passion and literary skill eventually conferred legendary status on the life and work of the great architect. Over half the manuscript is devoted to the Cupola. The successive stages in the extraordinary accomplishment of an 'impossible' work are emotionally and powerfully described in Manetti's *Life*, with an intensity that renders it something different from a purely scholarly account. The book covers the following phases in Brunelleschi's work on the Cupola. In 1417 Brunelleschi is back in Florence from one of his visits to Rome, where he had gone to study the buildings of classical antiquity; summoned by the *operai* to explain his ideas for vaulting the dome, he arouses interest, but also many doubts; he then asks permission to leave Florence and returns to Rome, where he continues his study of the vaulting techniques of the ancient Romans, without giving much thought to expenses, "because he had the construction of the aforesaid church in Florence continually on his mind"; he is called (it is now 1419) to take part in the commission for the building of the dome; he, alone among the members, maintains the feasibility of building the dome without centring; the discussion lasts several days; in the face of his obstinate insistence on an apparently impossible solution, the *operai* several times "have him physically expelled, as though he were talking nonsense and making a fool of himself"; he builds the Ridolfi chapel in the church of San Jacopo Sopr'Arno as a practical demonstration of his technical hypothesis; he draws up the building programme for the Cupola (which appears as an appendix to the Opera's 1420 resolution); he is appointed *capomaestro*; he agrees to a lower salary and to the limitation of the height at 14 *braccia* as a trial, in order to cut short the discussion and silence the opposition; he accepts Lorenzo Ghiberti as his partner, though he alone is called the "inventor"; work on the Cupola begins according to his instructions; fear and misgivings multiply, opposition increases; by feigning sickness he demonstrates Ghiberti's incompetence and the necessity of his own presence; he thus succeeds in defining and dividing their respective roles; he builds new models; he is the object of intense public curiosity (about which he complains) and of practical jokes; when the Cupola reaches the height of 7 *braccia* he is awarded the commission to complete it as far as the lantern; he is requested to assign a 'master mason' (*maestro di cazuola*) to each of the eight segments; he ends a strike of the building teams, who refuse to be completely subordinate to him, by showing himself capable of proceeding with new workmen, trained and supervised by him; he devises various "measures" and "procedures" to deal with specific problems in the construction (winds, earthquakes, the dead weight of the Cupola); he continually makes new models of details, and explains them practically to the workmen, using clay, wax, wood and even large turnips sliced with a knife; he attends to the safety of the workmen—"not only the dangers, but also the fears and discomfort of the bricklayers and of those who assisted them"; he sees that "there be those who sell wine and bread, as well as cooks" up on the work platforms, in order to save working time; he personally selects and checks the materials, and examines the workmanship; the work is by now perfectly organised, and proceeds smoothly until completion.

It is clear from this narrative, which makes only a few concessions to fiction, that Brunelleschi was no longer the architect acting within or delegated by the community, but rather an individual who interpreted and shaped collective action according to his own vision. Brunelleschi's technical and formal discoveries presupposed the need to move beyond traditional building practices, with the architect now having sole responsibility for the project and the building teams merely carrying out his orders. This explains Brunelleschi's clashes with the Opera, with Ghiberti and with the builders, attested by biographers but only partly documented in the sources. The position assumed by Brunelleschi was at variance with the corporate management of working relations. We have seen that in 1434 he refused to pay his dues to the Guild of Stonemasons and Woodworkers and was therefore imprisoned, being released only after the chapter of the Opera intervened on his behalf.

*   *   *

Many 15th- and 16th-century architects were inspired by Brunelleschi's Cupola. Giuliano da Sangallo (*c.* 1445–1516), who in the late 15th-century was one of the most faithful and brilliant interpreters of Brunelleschi's legacy, used the Florentine Cupola as the model for the shrine of the Holy House at Loreto (1498–1500), which however has only one shell (the lantern, similar to the one in Florence, was added by Giuseppe Sacconi in 1889). Like Giuliano da Maiano before him, Sangallo studied and employed herringbone brickwork.

Great interest in the Florentine Cupola was shown by other members of the Sangallo 'clan', who were all capable and indefatigable builders, designers and entrepreneurs. Antonio da Sangallo the Younger (1483–1546), a tireless student of ancient and modern architecture, examined (also with a view to his own design of the lantern for St Peter's in Rome) many facets of the geometry and construction of the Cupola in a wonderful series of drawings—a thorough investigation of the geometry of the vault, structural solutions, details of construction and form, and (following in the footsteps of his uncle Giuliano) of Brunelleschi's machinery. In some of his buildings he employed the herringbone pattern, which in the 16th century was to enjoy wide currency. Aristotile da Sangallo (1481–1551) produced a mannerist drawing showing his proposed solution for the exterior gallery (developing Brunelleschi's idea of two uncovered walkways) and for the marble facing of the drum.

Michelangelo Buonarroti (1475–1564), who criticised the exterior gallery designed by Baccio d'Agnolo, made various drawings for an alternative version of the gallery and of the facing of the drum. He carefully studied the structure of Brunelleschi's Cupola and the decoration of the lantern, reinterpreting them in powerful and monumental terms for the dome of St Peter's, which makes use of the double shell.

The influence of Brunelleschi's Cupola on Leonardo da Vinci (1452–1519) appears in many of his designs for churches.

Arduino Arriguzzi (documented 1482–1531) visited the Cupola several times, and reinterpreted it in late-Gothic style in a wooden model (*c.* 1514) for the church of San Petronio in Bologna. The Sienese architect and painter Baldassarre Peruzzi (1481–1536) visited Florence in the 1530s and made drawings of both the Cupola and the Baptistery.

Giorgio Vasari (1511–74) admired Brunelleschi's Cupola and used it as a model for the Basilica of the Madonna dell'Umiltà (Pistoia) and the *tempietto* of Santo Stefano alla Vittoria (Foiano). In his famous *Lives of the Artists* he devotes considerable space to the building of the Cupola. Making substantial though unacknowledged use of Manetti's biography, he accentuates traits of character (especially Brunelleschi's cunning) and the dynamics of human relations (especially the rivalry between Brunelleschi and Ghiberti, already stressed by Manetti). His account amounts to a veritable historical novel, highly intelligent and fascinating to read, opening and closing with rhetorical flourishes: "The world having for so long been without artists of lofty soul or inspired talent, heaven ordained that it should receive from the hand of Filippo the greatest, the tallest, and the finest edifice of ancient and modern times, demonstrating that Tuscan genius, although moribund, was not yet dead"; "and it can be confidently asserted that the ancients never built to such a height nor risked challenging the sky itself, for it truly appears that this building challenges the heavens, soaring as it does to so great a height that it seems to measure up to the mountains around Florence".[6]

Vasari's nephew, Giorgio Vasari the Younger (1562–1625), drew a somewhat inaccurate section of the Cupola as part of a series of plans of Tuscan and Italian churches, palaces and villas (now in the Gabinetto Disegni e Stampe degli Uffizi). His drawing probably follows an early-16th-century one, possibly the earliest measured section drawing of the Cupola.

Also possibly derived from an earlier original is the section drawing of the Cupola and apse, possibly intended for printing, made by Ludovico Cardi da Cigoli known as Cigoli (1559–1613), who traced on the same sheet a comparison with the Pantheon and St Peter's in Rome. As has been noted, this drawing and the comparison with the other two domes reflect the experimental approach promoted by the studies of Galileo.[7]

With their fondness for virtuoso manipulation of the canonical rules and proportions, the mannerist architects of the 16th century showed great interest in the Cupola. Santi di Tito (1536–1603) even built a reduced version of it—one eighth of the Cupola's size—in the chapel of San Michele outside Barberino Valdelsa, completed in 1597.

Ferdinando (*c.* 1691–1741) and Giuseppe (d. 1772) Ruggieri's plan for the dome of the Princes' Chapel at San Lorenzo in Florence (1740) involved an octagonal pavilion with marble ribs, crowned by a lantern.

5.2. The Development of Scientific Studies

In the course of the 17th and 18th centuries, with the spreading influence of Galileo's scientific revolution, studies of the Cupola could no longer be limited to making drawings of it. Its form and properties (notably its cracks) were scientifically investigated, especially in connection with interventions on the structure. This marked the beginning of modern historical analysis and research.

We have no certain documentary evidence on when the cracks first appeared. Already in 1491 Luca Fancelli was called to Florence from Milan to study the fissures. In 1639 the architect of the Opera Gherardo Silvani (1579–1675) wrote a report on the Cupola's condition: the fissures, he judged, were not serious, and could be remedied by plastering and the use of metal brackets. On the same occasion the vertical drainpipes at the corners of the drum were replaced by new ones, covered with masonry and located along the two edges of the corner pilasters. According to Filippo Baldinucci, Silvani also replaced "in many places the big oaken chains which encircle the great Cupola, [and] which had suffered considerably" from the rainwater.[8]

In the late 17th century, amid growing fears for the stability of the structure (aroused by the new attention paid to the lesions, which were particularly extensive in the segments above the two sacristies), it was decided that maintenance repairs were not enough and that direct structural intervention would be necessary.

Giovan Battista Nelli (1661–1725), a member of an ancient Florentine family of lawyers and notaries, pupil of the Florentine scientist Vincenzo Viviani, made, from 1688 onwards, a series of technical drawings of the Cathedral and the Cupola, which were later published as copperplates by Bernardo Sansone Sgrilli in 1773 (*Descrizione e studi dell'insigne Fabbrica di S. Maria del Fiore*, 'Description and Studies of the Illustrious Edifice of Santa Maria del Fiore') and in later editions in 1755 and 1820. In 1695 a commission was appointed by Grand Duke Cosimo III, consisting of Nelli, Giovan Battista Foggini (the architect in charge of San Lorenzo and the Uffizi), the German-born craftsman Filippo Sengher, the physician and mathematician Vincenzo Viviani, and Father Guerrino Guerrini. The commission's report advocated encircling the Cupola with four iron chains. In January 1696, Nelli was appointed *provveditore* of the Opera di Santa Maria del Fiore. The need for intervention was also urged by Carlo Fontana and Filippo Baldinucci, but immediately af-

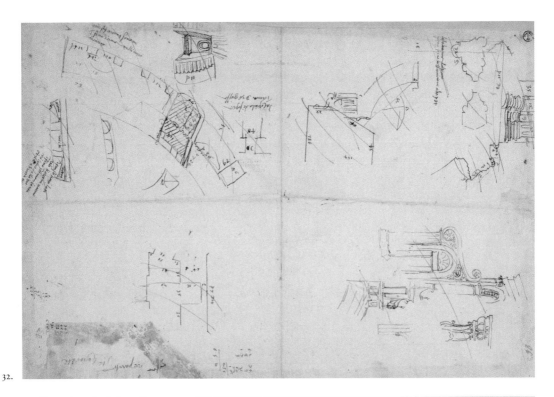

32.

32. Above, Antonio da Sangallo
the Younger, architectural sketches
of various details of the shape and
structure of the Cupola, *c.* 1520–1
(Florence, GDSU, 1130 A).

33. Right, Antonio da Sangallo
the Younger, drawing illustrating
the technique used for the "domes
of half-bricks (*mezzane*) such as are
built without centring in Florence",
c. 1520–1 (Florence, GDSU, 900 A).

34–5. Opposite, Antonio da Sangallo
the Younger, architectural sketches
of various details of the shape and
structure of the Cupola, *c.* 1520–1
(Florence, GDSU, 1164 A). Note
the detail featuring the special tiles
fixed to the shell with two nails.

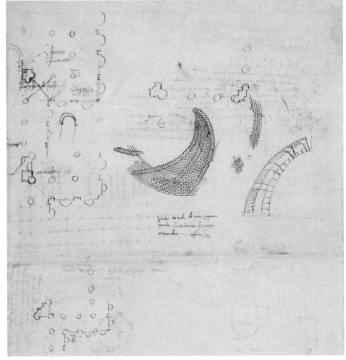

33.

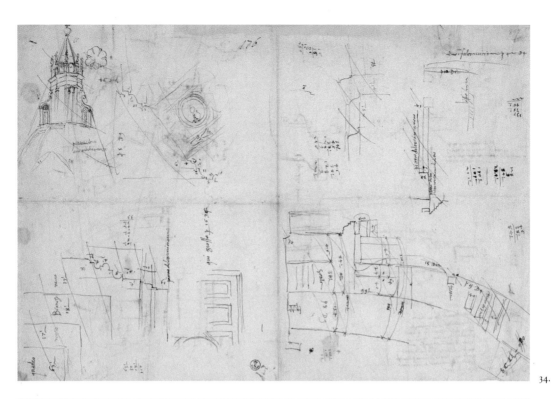

34.

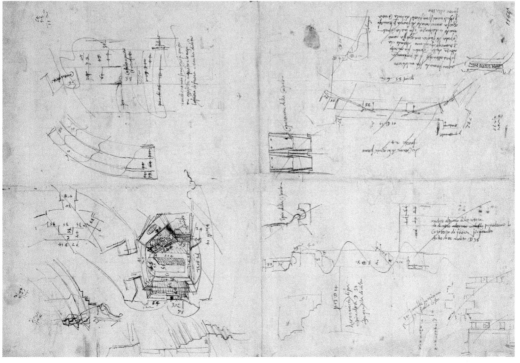

35.

36.

36. The chapel of San Michele Arcangelo in Val d'Elsa (1597), designed by Santi di Tito and based on Brunelleschi's Cupola on a scale reduced to one eighth.

37. Opposite, Giorgio Vasari the Younger, section of the Cupola, *c.* 1600 (Florence, GDSU, 4878 A).

38. [p. 68] The lantern damaged by lightning in 1601, in a drawing attributed to Alessandro Allori (Biblioteca Nazionale Centrale di Firenze, BNCF, MS II.I.429, fol. 33r).

39. [p. 69, top] The Cupola struck by lightning on 27 January 1601: in this fanciful representation, the bolt of lightning is launched by Zeus (Oxford, Ashmolean Museum).

40. [p. 69, bottom] Jacques Callot, *Grand Duke Ferdinando I Examining the Plan of the Lantern for the Cupola of Florence Cathedral*, burin engraving after a drawing by Matteo Rosselli, *c.* 1619–20 (BNCF, "Battaglie dei Medici", Cappugi 486, Plate 1).

37.

38.

39.

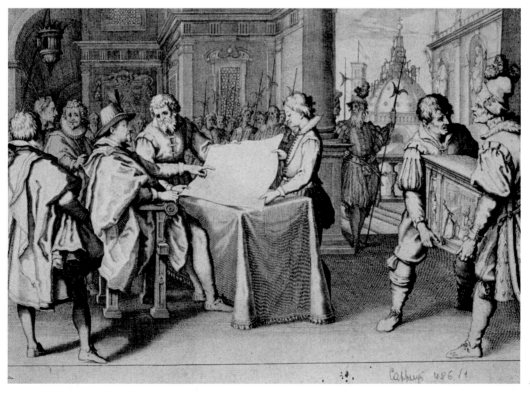

40.

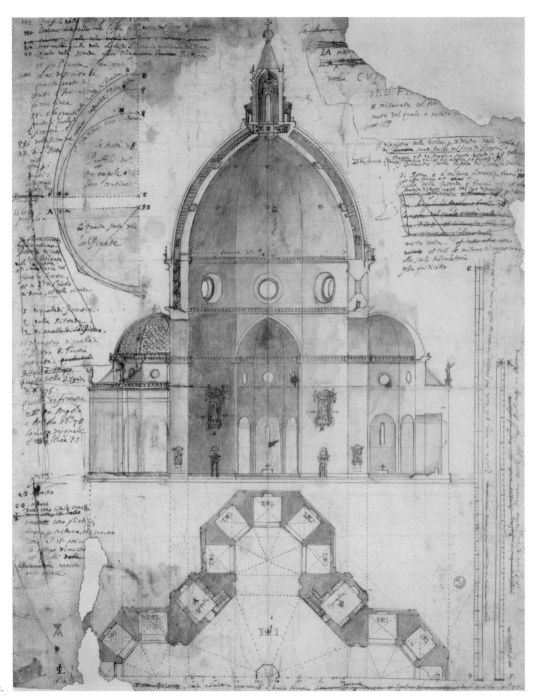

41.

42.

41. Opposite, Ludovico Cardi known as Cigoli, plan and section of the Cupola and apse, 1610 (Florence, GDSU, 7980 Ar). In the top left of the illustration, the Cupola is compared with the Pantheon and with St Peter's in Rome (plan and profile).

42. Above, Giulio Parigi, panel in semi-precious stones, gold and diamonds depicting Grand Duke Cosimo II in prayer, ex-voto for the altar of St Charles Borromeo in Milan Cathedral, *c.* 1617–24 (Florence, Pitti Palace, Silver Museum, inv. Gemme 488).

43. [p. 72] The Cupola seen from the Uffizi piazza in a drawing by Justus Suttermans, *c.* 1620–30 (Florence, GDSU, 2653 S).

44. [p. 73, top] The image of the Cupola used as a demonstration of the camera obscura, in a drawing attributed to Stefano della Bella and forming part of a manuscript about military fortifications, *c.* 1650 (Washington, Library of Congress, Rosenwald Collection).

45. [p. 73, bottom] The view of the Cathedral introducing *Firenze città nobilissima illustrata*, the first guide to Florence for visitors but also for local scholars and enthusiasts; the volume was dedicated by its author, Ferdinando Leopoldo Del Migliore, to Cosimo III in 1684. The use of a distorted, wide-angle perspective to take in a monument which, due its topographic position, is never visible in its entirety from the streets and the piazza, was to become a recurrent feature in the 18th and 19th-century urban iconography of Florence, and was also adopted by some of the pioneers of photography (→ Fig. 100).

43.

44.

45.

46. Below, Valerio Spada, *View of the City of Florence from the Field of the Fathers of San Francesco al Monte*, *c.* 1650 (this perhaps marks the first use of the Italian word *veduta*). The viewpoint from this church (now known as San Salvatore) later became popular with tourists, and ultimately led to the construction of Piazzale Michelangelo.

47. Opposite, Israël Silvestre, rear view of Santa Maria del Fiore (private collection).

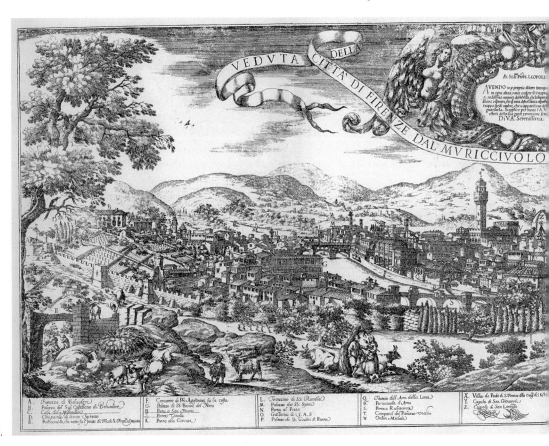

46.

47.

ter the proposed measures for encircling the Cupola had been officially approved, Alessandro Cecchini had two unsigned manuscripts delivered to the Grand Duke: they would be published only in 1753 by Giovan Battista Clemente Nelli, Giovan Battista's son, under the title *Due Ragionamenti sopra le Cupole di Alessandro Cecchini Architetto* ('Two Considerations Concerning Domes by Alessandro Cecchini, Architect'), together with the *Discorsi di architettura del Senatore Giovan Batista [sic] Nelli* ('Architectural Discourses of Senator Giovan Battista Nelli'). Cecchini attributed the fissures to subsidence of the foundations, arguing that the weight of the shells was pressing inwards and not outwards, so that encircling them with chains would prove useless, and might actually make matters worse. Work was suspended, and Nelli 'repented' of his earlier views; after an official investigation ordered by the Grand Duke in 1697, he produced a new report with conclusions opposite to those of 1695.

In 1748 the Paduan mathematician and engineer Giovanni Poleni, who had studied the lesions of the dome of St Peter's, was invited by Domenico Maria Manni to examine the Florentine Cupola. He ascribed the fissures primarily to the action of the Cupola's dead weight and not to foundation subsidence, and he therefore reiterated the need to encircle the structure with chains. In addition he studied the curvature of the Cupola with original methods which led him to define it as a 'catenary' (→ Glossary). His studies and intuitions regarding the structure of the Cupola remain of the greatest interest to this day.

In 1757 the Jesuit astronomer Leonardo Ximenes measured and catalogued the fissures. As regards the statics of the Cupola, he attributed an active function to the horizontal arches and clarified the structural role of the *macigno* stone chains. Ximenes also noted the 'slack-line' course of the brickwork.

In 1812, Domenico Moreni published for the first time the anonymous *Life of Brunelleschi*, later attributed to Manetti, together with Filippo Baldinucci's interpretation. The foundations for Brunelleschi scholarship had been laid.

In 1857 Cesare Guasti—a scholar from Prato who in 1850 had been appointed archivist to the Opera del Duomo and later became director of the local State Archives and member of the Accademia della Crusca—published a massive quantity of documents from the archives of the Opera in *La Cupola di Santa Maria del Fiore*. These documents offered the basis for a scholarly reconstruction of the history of the Cupola to set against the anecdotal tradition derived from Manetti. In 1885 the architect Aristide Nardini Despotti Mospignotti, from Livorno, published *Filippo di Ser Brunellesco e la Cupola del Duomo di Firenze*, which sought to reconstruct the building's history on the basis of the Opera's documents. Following the earthquake of 18 May 1885, Luigi del Moro, architect to the Opera, produced a report in which he noted an increase in the lesions of the Cupola as a result of the seismic disturbance. Some small-scale repair work was carried out as a result.

Surveys and technical drawings of the Cupola were made in the 1880s. The plates published by Paul Laspeyres in *Die Kirchen der Renaissance in Mittel-Italien* (Berlin–Stuttgart 1882) are substantially derived from those of Nelli. Of more interest is the contribution of Josef Durm, professor of architecture at the Technische Hochschule in Karlsruhe, who in his 1887 article on "Die Domkuppel in Florenz und die Kuppel der Peterskirche in Rom" cast light on aspects of the construction of the Cupola. Carl von Stegmann, collaborating with Heinrich von Geymüller on the monumental work *Die Architektur der Renaissance in Toscana*,[9] produced an elegant series of drawings of the Cupola. In 1892

Cornelius von Fabriczy published a major monograph on Brunelleschi (*Brunelleschi, sein Leben und seine Werke*) where he confirmed, with some qualifications, Karl Frey's reappraisal of Ghiberti's role in the planning of the Cupola.

In the late 1930s Hans Siebenhuber made a series of metric drawings of various portions of the Cupola, and in 1941 Piero Sanpaolesi published *La cupola di Santa Maria del Fiore*, in which he advanced theories on certain aspects of the building technique, demonstrating them with drawings.

Between 1934 and 1937 a commission headed by the Opera's architect, Rodolfo Sabatini, and including Pier Luigi Nervi, produced a detailed study of the statics of the Cathedral, Campanile and Baptistery.[10] Accurate drawings of the structure and its lesions were made by Giulio Padelli. The first sensors for measuring the cyclical movement of the lesions were installed; the yielding of the octagonal ring at the base of the Cupola and the consequent development of lesions in the segments were generally attributed to thermal factors. It became clear that it would be necessary to extend the investigation, hitherto restricted to the lesions, to the overall structure of the Cupola. These studies were carried out by the commission operating between 1950 and 1953, and, from 1975, by a ministry-appointed commission headed by Guglielmo De Angelis d'Ossat.

In 1970 Frank D. Prager and Gustina Scaglia published *Brunelleschi. Studies of his technology and inventions*, a study of some technological features of the Cupola. In 1971 a careful photogrammetric survey was carried out.[11] In 1977 Salvatore Di Pasquale published "Una ipotesi sulla struttura della cupola di Santa Maria del Fiore", in which, stressing the importance of the 'slack-line' brickwork, he emphasised the analogy between the octagonal dome and a rotationally symmetric vault.

In 1983, following further concerns given a prominent airing in the local press, the Ministry of the Cultural and Environmental Heritage reactivated the commission headed by Guglielmo De Angelis d'Ossat, dividing it into three sub-committees for paintings, surveys and structures, the latter headed by Carlo Cestelli Guidi. This commission, together with the CRIS–ENEL (the national electricity board's centre for hydraulic and structural research) and in collaboration with the Faculty of Engineering of the University of Florence, carried out extensive structural analysis, making use of sophisticated mathematical models. Then a permanent monitoring system was installed by the ISMES (the experimental institute for models and structures), and a further *in situ* survey was carried out on the mechanical characteristics of the Cupola and on the tensional state of the brickwork. A report produced in 1985 gave detailed information on the extent and location of the fissures, and an innovative interpretation was given of their cause (in terms of the nature and origin of the building) and of their development from the point of view of structural mechanics. Emphasis was placed on the fact that ever since its construction the Cupola has exercised a uniformly distributed pressure on the drum, which, assuming 'deep-beam' behaviour (→ Part Two), in turn receives pressure from below, concentrated in the area of the four supporting piers. As the result of tensional forces, the lesions have appeared above the round windows on the even sides and below the round windows on the odd sides of the octagon. The development of fissures has been caused, secondarily, by the recurrence of thermal forces and exceptional events.

48. Giovan Battista Nelli, survey sketch of one of the cracks in the Cupola, 13 June 1690.

49–51. Below and opposite, report on the condition of the cracks in the Cupola drawn up by Pietro Guerrini, Superintendent of Fortresses, in January 1691 (ASF, Miscellanea Medicea 366 II, fols. 1352r, 1353r and 1354r). The report includes drawings and plans: a section; a plan showing the horizontal arches linking the spurs, drawn as an unbroken span from one corner to the next; a partial section of a segment, where "certain junctions of stone" are indicated with the letter O; details of the "cornerpieces", showing the rotten wooden chains. Guerrini remarks that some of the cracks are old, and that they are a cause for concern not so much in normal conditions as in the event of earthquakes or lightning strikes. He also reports on the state of the wooden chains. His hypothesis that there are unbroken horizontal arches from one corner to the next appears unfounded.

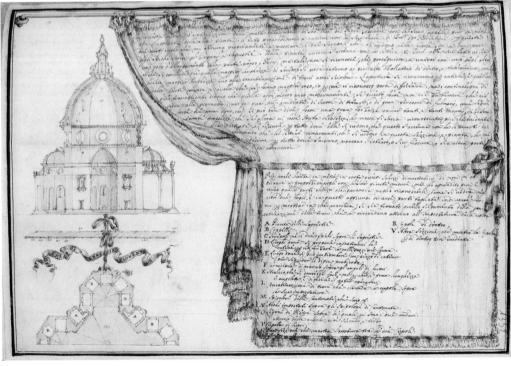

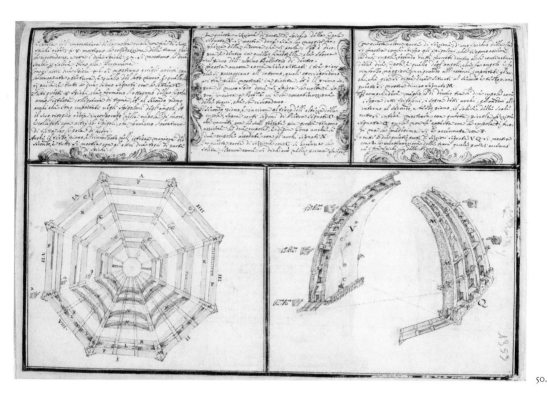

50.

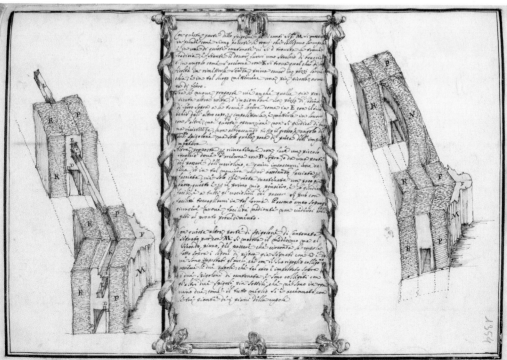

51.

52. Vincenzo Viviani, sketch showing two damaged areas of the Cupola (BNCF, MS Gal. 222, fol. 112r). Viviani was a member of the commission which argued in its 1695 report that it was necessary to encircle the Cupola with four iron chains at different elevations.

53. Opposite, "Measures to be taken regarding the principal cracks in the Cupola" (BNCF, MS Gal. 222, fol. 120r). The document proposes a method for investigating whether the cracks are due to subsidence of the foundations or to the weight of the structure.

52.

Diligente da farsi d'nuovo intorno agli terzoli
maggiori della Cupola.

Perchianisi senza che possa darvisi eccessione, et avvenir d'quen
dubbio, tanto delle due parti volte, delle due facce dell ottagono
tanto nella Cupola esterna che nell'interna, o sia moto all'ingiù
o per cagione d'abbassamenti et fendo, a quella soprapposta o se l'abbia all'infuori
per cagione della spinta del persuagione si potrebbe o per ciò.

Verso sia massima larghetta d'tali terzoli

Figuriamori che la ABCD sia una
faccia interna della Cupola esterna sia A
e che la EFGH sia l'esterna faccia
della Cupola interna nelle quali
siano gli terzoli GI, KL
corrispondenti, e che alla
medesima dal primo dellandito
resasi tre l'an e le l'al
faccia sia scalizato uno
spazio retangolo di larghezza

grandezza d'un braccio in
e a le si d'un ... si voleva da qual rettagoli pigli, e qual
della anno dell'ottone ... meno facevi due s dallo terzoli
e scoperto che questo sia più sì come alla più delle nettere ong... lo
facciasi questo annotare in modo che non essendosi ella direti
dare quello n'tavoli un effetto piano, e quanto sia possibile
e fecisi benele d'un s da d'terzolo. Di poi sopra amen
due questi piani annotati e lisci, con un regolo d'un
metallo lungo almeno un braccio si segni le due linee rette
ST, le quali appunto si però, tornino su un medesimo piano ortì
segnate l'una e l'altra faccia ABCD, EFGH e tagli d'sorindi
queste rette si facciano ... graffite o coll'inchiostro
... ... inscrissioni in S T. Di poi ... tutto
sotto lo se appuntati na'buoi esterni e da fermati in tutti quando
e coglia, si piglino in croce le due d'ittuale da 1. a 4.
si come le altre due da 3 a T. Le quali si non smer
vi sie, si trasporto d'nolla in volta sopra bree rette
primer, sopra quella lamina d'ottone o d'rame, continuando le
... ... Venisi su la nettera, con la mettera
ST. Fatti ciò, si semi tre chiavi d'uno da tenersi di più d'uso
et fatto e l'adito si che niun altro potria veder tali segni non che potere
li e poi d'mese in mese si veda e per la ricognitione d'tali d'ittuale prese
che se non si trovera mutasione, in alcune, si potrà affermar che in tali terzoli
ancora ella sia seguita.

53.

54. Opposite, *Descrizione e studi dell'insigne Fabbrica di S. Maria del Fiore, Metropolitana Fiorentina in varie carte intagliati da Bernardo Sansone Sgrilli architetto e dal medesimo dedicati all'Altezza Reale Gio. Gastone I Granduca di Toscana* ('Description and Studies of the Illustrious Edifice of Santa Maria del Fiore, the Metropolitan Cathedral of Florence, Produced in Various Sheets by Bernardo Sansone Sgrilli, Architect, and Dedicated by Him to His Royal Highness Gian Gastone I, Grand Duke of Tuscany': Florence, 1733), Plate I. In 1688 Giovan Battista Nelli (1661–1725)—who belonged to an ancient Florentine family of lawyers and notaries, and studied philosophy at the University of Pisa and later, in Florence, became a student of the scientist Vincenzo Viviani and the sculptor and architect Giovan Battista Foggini—produced a series of drawings of the Cathedral and the Cupola, subsequently copper-etched and published by Bernardo Sansone Sgrilli in 1733, together with some of his own drawings. This splendid work is still invaluable today. In 1687 Nelli had realised a series of drawings (now housed in the Uffizi) of Michelangelo's architectural work in the church of San Lorenzo, which was close to his family's properties. Nelli's original drawings of the Cathedral and the Cupola have not survived, possibly because they were used in the etching process. As represented here, the irregularities in the Cupola have been corrected: for instance, the sides of the drum are all the same length in the drawings, and the 'slack-line' course of the brickwork in the segments is not depicted. It is also worth pointing out that Sgrilli etched five of Zocchi's twenty-four views of Florence, including the one depicting Piazza del Duomo (→ Fig. 76).

55. [p. 84] *Descrizione e studi*, Plate II. Note the substantial walls in the apse beneath the Cupola; built inside these walls are the stairways climbing to the apsidioles. The planes of the sections in the following plates are visible.

56. [p. 85] *Descrizione e studi*, Plate III. Note the stairways emerging in the apsidioles and the ones built in the four massive supporting sides of the drum, which lead to the springing line of the Cupola.

57. [p. 86] *Descrizione e studi*, Plate IV: longitudinal section of the Cathedral along the midline of the Cupola and the east apse (the A–B line in Plate II). At the top right, the Cupola's plan and profile are compared to the Pantheon and St Peter's, as had already been done by Cigoli (→ Fig. 41). The illustration does not feature the pointed blind windows in the two arches adjacent to the façade, because they were built at a later date.

58. [p. 87] *Descrizione e studi*, Plate V: cross-section of the Cathedral along the midline of the Cupola and the north and south apses (the I–K line in Plate II).

59. [p. 88] *Descrizione e studi*, Plate VI: north elevation of the Cathedral. The exterior gallery at the base of the Cupola, designed by Baccio d'Agnolo, is depicted as if it had been realised on all sides of the octagon, as in Zocchi's views (→ Figs. 75–6).

60. [p. 89] *Descrizione e studi*, Plates VII and VIII. The plan shows the top of the drum. The paler-shaded areas indicate empty spaces in the underlying piers and the stairways leading to the internal walkway.

61. [p. 90] *Descrizione e studi*, Plate IX: in the drawing the two shells start to close in simultaneously at the level of the wooden chain, while this actually happens a little above the chain; it is also possible to see the inner shell closing in between the third and fourth walkway, whereas the closing in of the outer shell between the second and third walkway is not indicated. The M–O line represents the radius of the pointed fifth, but in actual fact this curvature can only be found in the angles of the octagon, while the section line

of the segments tends to an ellipse. In 1970 a working group headed by Mario Fondelli ascertained that the profiles of the external ribs and of the internal edges are not parallel, as the ellipses are different. The exterior gallery at the base of the Cupola is depicted as if it had been realised along the entire perimeter of the octagon, and not, as is actually the case, along just one side.

62. [p. 91] *Descrizione e studi*, Plate X: the drawing does not depict the 'slack-line' course of the platform at the base of the lantern.

63. [p. 92] *Descrizione e studi*, Plate XI.

64. [p. 93] *Descrizione e studi*, Plate XII: once again, the drawing does not depict the 'slack-line' course of the brickwork in the segments.

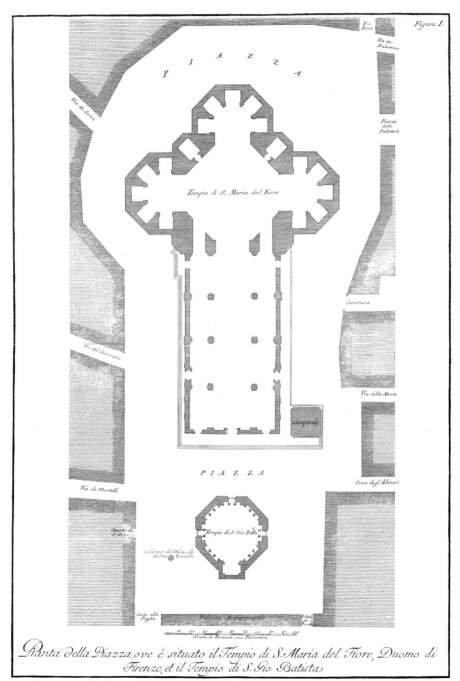

Figura I.

Pianta della Piazza, ove é situato il Tempio di S. Maria del Fiore, Duomo di Firenze, et il Tempio di S. Gio. Batista

54.

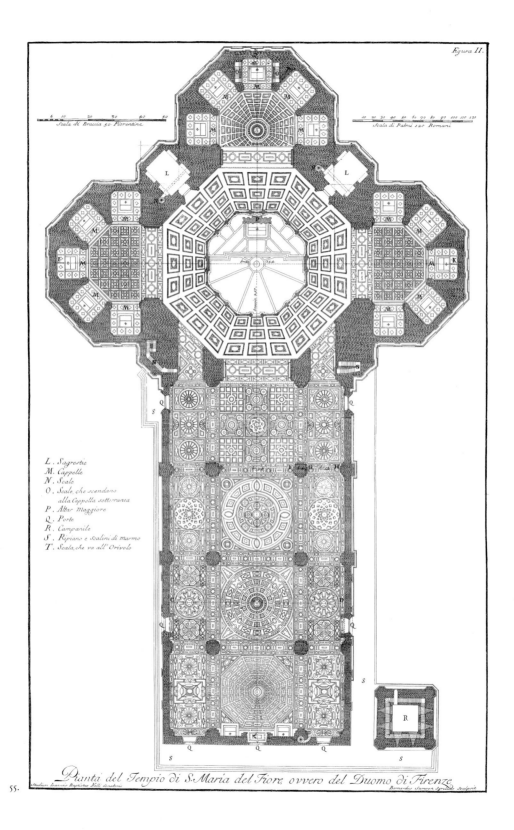

Figura II.

Scala di Braccia 50 Fiorentine

10 20 30 40 50 60 70 80 90 100 110 120
Scala di Palmi 120 Romani

L . Sagrestie
M . Cappelle
N . Scale
O . Scale che scendono
     alla Cappella sotterranea
P . Altar Maggiore
Q . Porte
R . Campanile
S . Ripiano e scalini di marmo
T . Scala che va all'Orivolo

Pianta del Tempio di S.Maria del Fiore, ovvero del Duomo di Firenze

55.

Studium Joannis Baptistæ Nelli senatoris

Bernardus Sansone Sgrilli Sculpsit

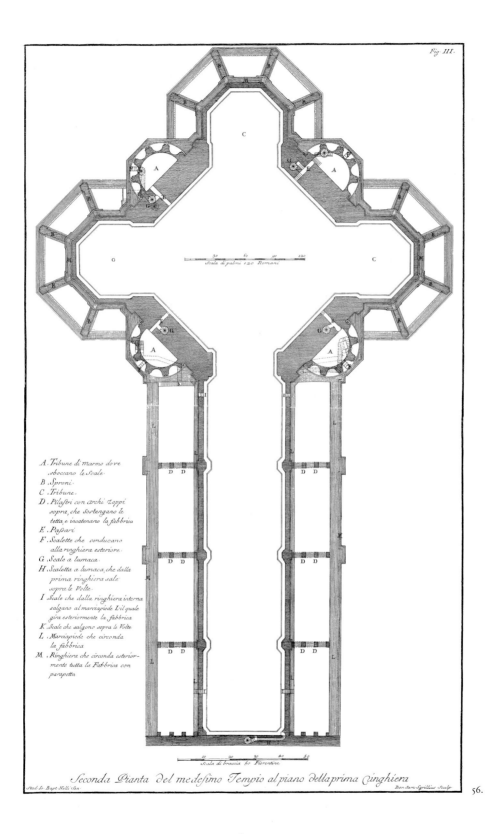

Fig. III.

A. Tribune di marmo dove
   sboccano le Scale.
B. Sproni.
C. Tribune.
D. Pilastri con archi zioppi
   sopra, che sostengano le
   tetta, e incatenano la fabbrica
E. Passari
F. Scalette che conducano
   alla ringhiera esteriore.
G. Scale a lumaca.
H. Scaletta a lumaca, che dalla
   prima ringhiera sale
   sopra le Volte.
I. Scale che dalla ringhiera interna
   salgano al marciapiede L'il quale
   gira esteriormente la fabbrica
K. Scale che salgono sopra le Volte
L. Marciapiede che circonda
   la fabbrica
M. Ringhiera che circonda esterior-
   mente tutta la Fabbrica con
   parapetto

Scala di palmi 120 Romani

Scala di braccia 50 Fiorentine.

Seconda Pianta del medesimo Tempio al piano della prima Cinghiera

Stud. Io. Bapt. Nolli Sen.   Ben. Sam. Sgrillius Sculp.   56.

85

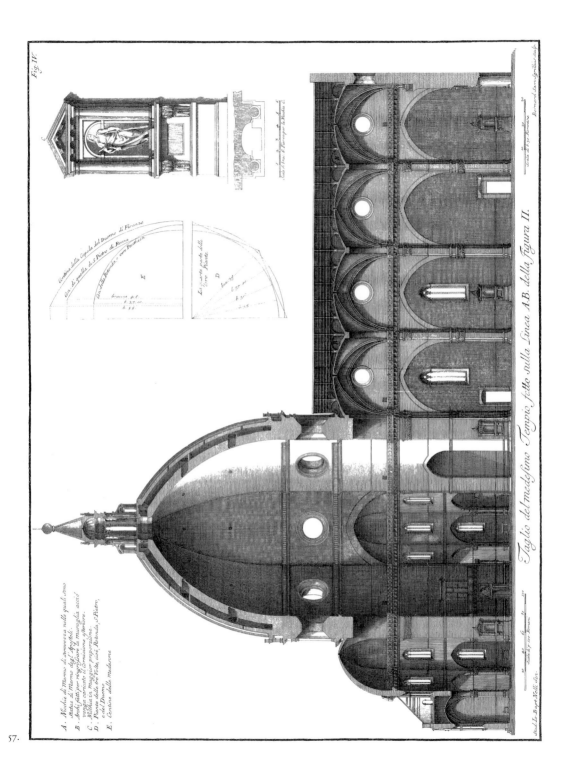

Fig. IV.

A. Nicchia di Marmo di domestica nelle quali sono
　fatte di Marmo degli Apostoli.
B. Archi fatti per rispondere la muraglia acciò
　venga caricata la Cornione ulteriore.
C. Nicchia in maggior proporzione.
D. Pianta delle tre Volte, cioè, Rotonda, S. Pietro,
　e del Duomo.
E. Centina della Madonna.

Centina della Cupla del Duomo di Firenze
Gr. di quella di S. Pietro di Roma.
Gr. della Rotonda, ovvero Pantheon.

Taglio del medesimo Tempio fatto sulla Linea A.B. della Figura II.

Fig V.

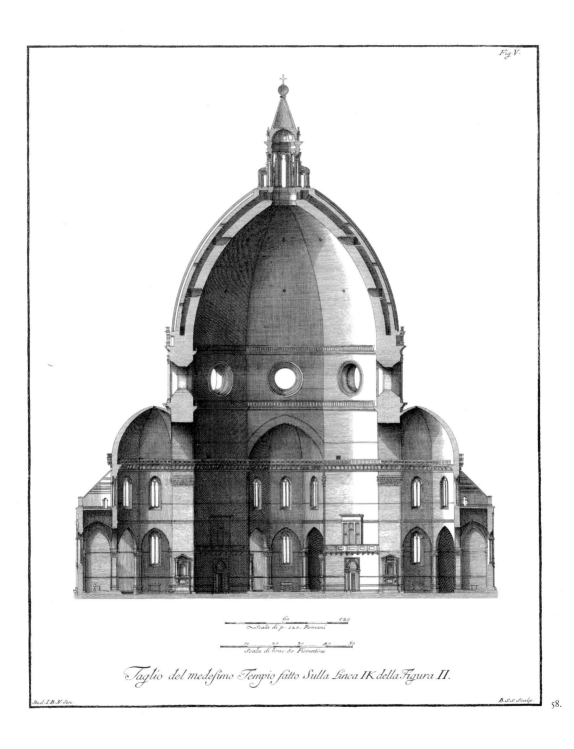

Scala di p. 120. Romani

Scala di brac 50 Fiorentine.

Taglio del medesimo Tempio fatto Sulla Linea IK della Figura II.

Stud. I.B.N. Sen.

B. S. S. Sculp.

58.

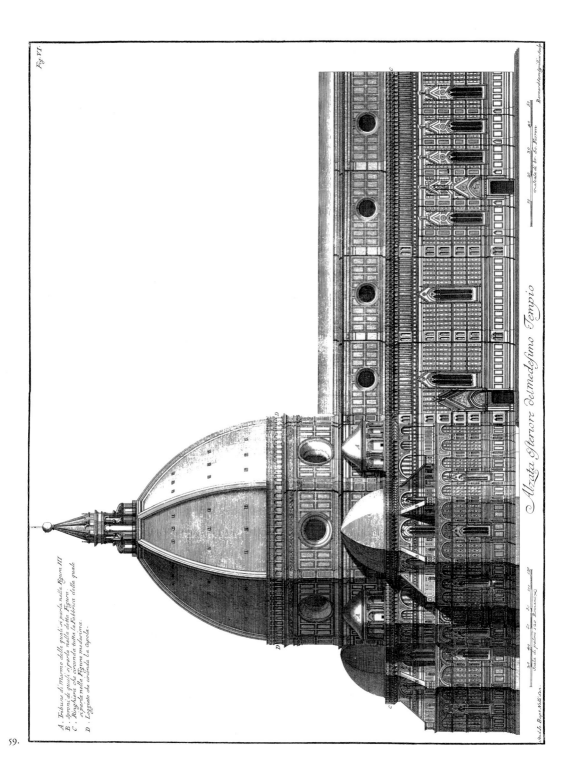

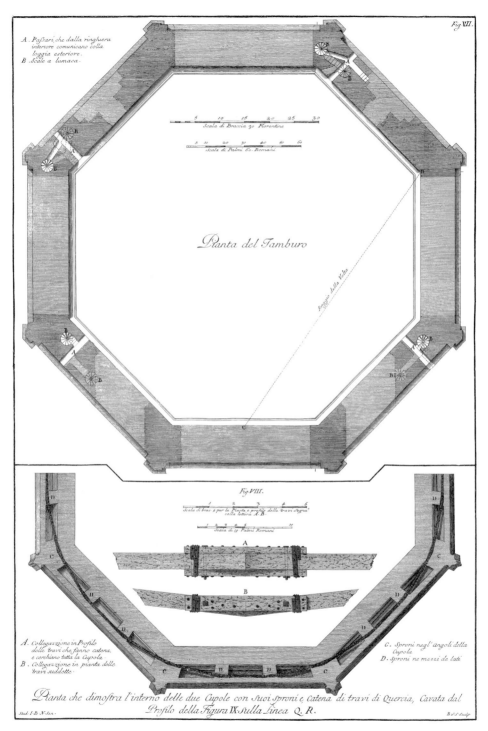

Fig.VII.

A. Passari, che dalla ringhiera
interiore comunicano colla
loggia esteriore.
B. Scale a lumaca.

5   10   15   20   25   30
Scala di Braccia 30 Fiorentine

5   10   20   30   40   50   60
Scala di Palmi 60. Romani

Pianta del Tamburo

Reggio della Volta

Fig.VIII.

1   2   3   4   5
Scala di brac. 5 per la Pianta, e profilo delle travi segnia
colla lettera A. B.

1   5   10
Scala di 15 Palmi Romani

A

B

A. Collocazzione in Profilo
delle travi che fanno catena,
e cerchiano tutta la Cupola.
B. Collocazzione in pianta delle
travi suddette.

C. Sproni negl'angoli della
Cupola.
D. Sproni ne mezzi de lati.

Pianta che dimostra l'interno delle due Cupole con Suoi Sproni e Catena di travi di Quercia, Cavata dal
Profilo della Figura IX. sulla Linea Q. R.

Stud. I. B. N. Sen.

B. S. S. Sculp.

60.

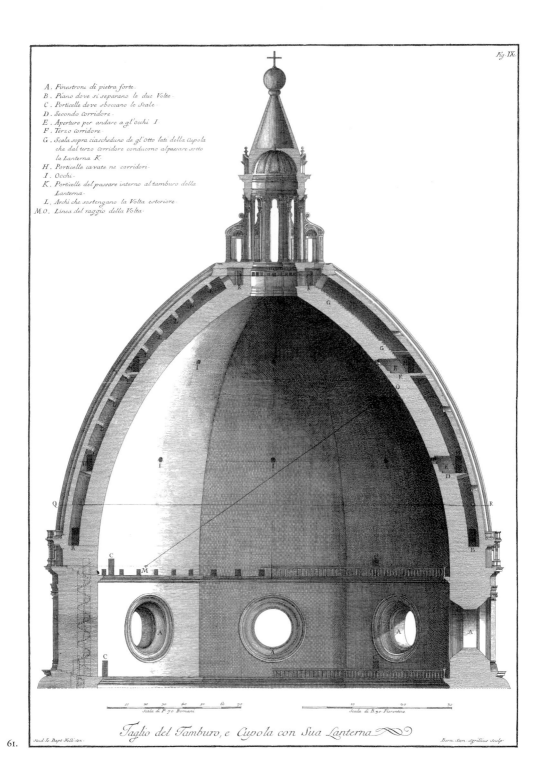

Fig. IX.

A . Finestrone di pietra forte.
B . Piano dove si separano le due Volte.
C . Porticelle dove sboccano le Scale.
D . Secondo corridore.
E . Aperture per andare a gl'occhi I
F . Terzo corridore.
G . Scala sopra ciascheduno de gl'Otto lati della Cupola
    che dal terzo corridore conducono al passare sotto
    la Lanterna K.
H . Porticelle cavate ne' corridori.
I . Occhi.
K . Porticelle del passare interno al tamburo della
    Lanterna.
L . Archi che sostengano la Volta esteriore.
M.O . Linea del raggio della Volta.

Scala di P. 70 Romani

Scala di B. 30 Fiorentina

Taglio del Tamburo, e Cupola con Sua Lanterna

Stud: Io: Bapt: Nelli del.

Bern: Sam: Sgrillius sculp.

61.

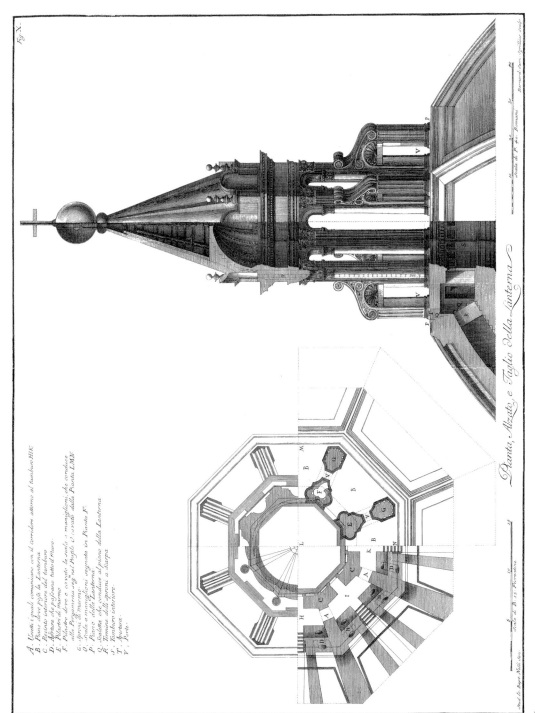

Fig. X.

A. Uccelli i quali comunicano con il corridore attorno al tamburo HIK
B. Piano dove posa la Lanterna
C. Recinto interiore del tamburo
D. Apertura che passano tutto il muro
E. Pilastri di marmo
F. Pilastro dove e cavato la scala i maniglioni, che conduce
   alla Pergomena veg nel Profilo e s'orato dalla Pianta LMN
G. Apertura di marmo.
O. Scala a maniglioni vegnata in Pianta F.
P. Piano della Lanterna.
Q. Scaletta che conduce al piano della Lanterna
R. Termine delle apertura a scarpa
S. Tamburo interiore
T. Apertura
V. Porte.

Pianta, Alzato, e Taglio della Lanterna

Scala di B. 15 Fiorentini

Scala di P. 40 Romani

Prod. G. Bapt. Nolli Gro.   Bernard Sans Spolino Sculp

62.

Fig XI

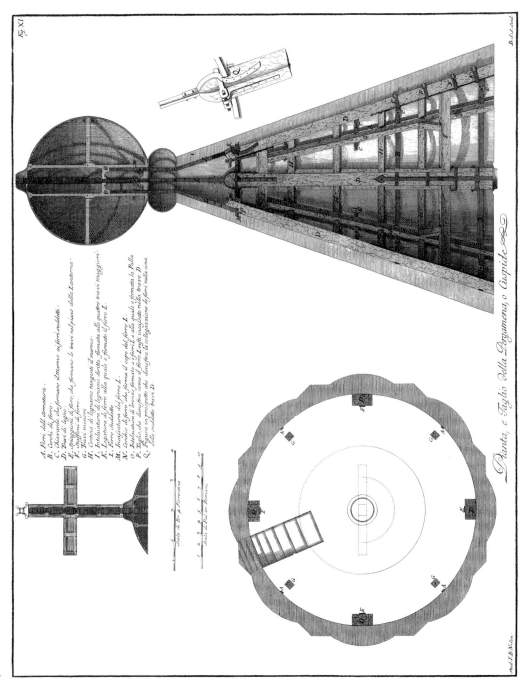

A. Ferri dell'armatura.
B. Cocchi del ferro.
C. Chiavardo che formano il Marmo ai fori suddetti.
D. Travi di legno.
E. Spranghe di ferro, che formano le travi nel piano della Lanterna.
F. Staffone di ferro.
G. Travi minori.
H. Cantoni di legname tangenti al marmo.
I. Intelaiatura di legname diritto, formata alla quattro tra vi maggiori.
K. Ligatura di ferro alla quale è formato il ferro I.
L. Ferro suddetto.
M. Inchiodatura del ferro I.
N. Cocchio di ferro che forma il capo del ferro I.
O. Intelaiatura di travesi formata a spirale alla quale è formata la Palla.
P. Ferro di destra come il ferro I, retto incaficato nella trave D.
Q. Taglio che dimostra come il ferro I, sia incaficato nella trave D.
   nella suddette travi D.

Scala di Br. 4 Fiorentine

Scala di Pal.10 Romani

Pianta, e Taglio della Pergamena, o Cuspide

incid.I.B.Nolin.

B.C.c.del.

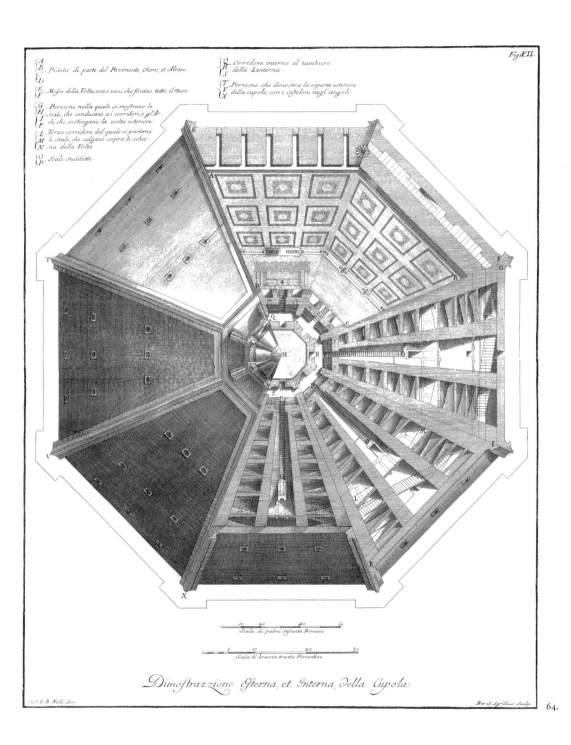

Fig.XII.

A
B .. Pianta di parte del Pavimento, Choro, et Altare.
D
E
F .. Mossa della Volta, con i vani che forano tutto il muro.

G
H .. Porzione nella quale si mostrano le
I .. Scale, che conducano a'i corridori, e gl'Ar-
L .. chi che sostengano la volta esteriore.

L .. Terzo corridore, dal quale si partono
M .. le Scale, che salgano sopra la schie-
N .. na della Volta.

O
P .. Scale suddette.

Q
R .. Corridore intorno al tamburo
S .. della Lanterna.

T
V .. Porzione, che dimostra la coperta esteriore
X .. della cupola, con i costoloni negl'angoli.

Scala di palmi sessanta Romani.

Scala di braccia trenta Fiorentine.

Dimostrazzione Esterna, et Interna della Cupola

Dis.Io.B.Nolli Sen.   Ben.S.Sgrillius Sculp.

64.

93

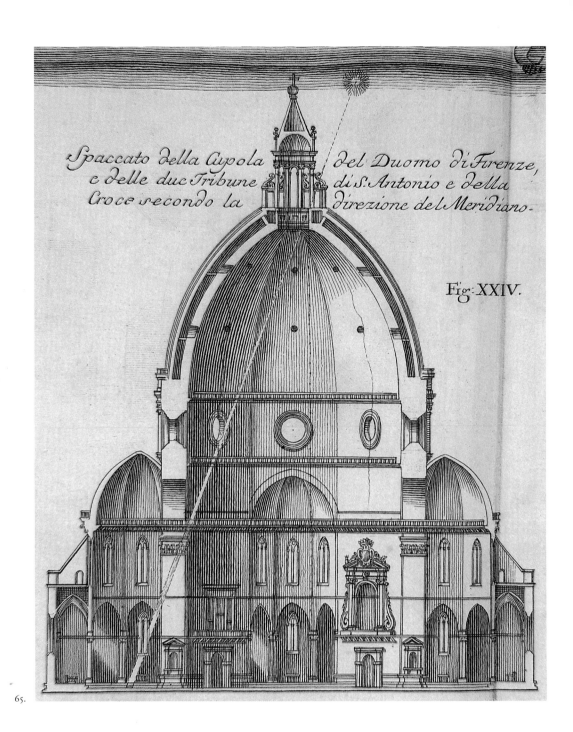

Spaccato della Cupola del Duomo di Firenze,
e delle due Tribune di S. Antonio e della
Croce secondo la direzione del Meridiano.

Fig. XXIV.

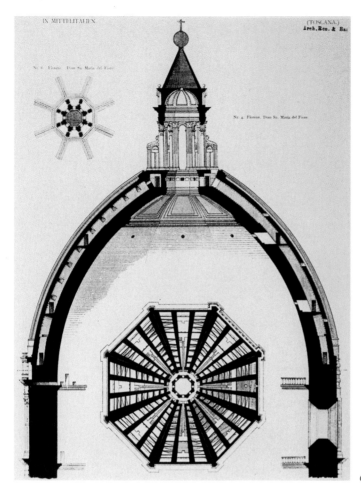

66.

65. Opposite, Leonardo Ximenes, section of the Cupola, viewed from the east, showing the ray of sunlight required to conduct the astronomical experiment, from *Del vecchio e nuovo gnomone Fiorentino* (Florence, 1757). Two of the cracks in the inner shell are clearly indicated.

66. Above, Paul Laspeyres, section and plan of the Cupola, from *Die Kirchen der Renaissance in Mittel-Italien* (Berlin–Stuttgart, 1882).

67. [p. 96] Carl von Stegmann, view of the Cupola, 1885.

68. [p. 97, top left] Carl von Stegmann, section and elevation of the Cupola, from *Die Architektur der Renaissance in Toscana* (Munich, 1885–1909).

69. [p. 97, top right] Josef Durm, "Die Domkuppel in Florenz und die Kuppel der Peterskirche in Rom", *Zeitschrift für Bauwesen* 37 (1887), Plate 43.

70. [p. 97, bottom] Giovanni Battista Milani, comparison between the double-shell structures of the Baptistery and the Cupola, from *L'ossatura murale: studio statico-costruttivo ed estetico-proporzionale degli organismi architettonici, con speciale riferimento alle strutture elastiche nelle loro varie e moderne applicazioni pratiche* ('The wall structure: a study of the statics, construction, aesthetics and proportions of the architectural members, with special reference to the various and modern practical applications of elastic structures'; Turin, 1920–6).

67.

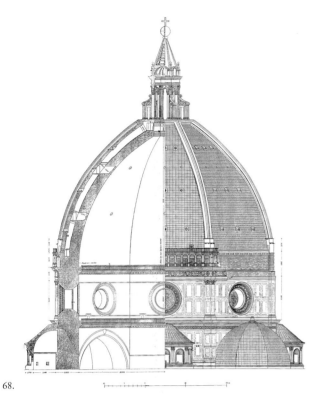

68.

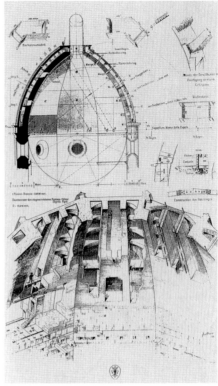

69.

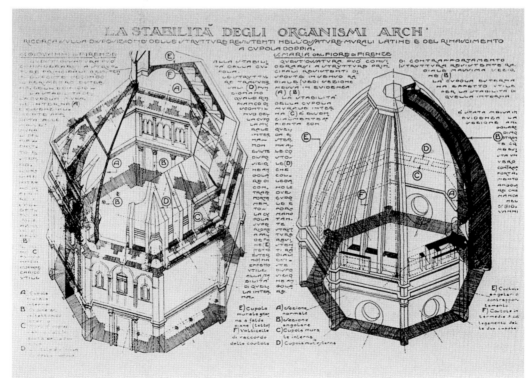

70.

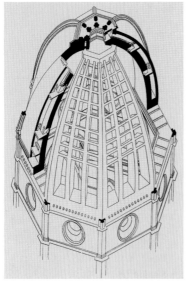

71.   72.

71–2. Above, Piero Sanpaolesi, axonometric view of the structure of the Cupola and detail of a corner between two sides, with a hypothetical rendering of the herringbone brickwork, from *La cupola di Santa Maria del Fiore: il progetto, la costruzione* (Rome, 1941).

73. The extrados of one of the Cupola's segments in the course of work to restore the roof tiling: note the 'slack-line' course of the brickwork in the segment and the curvature of the cornice at the base of the lantern (photograph by Salvatore Di Pasquale, *c.* 1980).

73.

THE IMAGE OF THE CUPOLA:
MOUNTAIN OR LIVING BEING?

6.1. Iconography of the Cupola

The Cupola inspired painters from the moment it was finished, especially in relation to the new science of perspective developed by Brunelleschi himself. Technical innovations in the arts followed one another in quick succession, especially from the mid 15th century. The invention of oil paints, the widespread use of large canvases, the employment of preparatory cartoons for frescoes, the extensive use of woodcuts, and the invention of metal engraving (attributed by Vasari to the Florentine Maso Finiguerra) all reflect the newly developed taste for perspectival, graphic composition and permitted the widespread circulation of visual images. For a long time the Cupola would not be depicted on his own, but as part of a bird's-eye view of the city, widely used as a background for religious paintings or portraits, in which Florence appears as the ideal city clustered around it—e.g. in works by Verrocchio, Filippino Lippi (→ Fig. 19), Jacopo del Sellaio, Piero del Pollaiolo (→ Fig. 16), Sandro Botticelli (→ Fig. 22)—, or else as a work of art in its own right, beginning with the famous view known as *della Catena* ('of the Chain'), attributed to Francesco Rosselli and dating to the period between 1471 and 1482. This view is one of the highest achievements of the Florentine perspectival tradition, and marks a fundamental advance in the history of the iconography of Florence, and more generally in the representation of the city in western culture.

If we exclude simple, stylised images such as the miniature by Giovanni di Paolo (→ Fig. 13) dating from around 1435, the first painted representation of the Cupola is perhaps the one that appears in the background of the painting celebrating Dante Alighieri and his *Commedia*, painted for the Cathedral in 1465—with daring anachronism—by Domenico di Michelino (→ Fig. 14) after a drawing by Alessio Baldovinetti. It is a realistic, readily visible depiction which has been highly influential.

In a painting showing the *Archangels Michael, Raphael and Gabriel with young Tobias* and dating from around 1471 (→ Fig. 15), Biagio d'Antonio (*c.* 1446–1516) introduces a new vantage point—Florence seen from the hill of Montughi—later adopted by Piero del Pollaiolo; the greatest exponent of this tradition would be Giuseppe Zocchi with the opening plate of his celebrated collections of Florentine panoramic views (→ Fig. 75).[1] Biagio d'Antonio's view also provides us with a valuable glimpse of the great wooden scaffolding used for the construction of the lantern.

The drawn or painted image of the Cupola took on a new lease of life in the 17th and 18th century—the age of view painters (*vedutisti*) and the camera obscura (→ Fig. 44 and Glossary). In this period the panoramic view (from Monteoliveto, Bellosguardo, San Miniato or Montughi) enjoyed considerable success, and the Cupola was portrayed also from vantage points within the city itself, such as streets and squares.

The views of Florence by the French artist Israël Silvestre (1621–91) are remarkably similar to the images of pioneer photographers active in Florence, and reveal that he undoubtedly made use of a camera obscura with a short-focus lens. Silvestre's rear view of the Cathedral (→ Fig. 47)—to be compared with that by Jacques Stella (1596–1657), the result of a typically Baroque interest in the volumetric relations between the dome and the apses—is the first example of the vantage point that was to be taken up by Eugène Emmanuel Viollet-le-Duc (1814–79) in the 19th century and by Ottone Rosai (1895–1957) in the 20th century (→ Figs. 82 and 124).

Artists of the Macchiaioli group—Giovanni Fattori (1825–1908), Giuseppe Abbati (1830–68), Raffaello Sernesi (1838–66), Silvestro Lega (1826–95)—frequently portrayed the Cupola in the backgrounds of their paintings and drawings, where the interplay between the imposing presence of architecture or landscape and a lyrical atmosphere is an integral component of their poetic search for the universal within the particular (→ Figs. 101–3).

The discovery of photography further extended the range of panoramic or close-up vantage points, whether inside or outside the city. The pioneers of the new art—the Alinari brothers, John Brampton Philpot (1812–78), Anton Hautmann (1821–62), Alphonse Bernoud (1820–89), Giorgio Sommer (1834–1914), Giacomo Brogi (1822–81), James and Domenico Anderson, to mention only the most important and the most committed to the widest possible circulation of their works, also in the commercial context of the Grand Tour—competed with one another in photographing the Cupola from the slopes of San Miniato, Bellosguardo and Fiesole, but also from Orsanmichele, from Palazzo Vecchio, from medieval towers, from the *campanili* of churches (Santo Spirito, San Lorenzo, Santa Maria Novella) and from the Boboli Gardens. Stereoscopic photography, pioneered in Florence by Bernoud and Hautmann,[2] allowed the Cupola's sculptural qualities to be appreciated as never before (→ Figs. 90 ff.).

6.2. The Literary Image

The feature of the Cupola which most caught the collective imagination from the time of Brunelleschi onwards was its astonishing size and majesty. The Florentines, as we have seen, call the Cupola of their cathedral the *Cupolone*.

The remarkable body of definitions and descriptions of the Cupola that literature has produced over the centuries attest to the multiplicity of the features and connotations that characterise this work of genius. Sometimes it is the power and mass that are emphasised—the Cupola as a huge, imposing mountain—and sometimes the lightness and levitation—the Cupola as a balloon. However, these analogies fail to convey the dynamic contrast between different and even opposite, yet coexisting properties, a contrast that distinguishes the Cupola as a structural and formal organism, living and breathing in its extraordinary dynamic equilibrium.

Among the images inspired by the Cupola in the history of culture and in the collective imagination, the most recurrent is that of a mountain, first used by Vasari: "and it can be confidently asserted that the ancients never built to such a height nor risked challenging the sky itself, for it truly appears that this building challenges the heavens, soaring as it does to so great a height that it seems to measure up to the mountains around Florence. Indeed, the heavens themselves seem to be envious of it since every day it is struck by lightning". And it is worth recalling that in Vasari's account Brunelleschi himself refers to the Cupola as *terribile* ('daunting').[3]

In his *Prodromo della corografia e della topografia fisica della Toscana* ('Introduction to the Chorography and Physical Topography of Tuscany'), the botanist and geologist Giovanni Targioni Tozzetti (1712–83) wrote somewhat critically that "the beautiful Dome of this noble Basilica is equivalent to a man-made mound, and therefore reflects and channels the winds, overshadows [the piazza], bounces back the heat, and also increases the risk of nearby buildings being struck by lightning".[4]

In 1764 the English historian Edward Gibbon (1737–94) noted—in French—in his travel journal that the Cupola "is impressive, simple, sublime [...] To see the exterior properly one must be very far off or very high up, so as to embrace in a single glance the entire form, which seems to me as perfect in its ensemble as it is irregular and defective in its parts".[5]

For the French philosopher and historian Hippolyte Taine (1828–93), the Cupola "carries its elongated form to an amazing height in the air [...] How to express in words the features, the face of a church? However, this has one; all of its parts appear together, combined in a single accord and a single effect".[6]

According to the Florentine poet and novelist Giovanni Papini (1881–1956), "the Cupola resembles a hill of red sandstone, reduced to a human scale and traversed by channels of snow. At its very summit a globe of antique gold looks like an ex-voto which the earth itself, for centuries, has been offering to the life-giving sun".[7]

In a letter addressed to his parents dated 8 October 1907, the French architect Le Corbusier (1887–1965) wrote from Florence: "This morning I climbed up the Cupola, and I came down amazed by such greatness; I take back all the stupid things I have thought and perhaps written about the genius who dared to build something so colossal and so strong". And in a letter to Charles L'Eplattenier, written from Venice on 1 November 1907, he quotes Vasari and Taine, and recalls the Cupola dissolving into a surreal atmosphere, distilling within it the contents of the place and of history: "On the eve of my departure I climbed up the Cupola and became aware of its extraordinary greatness. This confirmed a hundred times over the impressions I had had a few days previously from San Miniato. But to actually *see* the Cupola from Piazza del Duomo, leaping constantly from side to side to avoid a tram, a hackney-coach, a bicycle or a funeral, and to *see* the Cupola from the surroundings of Florence, to see it as medieval travellers saw it when they reached the top of a hill and it suddenly emerged out of the blue haze of morning, this stone monster, a hill bigger than the ones surrounding it, organised and calculated—these are two completely different things".[8]

According to Carlo Ludovico Ragghianti, Frank Lloyd Wright (1869–1959) referred to the Cupola as "the animal", grasping in a single word its dynamic and powerful nature. Bearing in mind Wright's illuminating definition, Ragghianti has written: "even the closest description—a possible anatomy or laparotomy of the building, pushed far beyond the investigations that have been carried out, and capable of giving satisfactory answers to the many persistent questions, both structural and functional, would not succeed in explaining this architecture, continuing to regard it [...] as a static entity, orderly, immobile, an object reduced and consigned to the condition of solidified and perhaps immortalised matter; indeed, one often hears the Cupola admiringly called a mountain, which is something that applies only to its mass. An authentic perception of the Cupola can be attained only by expressing oneself through 'dynamological' imagery, as of a self-propelled vehicle where the propulsion forces capable of producing and modifying states of motion, of equilibrium, of repose, the *vis viva* or kinetic action, the *impetus* or power, can be continually found, in their inexhaustible generation, in a diagram or parallelogram of impulses. The Cupola is not a fantastic crystal, it is an organism—alive, cosmic, natural energy set in motion and perpetually in act. It is a reality as activity, a living being".[9]

Very often in the writings of travellers the arrival in Florence coincided with a sighting of the Cupola, notably with the view glimpsed as one approached the city along the Via Bolognese. Thus Stendhal (1783–1842), in 1817: "descending the Apennines to reach Florence, my heart was beating fast. What puerility! Finally, at a bend in the road, my glance swept the plain and I discerned in the distance a dark mass, Santa Maria del Fiore and its famous dome, Brunelleschi's masterpiece".[10] And the German composer Felix Mendelssohn-Bartholdy (1809–47) wrote in his travel journal: "The coachman pointed to a place between the hills, suffused with a bluish mist, and said: 'Ecco Firenze!' I looked anxiously in the direction he was pointing, and saw the rounded dome appearing out of the haze, and the wide valley in which the city lay".[11]

In the many 19th- and 20th-century novels that are set in Florence, the characters' arrival in the city is frequently introduced by a sighting of the Cupola. Thus Somerset Maugham (1874–1965) in *Then and Now* (1946): "'Look, Messere,' cried his servant Antonio, riding up to come abreast of him. 'Florence.' Machiavelli looked. In the distance against the winter sky, paling now with the decline of day, he saw the dome, the proud dome that Bramante [!] had built".[12]

In a letter to his father sent from Florence on 3 October 1836, the French architect Eugène Emmanuel Viollet-le-Duc (1814–79) wrote: "Here I have worked with great diligence on the monuments of Brunelleschi, and for the time being this architect is my man; so great is the daring and at the same time the constant prudence of his works; he is grave, sweet or brilliant as it pleases him, he terrifies with his immense conceptions or else he reveals the most graceful and least affected simplicity".[13] He also made a drawing, magnificent in its accuracy and power, of the Cupola and apsidal complex seen from behind.

Charles Dickens (1812–70) mentions Brunelleschi's "shining dome" in *Pictures from Italy*.[14] Finally Mark Twain (1835–1910), writing of his sojourn at Villa Viviani in Settignano in 1892, describes the "rusty huge dome" dominating the centre of the city as a "captive balloon".[15]

74.

74. Giuseppe Zocchi, view of Florence from the river Arno, upstream of the weir at San Niccolò, oil on canvas, c. 1741 (New York, Grassi Collection).

75. [p. 104, top] Giuseppe Zocchi, *Scelta di XXIV vedute delle principali Contrade, Piazze, Chiese e Palazzi della Città di Firenze* (Florence, 1744), Plate 1: *View of Florence from the Capuchin Convent of Montughi* (etching). In keeping with his scenic taste, Zocchi opened his collection with a panoramic view of the city from a viewpoint that had not been used since the 15th century (→ Figs. 15–6), as artists had tended to favour viewpoints from the hills to the south. In the 18th century Friedrich Bernhard Werner was the only other artist to adopt this northern perspective, which would never become popular. Here the city assumes a simple, linear profile: the depiction of the urban fabric is kept to a bare minimum, broken only by the regular succession of vertically rising monuments, above all the Cupola.

76. [p. 104, bottom] Giuseppe Zocchi, *Scelta di XXIV vedute*, Plate 21: *View of Florence Cathedral and the Baptistery of San Giovanni with the Corpus Domini Procession* (etching by Bernardo Sansone Sgrilli). With an eye for scenic effect Zocchi

dramatically enlarges the space in the foreground, creating an illusionary point of view from the north in order to take in the whole piazza; in doing so, he reduces in perspective the buildings in the background. As in the overall view of the city, the gallery at the base of the Cupola is depicted as if it had been realised on all sides of the octagon, instead of just the short section actually built by Baccio d'Agnolo.

77. [p. 105, top] Thomas Patch, *View of Florence from Bellosguardo*, oil on canvas, 1767 (Florence, Cassa di Risparmio di Firenze Collection). After Botticelli (→ Fig. 22) the vantage point from Bellosguardo had been adopted in the 17th century by Israël Silvestre, but it was this view by Patch that heralded the success of this viewing point in Anglo-Florentine culture through to the 19th century.

78. [p. 105, bottom] Wilhelm Berczy, *Portrait of Peter Leopold of Lorraine with the Grand-Ducal Family*, 1781 (Florence, Pitti Palace, Silver Museum): in the background, the Cupola seen from the Pitti Palace.

75.

Joseph Zocchi delin. Floren.

Johan. Andreas Pfeffel S.C.M.Chalcogr. sculp. Svae Aug.Vind.

Veduta di Firenze dal Convento de P.P. Cappuccini di Montughi   T.I.

76.

Joseph Zocchi del. et Figuravit

B. Egid. Sculp.

Veduta della Metropolitana Fiorentina, e del Battistero di S. Gio. con la Processione del Corpus Domini.   T.XXI

77.

78.

79.

80.

79. Opposite, Louis Gauffier, *Portrait of Dr. Penrose*, oil on canvas, 1798 (Minneapolis, Institute of Arts): in the background, a view of Florence with the Cupola from the Boboli Gardens.

80. C. Giglio (drawing) and Ladislaus Rupp (etching), the interior of the Cathedral of Santa Maria del Fiore, aquatint, *c.* 1805.

81.

81. Friedrich Wilhelm Moritz (drawing) and Niccolò Angeli (etching), rear view of the Cathedral with the Cupola, aquatint, *c.* 1805.

82. Opposite, top, Eugène Emmanuel Viollet-le-Duc, rear view of the Cathedral with the Cupola, 22 September 1836 (Paris, Centre de Recherche sur les Monuments Historiques, n. 55). Unlike Stella and Silvestre (→ Fig. 47), Viollet-le-Duc shifts the viewpoint to the left in relation to the monument's longitudinal axis, thereby creating a more dynamic perspective.

83. Opposite, bottom, Luigi De Cambray Digny, the Cathedral and Via dei Calzaiuoli from the north, pen and watercolour, *c.* 1845–50 (Florence, Biblioteca Marucelliana, Disegni). In a compositional *tour de force* the artist isolates the monument, which he draws in precise detail, introducing at the same time various nonexistent features, such as the exterior gallery wrapped all the way

round the base of the Cupola and an imaginary façade. The perspective closely resembles the one adopted by Zocchi (→ Fig. 76).

84. [p. 110, top] Emilio Burci, view of Florence from Rusciano (south-east of the city), *c.* 1840 (Florence, GDSU). The artist adopts a new viewpoint, in which the Cupola stands out in relation to the urban fabric and the surrounding area.

85. [pp. 110–1, bottom] Luigi Garibbo, 360-degree panoramic view of Florence from the top of the Buondelmonti-Acciaioli tower in Borgo Santi Apostoli, pen and watercolour, *c.* 1840 (Florence, GDSU, 1949 P). Composed with the aid of an optical camera, this drawing combines topographic rigour and precise rendering of architectural details. The vantage point within the urban landscape permits a fresh depiction of the dynamics at play between the structural components of the historic city centre.

86. [p. 111, top] Luigi Garibbo, view of Florence with the Cupola from the Maglio gardens (the Maglio was a small tower near the city walls, situated at the northern end of the present-day Via Lamarmora), watercolour on paper, 1840–50 (Florence, GDSU, 12161 S).

82.

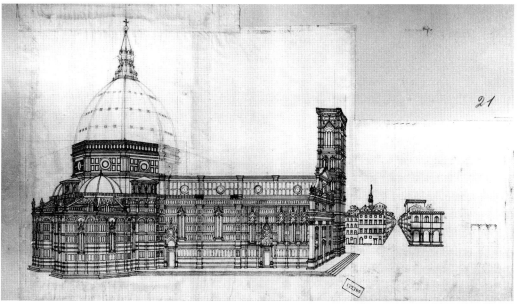

83.

84.

85.

86.

87.

87. Louis Cherbuin, panoramic view of Florence from the Boboli Gardens, aquatint from daguerrotype, *c.* 1843. The views by Cherbuin and Falkeisen were collected in a volume entitled *Recueil des Vues principales de Florence exécutées d'après le daguerréotype et gravées par J.J. Falkeisen et L. Cherbuin*, published in Milan by Artaria.

88. Opposite, top, Johann Jakob Falkeisen, panoramic view of Florence with the Cupola from the tower of Porta San Niccolò, aquatint from daguerrotype, *c.* 1843, from *Recueil des Vues principales de Florence*. This fine example of 19th-century visual taste combines the perspectival precision and richness of detail made possible by the daguerrotype with the etcher's extraordinary skill in obtaining a wide range of light effects.

89. Opposite, bottom, Alfred Guesdon, bird's-eye view of Florence (*Florence, Vue prise au dessus de S.ta Maria dell'Annunziata*), lithograph from *L'Italie à vol d'oiseau*, an extensive collection published in Paris by Hauser in 1849 and, in a second edition, in 1852. The use of the hot-air balloon opened up fresh possibilities for European urban iconography and Guesdon was one of the first to systematically exploit its potential. This view from above Santissima Annunziata was unusual at the time and reflects the 19th-century taste for chromatic balance and the regularity and uniformity of the streets and lines of buildings.

88.

89.

90.

91.

90. Opposite, John Brampton Philpot, the Cathedral and the Cupola from the Via dei Cerretani side of Piazza San Giovanni, bromide print from calotype negative, *c.* 1859 (Florence, Soprintendenza Speciale per il Polo Museale Fiorentino, Gabinetto fotografico, 2393). Not surprisingly, the advent of photography represented a fundamental step in the history of monumental iconography, including that of the Cupola. The daguerrotype, the calotype, the stereoscopic view, the *carte-de-visite* and the photographic postcard each have their own specific purpose, be it that of encapsulating an overall scene or narrowing down on a detail, which is reflected in the

choice of lens (wide-angle, zoom, etc.). The viewpoint and light give extraordinary emphasis to the solid yet airy mass of the Cupola.

91. Above, Giorgio Sommer, the Cathedral and the Cupola from the Via dei Pecori side of Piazza San Giovanni, albumen print from collodion negative, *c.* 1865. Adopting a viewpoint already used by the Alinari (from a window in the curtain of buildings formerly separating Via dei Pecori from Piazza San Giovanni), Sommer brings together the Baptistery, the Cathedral, the Campanile and the Cupola in a single, densely packed composition.

Compare the dimensions of the Cupola in this wide-angle shot with Brampton Philpot's photograph taken with a zoom lens.

92.

93.

92. Opposite, Anton Hautmann, panoramic view of Florence from Bellosguardo, stereograph, albumen print from collodion negative, *c.* 1861 (Florence, G. Hautmann Collection). The viewpoint adopted by Botticelli (→ Fig. 22), Silvestre, Patch (→ Fig. 77) was very popular with the 19th-century *vedutisti* and pioneering photographers such as Hautmann, Brogi and the Alinari brothers.

93. Alinari brothers, panoramic view of Florence from Bellosguardo, bromide print, *c.* 1872.

94.

95.

96.

94. Opposite, top, Anton Hautmann, panoramic view of Florence from a tower in Piazza San Biagio, stereograph, albumen print from collodion negative, *c.* 1861 (Florence, G. Hautmann Collection). The view of the Cathedral from the south-west, taken from a vantage point within the urban landscape, has an iconographical precedent in the view by Garibbo.

95. Opposite, bottom, Anton Hautmann, panoramic view of Florence from a tower in Borgo degli Albizzi, stereograph, albumen print from collodion negative, *c.* 1861 (Florence, G. Hautmann Collection). The unusual vantage point accentuates the dynamic equilibrium and plastic qualities of the Cupola towering over a sea of roofs.

96. Above, Anton Hautmann, the Cupola from Piazza della Santissima Annunziata, stereograph, albumen print from collodion negative, *c.* 1861 (Florence, G. Hautmann Collection). Anton Hautmann was the first photographer to take instantaneous views of urban scenes in Florence that included people.

97. [p. 120, top] Alinari brothers, view of the Cathedral from Orsanmichele, albumen print from collodion negative, *c.* 1865 (Florence, Accademia delle Arti del Disegno). This visually powerful image records the condition of the tile roofing (the areas where the tiling has been replaced are clearly visible) and of the marble ribs.

98. [p. 120, bottom] Vincenzo Paganori, view of the Cathedral from the *campanile* of the Badia Fiorentina, albumen print from collodion negative, *c.* 1865–70.

99. [p. 121, top] Giorgio Sommer, view of the Cathedral from Palazzo Vecchio, albumen print from collodion negative, *c.* 1865.

100. [p. 121, bottom] Giorgio Sommer, the Cathedral from the south, albumen print from collodion negative, *c.* 1865–70. By using a wide-angle lens and combining three shots, Sommer succeeded in encapsulating the entire monument in a single image, creating the illusion of a large expanse of empty space in the foreground.

97.

98.

99.

100.

101.

101. Odoardo Borrani, *Chatting on the Terrace*, 1873 (Montecatini, Piero Dini Collection).

102. Opposite, top, Silvestro Lega, *Real-life Scene*, view of the Cupola from Piagentina, on the outskirts of Florence, 1865 (Montecatini, Piero Dini Collection).

103. Opposite, bottom, Giovanni Fattori, the Cupola seen from Via Lamarmora, etching, *c.* 1900.

102.

103.

104.

105.

106.

104. Opposite, top, Giorgio Sommer, view of Florence from the *campanile* of the church of Santo Spirito, albumen print from collodion negative, *c.* 1865.

105. Opposite, bottom, Giorgio Sommer, view of Florence from Monte alle Croci, albumen print from collodion negative, *c.* 1865–70.

106. Above, Giorgio Sommer, view of Florence from the Uffizi, *carte-de-visite*, albumen print from collodion negative, *c.* 1865–70.

107. [p. 126, top] Giorgio Sommer, view of Florence from San Miniato, albumen print from collodion negative, *c.* 1865.

108. [p. 126, bottom] Alinari brothers, view of Florence from the Arcetri Observatory, albumen print from collodion negative, *c.* 1868.

109. [p. 127] One of a series of photographs of the Cupola taken in 1892 by Giorgio Roster with a powerful zoom lens.

107.

108.

110.

110. Anchise Mannelli, rear view
of the Cathedral, albumen print from
collodion negative, *c.* 1880.

III. Anchise Mannelli, view of the
Cupola from the south, albumen print
from collodion negative, *c.* 1880.

112.

112. Opposite, Alinari brothers, a detail of the south-east side of the drum and the lower section of the Cathedral, albumen print from collodion negative, *c.* 1880. According to Manetti, the extension of the cornice of the nave to include the drum, thereby cutting it in two and giving rise to two separate pilasters, one thicker than the other, ran counter to Brunelleschi's original design, which envisaged single, unbroken pilasters of equal thickness, a kind of ideal continuation of the marble ribs of the Cupola.

113. Above, Alinari brothers, detail of the north-west side of the drum, bromide print, *c.* 1940. Clearly visible are the protruding ends of the cross-beams of the first stone chain, the putlog holes and the marble cornice and gutter at the base of the vault face.

114. [p. 132, top] View of Florence from Palazzo Vecchio, postcard, collographic print, *c.* 1900 (photographer and publisher uncited).

115. [p. 132, bottom] Pictorial-style photograph of the urban skyline and the Cupola, postcard, bromide print, *c.* 1915.

116. [p. 133, top] Panoramic view of Florence from Fiesole, postcard, chromolithographic print, *c.* 1915 (Brunner & C., Como).

117. [p. 133, bottom] Hilde Lotz, view of Florence and the Cupola from Palazzo Dei-Guadagni in Piazza Santo Spirito, bromide print, 1943 (Florence, Kunsthistorisches Institut).

114.

FIRENZE - Panorama.

193

115.

116.

117.

118.

118. Aerial photograph of Florence
city centre, bromide print, 1935
(IGM, Florence).

119. Opposite, top, aerial photograph
of Piazza del Duomo from the east,
c. 1925.

120. Opposite, bottom, aerial
photograph of Piazza del Duomo
from the south-west, c. 1935 (Milan,
Fotografia Navigazione Aerea).

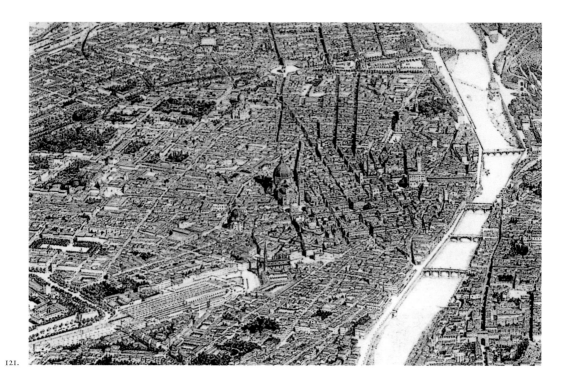

121.

121. Luigi Zumkeller, detail of
a bird's-eye view of Florence based
on aerial photographs, ink on paper,
1934–5 (Florence, Palazzo Vecchio,
offices of Florence City Council).

122. Opposite, top, aerial photograph
of Florence, bromide print, *c.* 1970.

123. Opposite, bottom, aerial
photograph of Florence, bromide
print, *c.* 1970 (Rotalfoto).
Compare with the view known
as "della Catena" (→ Fig. 17).

122.

123.

124.

124. Opposite, Ottone Rosai,
the Cupola of Santa Maria del Fiore,
oil on canvas, 1954 (Florence,
private collection).

125. Above, left, front cover of Anne
Rockwell's children's book *Filippo's
Dome* (New York, 1967), realised
by the author herself.

126. Above, right, Ugo Fontana's
cover for *Il cielo di pietra* ('The Sky
of Stone'), a children's book by Baccio
Maria Bacci, published in Florence
by Vallecchi in 1977.

127.

128.

127–8. Photomontages from the
booklet accompanying the exhibition
Brunelleschi anticlassico curated by
Bruno Zevi (Florence, 1977).

129.

129. Giovanni Fanelli, view of
Florence with the domes of Santissima
Annunziata and the Cathedral, seen
from the palace of San Clemente,
ink drawing on paper, 1991.

130.

130. Wooden model of Florence
Cathedral, *c.* 1900 (Florence, formerly
part of the Elia Volpi Collection).
The model features the 16th-century
gallery as if it had been built
all around the drum.

131. Franco Gizdulich, wooden model
of the Cupola (scale 1:20), 1995
(Florence, Istituto e Museo di Storia
della Scienza).

IMAGES OF THE CUPOLA

132.

132. Florence and the Cupola from above Candeli, south-east of the city.

133. Opposite, top, Brunelleschi's Cupola and the dome of Santissima Annunziata, designed by Michelozzo, at opposite ends of Via dei Servi, seen from Giotto's Campanile.

134–6. Opposite, bottom, the Cupola in natural light: in the morning, at midday, in the late afternoon.

133.

134.

135.

136.

137.

138.

137–8. Opposite, details of the drum. Clearly visible are the protruding ends of the cross-beams of the first stone chain, the putlog holes, the marble cornice and gutter (*ratta*), and the iron bars with eyelets (*occhi con rampo*) inserted to support the planned exterior gallery.

139. Above, detail of the marble facing of the drum and of one of the great round windows.

140.

141.

140. Opposite, *tribuna morta*
and great round window on one
of the sides of the drum.

141. Above, detail of a niche
in one of the *tribune morte*.

142.

142–3. The dynamic interplay of the ribs and vault segments.

144–6. [pp. 154–6] The "magnificent and swollen" Cupola seen from the Campanile.

147. [p. 157] The lantern seen from the Campanile.

143.

144.

146.

147.

148.

148–53. [pp. 158–62] The lantern:
full view and details of the buttresses
and windows.

149.

150.

151.

152.

153.

154.

154. The lantern buttresses and the vault segments.

155. [p. 164] Detail of the large roof tiles.

156. [p. 165] The interior of the apse and the intrados of the inner shell.

157–8. [p. 166] The interior of the lantern seen from the presbytery area.

159. [p. 167, top] The frescoed intrados of the inner shell.

160. [p. 167, bottom] View of the presbytery area from the lantern.

155.

156.

157.

158.

159.

160.

161.

161. The space between the inner
and the outer shell: on the left,
one of the passages through a spur
and the horizontal arches connecting
the corner and the intermediate
spurs; on the right, herringbone
brickwork.

162.

162. The flight of stairs connecting
the third and fourth walkways
in the space between the inner
and the outer shell.

163.

163. Opposite, a view of the first walkway in the space between the inner and the outer shell.

164. Above, a view of the wooden chain in the space between the inner and the outer shell, looking up from the first walkway.

165. Right, view of the stairs leading to the oculus ring from the third walkway.

165.

166. Passage through a corner spur and herringbone brickwork.

167. Below, a detail of the herringbone brickwork in the walkway at the base of the lantern; the eye gives on to the space between the two shells.

166.

167.

PART TWO

FOREWORD

The exercise of 'reading' and understanding the great building enterprises of the past is by no means straightforward. The difficulties do not relate so much to the different cultural context (historical and critical investigation is actually helpful to some extent), nor to changes brought about by advancing technology. The major obstacle is that we have a different conceptual perception of the life-span of great buildings. We often find it difficult to shake off certain mental habits acquired in the second half of the 20th century, foremost amongst which is the concept that a building will not last indefinitely but is something that has a finite life measurable in decades; this is coupled with a 'philosophy' of programmed obsolescence or rational planning of maintenance and periodic substitution.

Examination of Brunelleschi's modus operandi in building the Cupola reveals a number of surprisingly 'modern' aspects, and so it might not unreasonably be contended that considerable attention was paid even in those days to time-schedules, costs and productivity. However, while in the modern age the constraints of financial mechanisms, socio-economic expectations and rapidly evolving needs have resulted in an ingrained imperative to deliver fast, it is indisputable that these considerations could be overruled in the past by what were regarded as higher requirements. It is also worth recalling how in former times the conception and construction of any representative city building entailed a collective participation on the part of all citizens, and was accompanied by lively and often polemical debate about *how* to build. By contrast, the prevailing mood nowadays is one of sectorial, even individualistic fragmentation, the result of which is that analogous building projects are no longer seen from a cooperative perspective. Indeed, current debate often centres on *whether* and *why* one should build at all. Cultural continuity across generations and the long-term stability of the socio-cultural fabric, which have been replaced today by sudden fractures and incessant upheavals, made it possible to be fairly confident about entrusting the completion of great city buildings to subsequent generations—even those of later centuries.

Turning now to the more technical aspects of structural conception, it is possible to detect — alongside attitudes and practices not unlike modern ones—a profound discontinuity. This is not only a question of obvious differences in basic knowledge, analytical design tools, building materials, energy sources and mechanical equipment; a still more fundamental diversity regards what is usually called the structural insight of a builder. This is undoubtedly based on personal qualities which can be developed and reinforced through experience as well as by critical analysis of earlier buildings, and as such, it is not exclusive to any historical epoch. It can hardly be denied, however, that it needed to be more commonly found and sharply honed in the technical milieu of Brunelleschi's days than in our specialist elites. Apart from occasional peaks of excellence, contemporary professional builders suffer in general from the preference of our education system to adopt an analytical-mathematical approach, which inevitably atrophies structural intuition to some extent. Indeed, modern engineering faculties have chosen—out of necessity, but not entirely without negative side effects— to inculcate in their students an adroit use of the formalism inherent in modern mathematical tools. Instructing them in the use of the autonomous power of symbolic structural analysis according to codified procedures is preferred to the longer, more arduous process of cultivating other, less formalised qualities. By contrast, in the past an apprentice would be patiently initiated to manual drawing and encouraged to 'feel' intuitively the physical interactions of different structural elements. Such qualities were bound to lead to a grasp of the equilibrium and *firmitas* (i.e. solidity) of a building in instinctive rather than quantitative, formalised terms.

Moreover, the insight of a great builder cannot be limited to the comprehension—through synthesis or analysis—of the stress flow in a 'mental' model of the structure, conceived as a geometric body carved out of a faultless material continuum and subjected to an equally idealised system of constraints and forces. Such insight should also include a full awareness of the peculiarities, limitations and shortcomings of actual materials and building methods, in order to foresee their possible drawbacks. This allows builders to use all the means at their disposal to prevent (or at least minimise) the negative short- and long-term consequences of these limitations and shortcomings.

One can maintain—as will be shown in detail further on, on the basis of historical records and of the objective examination of the Cupola—that Brunelleschi was extraordinarily gifted with both these kinds of structural insight, as well as with outstanding organisational abilities. It is only fair to mention that the scientific and technical limitations of his day meant that he was unable to foresee some of the negative dynamics that subsequently became apparent in the form of cracks. However, this does not in the least detract from his merit in having undertaken and successfully executed an unheard-of endeavour requiring an unprecedented magnification of structural forms and building procedures. Besides, he went to such lengths in his design and construction methods that in all probability he mitigated the consequences of these negative dynamics, so that one is forced to wonder what might have happened in a less carefully controlled structure.

Poring over the many details of the Cupola's history, as well as of the internal articulation of its structural elements, one cannot avoid sensing the constant struggle of a genius against the limitations of the technology of his times. This is reminiscent of the attitude that would distinguish, a few years later, the work of another genius, Leonardo da Vinci. Studying Brunelleschi's greatest building is still of the utmost interest today and can yield surprising discoveries, a testimony to the vitality of his genius. This can be fully appreciated by all ages, because although the reading code may change down the centuries, the fundamental essence of the language has remained unaltered.

As is appropriate when studying any complex organism, the following study has been organised along distinct lines corresponding to successive stages in the life of the Cupola: conception and anatomy; physiology; ageing and pathologies; diagnosis and possible therapies. An effort has been made to express the conclusions of this study in as plain and non-technical a language as possible. Nonetheless, some recourse to the concepts of structural analysis is inevitable. The glossary at the end of the book will help the general reader to follow the thread of reasoning. To enable readers to skip the parts which they may find less interesting, an effort has been made to render each section basically self-contained; this has inevitably entailed a certain amount of repetition.

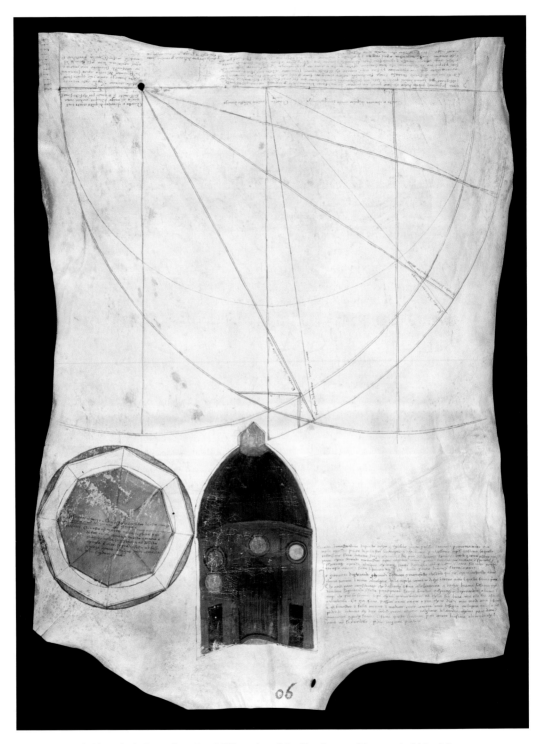

1.1.1. Giovanni di Gherardo da Prato, the pointed-fifth tracing of the Cupola, 1425. Florence, Archivio di Stato.

The Geometric, Functional and Structural Design of the Cupola

1.1. The Cupola: Its Components, Geometry, Dimensions and Mass

The Cupola matches the octagonal shape of the drum on which it rests; it is therefore formed by the union of eight cylindrical segments, the horizontal generatrices of their surfaces being straight lines. Adjacent segments intersect along curved edges; each pair of diametrically opposed edges is contained in a vertical plane passing through the Cupola's axis. In this plane, each edge of the inner surface is a circular sector whose radius is four fifths of the diagonal (or 'diameter') of the base octagon and whose centre is placed on the summit plane of the drum (the so-called pointed fifth, → Fig. 1.1.2). The circular sector springs from the drum corner with a vertical tangent and has an angular aperture close to 60°. The eight circular sectors thus defined form the converging intrados edges of the Cupola; between two adjacent edges lies the intrados of one of the eight segments, which is a ruled surface (a cylinder) generated by horizontal, parallel segments terminating on the two edges. In fact, the intrados surface of each segment is cut from the mantle of a cylinder that has an elliptical right section; the cylinder axis is horizontal and contains the two centres of curvature of the segment's circular edges. The eight segments thus belong to different cylinders, each of which has a distinct axis location and orientation.

* * *

Until now it has been implicitly assumed that the octagon which forms the base of both the drum and the Cupola is a regular polygon, but in fact its eight sides differ perceptibly in length. The average length is 16.956 m, the shortest side measuring 16.617 m and the longest one 17.240 m; the difference between the longest and short-

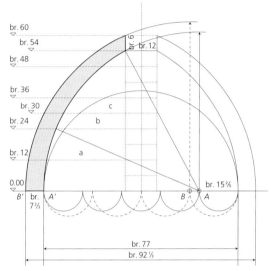

AA′ radius of curvature of the intrados edge (inner shell)
BB′ radius of curvature of the extrados edge (outer shell)
a: upper limit of the stone masonry; b: upper limit of the stone masonry envisaged in 1420; c: upper limit 'without centring' envisaged in 1420

1.1.2. Tracing of the intrados edge of the inner shell. The diagram indicates some of the heights laid down in the 1420 building programme.

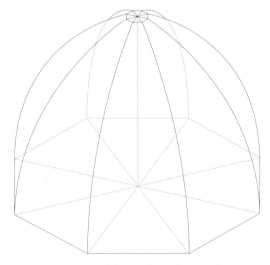

1.1.3. Isometric view of the intrados of the inner shell.

est lengths is 0.623 m, i.e. some 3.7% of the average side. Consequently, the eight inner angles also differ slightly, by different amounts, from the 135° of a regular octagon. For the sake of simplicity—unless specifically stated—an idealised geometry of the Cupola will be assumed from here on. Each side of the base octagon is taken to be 16.956 m long; this octagon is symmetrical with respect to the vertical axis passing through its centre. There are therefore sixteen vertical symmetry planes; eight of them pass through the edges, the other eight through the midlines of the segments, and all of them pass through the central axis (→ Fig. 1.1.3). The diameter of the circle circumscribed to this base octagon measures 44.308 m, and the radius of the vertical circles defining the edges is four fifths of the latter, i.e. 35.446 m. The above lengths are derived from a survey made during the 1930s, and correspond more or less to those that can be found on the famous parchment drawing by Giovanni di Gherardo da Prato (→ Fig. 1.1.1).

Starting from the intrados surface, three more reference surfaces can be defined: they correspond—apart from small offsets of about 10 cm each, intended to reduce the masonry thickness with increasing height—to the extrados of the inner shell and to the intrados and extrados surfaces of the outer shell. These reference surfaces are obtained by tracing straight lines perpendicularly to the first surface (the intrados of the inner shell) and marking on them, starting from this first surface, points at about 2.25, 3.45 and 4.25 m respectively. The reference surfaces thus defined coincide with the real surfaces at an elevation of about 3.40 m above the upper gallery of the drum; it follows that at this elevation the thickness of the inner shell, the inter-shell cavity and the outer shell are about 2.25, 1.20 and 0.80 m respectively. The first two offsets, one on the extrados surface of the inner shell and one on the intrados surface of the outer shell, are at an elevation of about 8.05 and reduce the thickness of both shells by an equal amount. More offsets can be found between the second and third walkway

for the outer shell and between the third and fourth walkway for the inner shell.

The two shells are connected by a system of twenty-four spurs or buttresses; eight of them (corner spurs) are located at the corners, so that their median planes coincide with the eight vertical edge planes, while the median planes of the remaining sixteen spurs (intermediate spurs, two for each segment), which also converge towards the central axis, divide into equal parts the dihedral angles comprised between the planes of each pair of corner spurs enclosing a segment. The lateral planes containing the masonry of the spurs are all radial vertical planes passing through the central axis of the Cupola.

The thickness of each intermediate spur—which is about 1.75 m at the base of the Cupola (instead of the 2.40 m envisaged in the original programme)—diminishes progressively as the spurs draw closer to each other as they rise towards the summit, down to a minimum thickness of about 0.40 m; the corner spurs are about twice as thick. Figure 1.1.4 represents the horizontal section of the Cupola at the elevation where the two shells spring from the underlying solid masonry, while Figure 1.1.5 represents the section of the Cupola with a vertical plane passing through two opposite vertices of the base octagon.

At the summit of the Cupola a special structure known as the oculus ring (*serraglio*), which is also octagonal in shape and symmetry with respect to the central axis of the Cupola, connects and closes the two shells and the relative spurs. When viewed in section in relation to one of the vertical edge planes, the oculus ring encloses a trapezoidal cavity about 5.65 m in diameter. The perimeter is pierced by eight doors (one for each segment) and by eight small windows giving onto the inner cylindrical cavity of the lantern; the masonry surrounding these apertures is reinforced by massive *pietra forte* frames. The inner cavity of the lantern is enclosed on each of its eight sides, internally by vertical walls, and externally by sloping walls joining the two vault shells. In other words, the contact surface be-

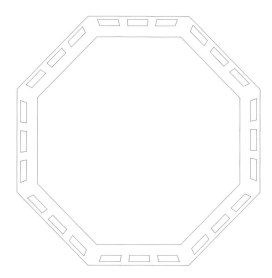

1.1.4. Horizontal section at the base of the Cupola at an elevation of 3.5 m above the summit of the drum.

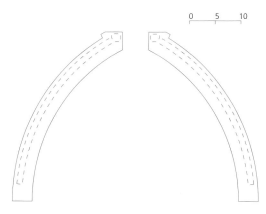

0   5   10

1.1.5. Schematic section of the Cupola with a vertical plane containing two opposing edges.

oculus, the inner shell abuts onto a massive octagonal stone ring: the compression ring sustaining the horizontal inward thrust of the eight segments of the shell. Each of the eight sides of this ring, with a square section 1.75 m wide and 1.75 m high, is formed by the juxtaposition of sixteen *macigno* beams with 0.44 m sides. Resting on the oculus ring is the base of the lantern that crowns the whole edifice of the Cupola.

The exterior of the outer shell is covered by about 30,000 large terracotta tiles (measuring 50 × 37 cm, laid on a bed of mortar and fixed to the extrados of the outer shell by iron hooks. This covering is interrupted at the junctions between the segments by white marble ribs; these ribs, with a roof-like section of constant size from bottom to top, accentuate the eight edges along the profile of the corner spurs.

The outer shell of the Cupola is pierced by seventy-two small circular apertures, or oculi. There are nine to each segment, positioned in groups of three at three different elevations in order to admit daylight into the space between the two shells. The inner shell is pierced by sixteen similar oculi, about 58 cm in diameter, each of which is carved out of a quadrangular block of *macigno*; they are arranged, two for each segment, along the midline of the segments, at the level of the second and third walkways. These sixteen oculi provide a breathtaking view of the inner space of the Cupola, and can be accessed via a rectangular recess cut into the masonry of the inner shell. The oculi may have been intended to give access to the intrados of the vault in order to work on decorative mosaics envisaged in the original plan.

The walkways and stairs which, together with the passages through the spurs, give access all around the eight segments to the space between the outer and the inner shell, are described elsewhere; it suffices to mention here that these walkways can be found at elevations of approximately 3.50, 11.90, 23.20 and 33.30 m above the springing of the Cupola (the last walkway winds around inside the oculus ring, as said above).

tween the oculus ring and the Cupola proper is a truncated pyramidal surface, with the vertex of the pyramid facing downwards. The space enclosed by the inner surface of the oculus ring is a straight, vertical-axis cylinder with an octagonal horizontal section the sides of which are about 2.95 m.[1] The axes of both pyramid and cylinder coincide with the central axis of the Cupola. The masonry of the oculus ring's trapezoidal section, enclosing the annular cavity (about 2 m high and 1 m wide at the floor, 1.75 m wide at the ceiling), is about 0.8 m thick. At the junction with the

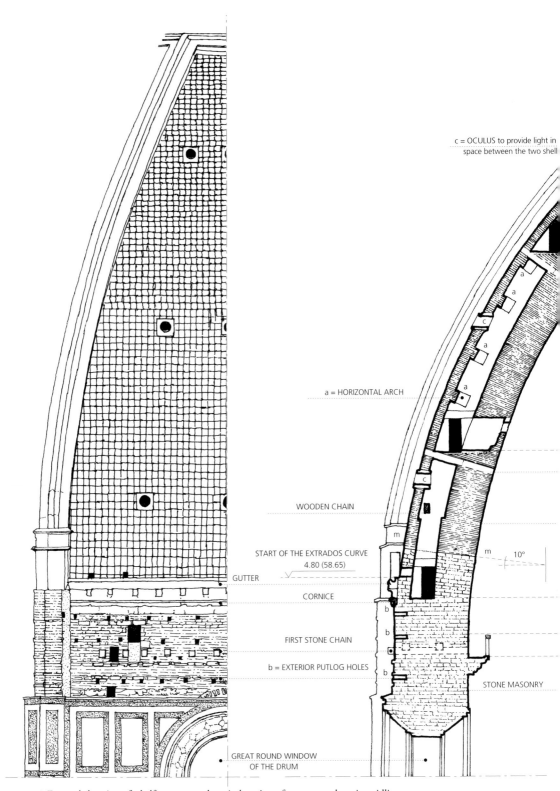

c = OCULUS to provide light in
space between the two shell

a = HORIZONTAL ARCH

WOODEN CHAIN

START OF THE EXTRADOS CURVE
4.80 (58.65)

GUTTER

CORNICE

FIRST STONE CHAIN

b = EXTERIOR PUTLOG HOLES

GREAT ROUND WINDOW
OF THE DRUM

10°

STONE MASONRY

1.1.6. External elevation of a half-segment and vertical section of a segment along its midline.

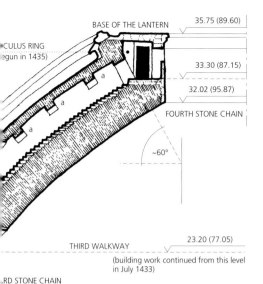

BASE OF THE LANTERN   35.75 (89.60)

CULUS RING
egun in 1435)

a

33.30 (87.15)

32.02 (95.87)

a

FOURTH STONE CHAIN

a

~60°

a

THIRD WALKWAY   23.20 (77.05)

(building work continued from this level
in July 1433)

RD STONE CHAIN

COND WALKWAY
ilding work resumed from this level   11.90 (65.75)
March 1426)

COND STONE CHAIN

derpinned by radially laid cross-members,
t also provide support for the second walkway)

CKWORK

e transition from stone masonry to brickwork
he m–m line—occurred in 1422)

ST WALKWAY   3.50 (57.35)

1.02 (54.87)

0.00 (53.85)

ERNAL GALLERY

SPRINGING LINE OF THE CUPOLA
(a circular wooden platform was
built at this level to act as a base for
the building work)

Another main component of the Cupola's structure are the 144 horizontal arches (eighteen of them to each segment) reinforcing the outer shell where it joins the corner spurs. These powerful half-arches, or consoles, are to be found at nine regularly spaced levels (about 2.5 m from each other) in the upper two thirds of the Cupola. Viewed in a section perpendicular to the two shells, they have a skew profile—i.e., the thickness jutting inwards from the outer shell varies. The thickness is at a maximum near the corner spur from which the arch springs (occupying practically all the space between the shells) and gradually decreases as it moves towards the adjacent intermediate spur, against which the arch abuts, its thickness diminishing almost to zero.

At each of the nine elevations the intrados of these arches, taken together with the intrados of the outer shell between the two intermediate spurs, nearly forms a circle. This has given rise to an interpretation of the static function of these arches, according to which they make it possible for the combined structure formed by the outer shell and the arches to behave like a circular shell. Some scholars claim that the intention was to build twenty-four-sided wooden chains below each of these arches, like the one actually installed about 2 m above the beginning of the Cupola's brick masonry (see below). This functional interpretation seems objectively untenable in the light of considerations that will be described in due course (→ § 2.3), and a different structural explanation of these peculiar components will be offered. It should be noted that the arches are a variant with respect to the 1420 building programme, where it was specified that the shells were to be connected by radial barrel vaults, which were never built.

The Cupola's masonry is reinforced by three pairs of *macigno* chains (→ Fig. 1.1.7), located at elevations 0.00, 10.50 and 21.00 m respectively above the springing of the Cupola. In actual fact only the existence of the lowest pair of chains has been ascertained beyond all doubt, since a few stretches of these chains can be discerned in the

1.1.7. A detail of the first *macigno* chain (Ippolito–Peroni, 1997).

space between the two shells; the other two pairs are hidden inside the brickwork and their existence has been doubted by some scholars. It must be said, however, that these upper chains were contemplated in the original building programme—a fourth pair, possibly to be located at the summit of the Cupola, was added in the 1426 modifications—, and that some parts of the second pair are also visible. Indeed, in some of the passages between the two shells, it is possible to see the stone cross-beams forming a 'bed' on which the chains in question rest (see below). Each chain forms an octagon whose sides run inside the masonry parallel to the sides of the segments, and is composed by stone blocks (2.65 m long, with a square section of 0.44 m; in the original programme the cross-section was to have been considerably larger, namely 1.16, 0.78 and 0.58 m for the lowest, intermediate and upper pair respectively). The blocks are joined by iron clamps; under the two parallel courses of longitudinal beams and transverse to their alignment are located more *macigno* beams with the same cross-section (formed by blocks ranging from 0.80 to 1.15 m, also joined by iron clamps). The

whole construction forms a stout lattice, the longitudinal and transverse beams being dovetailed by means of carefully carved indentures. This entails that the shaping in the workshops and the subsequent positioning on site had to be carried out with great precision. Special angular pieces, located at the corners of the octagon, ensure the continuity of each longitudinal course. At the lowest level the transverse beams, twelve to each side of the octagon, are perpendicular to the longitudinal ones and jut out of the Cupola to form cantilevers that were intended to support the exterior gallery (later built on just one side by Baccio d'Agnolo). At the upper levels they follow, in all probability, radial alignments, thus conforming to the general masonry layout at those elevations; moreover, the planes defined by the lattices of transverse and longitudinal stone beams had to follow the inward inclination of the brick beds.

The static function of these *macigno* longitudinal and transverse chains can now be interpreted as a *local* system for bonding the masonry, while at the time of the raising of the Cupola they were probably intended to strengthen the *global* equilibrium of the Cupola, the idea being that the longitudinal chains were a sort of hoop of reinforcing bars helping to contain the outward thrust of the segments, or, in modern terms, to absorb the tensile stresses in the lower 'parallels', just like the steel bars used in reinforced concrete. Needless to say, their effectiveness in performing this kind of structural role is quite negligible, even for completely unbroken chains; besides, after construction the chains broke along the cracks, and the lowest one was even interrupted from the outset by four passages left between the inter-shell cavity and the upper gallery of the drum, thus losing what little effectiveness it might have had as a containing hoop.

Some scholars maintain that there are also iron chains inside the masonry; however, investigations with metal detectors have failed to yield conclusive evidence either for or against this view. What is certain is that considerable sums of money—in the order of a thousand *lire* each year—were spent on the purchase of iron parts, the total weight of which amounted to thousands of Florentine pounds (1 pound = 0.34 kg). In this context it is worth mentioning the many massive iron rings anchored—by means of long iron bars embedded in the brickwork—on five levels of the intrados of the inner shell at the eight corners in order to provide support for the suspended work platforms ($\rightarrow$ § 1.8). Beside these big rings, many more lines of smaller hooks can be found along the surface of the segments; moreover, metal brackets were used in the edges, probably to position the templates used to trace their profile. Lastly, iron rings were also found on the extrados of the outer shell when the cover of terracotta tiles was partially removed.

Beside the three stone chains, a single wooden chain was also installed in the Cupola; the original building programme envisaged the in-

stallation of three more wooden chains, overlaid by iron chains, at progressively higher elevations. The cross-section of the wooden chain is about 0.35 by 0.35 m; on a horizontal plane 7.75 m above the springing of the Cupola, its layout has the outline of a regular, twenty-four-sided polygon: eight sides run adjacent to the outer shell between each pair of intermediate spurs, while the remaining sixteen sides run obliquely across the inter-shell space between each corner spur and the neighbouring intermediate ones, passing through the corner spurs close to the extrados of the inner shell. The shape of the wooden chain is much closer to a circle than to an octagon. The chain consists of long chestnut beams (the original programme envisaged the use of oak) that make up the twenty-four sides of the polygon. The adjacent sides of the polygon are joined by means of oak angle pieces laid above and below the two ends and attached to them by iron pins; the whole junction is fastened to-

1.1.8. View of the horizontal arches from the second walkway (looking upwards).

gether by nailed iron bands. A large portion of the wooden chain is clearly visible because it crosses the inter-shell space between the first and second walkways; inside the masonry it is reinforced by overlaid iron chains, connected to the wood beams by pins that meet the eyes of the iron chains; a close fit between pins and eyes is assured by wedges. The wooden chain has a stiffness and resistance that makes it quite inadequate to fulfil the role of containing hoop that may have been intended for it.

As regards the total weight of the Cupola, it has been variously evaluated by different scholars, with figures ranging from 20,000 to 35,000 metric tons. While the first figure is probably an underestimate, the second appears rather too large. Computing from the known geometry the total volume of the masonry, to which a specific gravity of about 2 t/m³ can be assigned, and assuming the total weight of the tiles and marble mouldings, augmented by the excess weight of the stone masonry as compared to the bricks, to be approximately one fourth of the weight of the outer shell, the most likely figure appears to be about 29,000 metric tons (18,000 for the inner shell, 8,500 for the outer shell with the tiles and marble, and 2,500 for the spurs). Another 800 tons have to be added to this to account for the lantern. It is also worth noting that the presence of the inter-shell space reduces the total mass by about 20%, as compared to the total mass of a hypothetically solid Cupola with the same inner and outer surfaces. As a reference, a hemispherical dome with the same diameter as the circle circumscribed to the base octagon and made up by two shells as thick as those of the Cupola would weigh about 24,000 metric tons.

* * *

In order to achieve an adequate understanding of the structural behaviour of the Cupola, as well as of the causes of the cracks, it is important to take into account the Cupola's interaction with the underlying and surrounding structures—above all the drum, the four massive piers carrying the

weight of the drum, and the apses. These structures determine the boundary conditions affecting the stress and deformation regime of the Cupola proper. (The lateral structures, namely the three apses and the four apsidioles or *tribune morte*, might have been conceived as sorts of buttresses intended to contain the outward thrust of the great vault, but in all probability they only make a small contribution to this.)

It seems useful, then, to add (→ §§ 1.2–4) to this description of the Cupola a short reminder of the main features of these other structures, together with a few preliminary comments on their interactions with the Cupola. These interactions will be analysed in more detail in the following chapter.

1.2. The Drum

Most scholars consider the drum to consist only of the upper octagonal wall, about 10.5 m high, between the two internal galleries, that is between the summit of the four great arches on the north, east, south and west sides and the springing of the Cupola. From a functional point of view, however, it is preferable to use the term 'drum'—as will be done from here on—to include all the parts between the summit of the piers (28 m from the ground) and the springing of the Cupola (52.5 m from the ground).

Thus defined, the drum can be described as a huge deep beam, made of *pietra forte* masonry, octagonal in plan, about 24.5 m high and some 4.65 m thick. Its upper edge—on which the Cupola rests—lies on a horizontal plane, while the lower edge is regularly mixtilinear in profile; indeed, the north-west, north-east, south-east and south-west lower sides of the drum rest directly on the four imposing piers located at the corners of the presbytery area, whereas on the north, east, south and west sides the lower edge is formed by the intrados of the four imposing pointed arches, which have a span of about 17 m and whose end abutments also rest on the piers (→ Fig. 1.2.1).

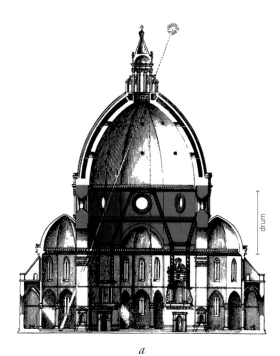

Imagine that the Cupola consists of highly deformable, heavy material. The pattern of particle displacement would be as illustrated below: above the solid supports the particles tend to diverge from the mid-vertical plane, while above the arches they tend to converge towards it.

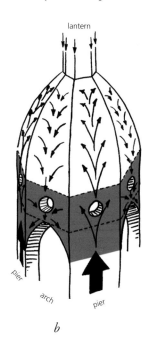

a

b

1.2.1. Section of the drum and intuitive representation of the stress flow.
a. Functioning of the lower part of the structure, viewed as a truss.
b. Particle displacements occurring during deformation caused by the Cupola's dead weight and the corresponding reaction of the four solid piers.

Located between the extrados of the arches and the upper edge of the drum are eight splayed great round windows, which admit daylight into the presbytery area. The diameter of the inner circular openings is about 4.65 m, while the diameter at the outer edge of the splay is about 6.95 m. The mass of the drum may be estimated at some 39,000 metric tons.

One important aspect of the static behaviour of the whole structure is self-evident: the weight of the Cupola (including the lantern), which is evenly borne by the eight upper sides of the drum (approximately 3,600 metric tons per side), is carried to the summit of the piers in two different ways. The four segments directly above the piers transmit their weight along a direct vertical path; the other four transmit their weight to the four big arches, and only indirectly, through the arches' abutments, are these weights carried to the four piers together with the weight of the drum itself. Each pier summit thus receives a total weight (direct plus indirect load) of some 17,000 metric tons (→ Fig. 3.2.5).

A further observation can also be made on fairly intuitive grounds: the four sides of the drum resting directly on the piers are much stiffer, in their vertical plane, than the four with the big arches. This means that the latter bend, in their middle vertical plane, under the vertical loads transmitted by the Cupola's segments, while the former suffer much smaller deformations. The four sides with the arches therefore demand from the other four, by which they are constrained, a fixed-end moment causing tensile stresses along the upper fibres, while in the centre of the span (above each arch's summit) a bending moment of opposite sign will cause tensile stresses along the lower fibres.

The presence of the great round windows intensifies these tensile stresses—quite uniformly distributed across the thickness of the drum—along the upper or the lower rim, respectively, of the round windows above the piers or above the summit of the arches. In due course (→ § 3.2), and with the help of detailed numerical analyses, it will become clear how the situation briefly outlined here may have played a fundamental role in the genesis of the cracks.

1.3. The Piers

The stone piers soar to a height of 28 m above the Cathedral floor. These piers have a complex structure, because their cross-section varies with elevation. Furthermore, the two apsidal piers (north-east and south-east) differ from the other two (north-west and south-west): the cross-section of the lower part—from the ground to a height of 20 m—of each of the apsidal piers is split into two separate quadrangular parts (→ Fig. 3.4.1) resembling a kite in shape. The two sides of each quadrangle enclosing an obtuse angle (135°) are about 5 m long, while the two sides enclosing the opposite acute angle (45°) measure about 10 m. The total surface of each pier's horizontal section thus amounts to $50 \times 2 = 100 \text{ m}^2$. Between the 20 and 28 m elevations, the two separate half-sections merge into a single cross-section with a surface of about 170 m², since a huge block of stone masonry (with a hexagonal section in which the pair of opposite sides measure respectively about 7 and 17 m, 10 and 5 m, 10 and 5 m) straddles the two underlying half-piers and is aligned with their outer edges. Erected on these two blocks are the north-east and south-east apsidioles.

The cross-section of the two piers (the north-west and south-west ones) adjacent to the nave also varies with elevation, and the lower segment is divided into two separate parts. These parts differ in shape from the apsidal piers, insofar as

they must accommodate a prismatic passage in between, with walls parallel to the main Cathedral axis, connecting each side aisle with the presbytery area (→ Fig. 3.4.1). Indeed, between the floor and the 20 m elevation the two separate parts of the cross-section are non-symmetrical: the part nearest to the Cathedral's longitudinal axis is markedly smaller than the other part; nevertheless, the total surface of the two parts is practically the same as that of the apsidal piers. Between elevations 20 and 28 m these piers are crowned by massive blocks, like those previously described for the apsidal piers, above which rise the north-west and south-west apsidioles.

* * *

NB: In the simplified model used for the structural analysis, it was assumed that all the piers were identical. Therefore, while the structure formed by the union of Cupola, drum and piers is symmetrical—as is the whole of the Cathedral—only with respect to the east–west plane, the simplified structural model is symmetrical also with respect to the north–south plane.

* * *

The exterior of the four piers was built of carefully dressed and interlaced *pietra forte* blocks. The interior was filled with rubble masonry consisting of small stones embedded in mortar with small, wide-spaced voids. This was shown by investigations carried out using camera probes inserted into boreholes and subsequent examination of the recovered cores; these investigations were conducted by ISMES (Istituto Sperimentale Modelli e Strutture, 'Experimental Institute for Models and Structures'), a research institute of the Italian national power board (ENEL) at the beginning of the 1990s (→ § 3.3).

Little is known about the pier foundations, beyond the fact that they rest on gravel strata. Ancient chronicles record that considerable water seepage occurred during excavation work for the south-west pier, to the point that the area had to be drained (→ § 2.3).

Each pier has a mass of about 9,000 metric tons; therefore, taking into account all of the above-mentioned figures, the mass of the overall structure formed by the Cupola, lantern, drum and piers is probably 100,000 tons or more.

1.4. The Structures Surrounding the Cupola: the Nave, Apses and Apsidioles

The apses that rise on the east, north and south sides of the octagon were completed in 1420, before work began to raise the Cupola, and it is worth bearing this in mind when interpreting the interaction of these structures with the Cupola itself. In order to raise the round domes crowning the apses, conventional formwork was used. The so-called *tribune morte* or apsidioles were raised directly above the four piers according to Brunelleschi's own drawings. The weight and stiffness of the apses and apsidioles was probably relied upon to counteract the horizontal outward thrusts of the Cupola, almost as if they were acting as buttresses. As will become clear, the junction between these structures and the Cupola was seriously damaged as a consequence not only of the above-mentioned thrusts, but also as the result of the vertical settling of the structures in question with respect to the octagon. Their buttressing function, if it ever existed, is now probably virtually non-existent.

In 1429 some cracks were detected in the side walls of the nave, maybe as a consequence of the horizontal, east-to-west thrust of the Cupola, which by then had reached an appreciable height. It was therefore decided to install a bidirectional system of chains across the spans of the arches and vaults, both in the nave and in the side aisles. These chains were realised under Brunelleschi's supervision.

1.5. The Masonry of the Cupola

The lower part of the Cupola is built out of big squared blocks of sandstone bound together by thin mortar beds. The pattern does not depart in any clear-cut way from that of ordinary, horizontal-layer masonry; to be more precise, the successive beds appear to be level, but perpendicular to the surface of the Cupola's segments, namely with a slight but increasing declivity towards the centre of the Cupola. This masonry is solid across the whole thickness of the Cupola to a height of about 3.50 m above the springing line (this elevation corresponds to an inclination of about 5° of the radius connecting the midline of the wall to the centre of curvature). Above this elevation, the sandstone masonry splits into the two shells and continues up to an elevation of about 7 m above the springing of the Cupola (this elevation corresponds to an inclination of about 10° of the radius connecting the midline of the wall to the centre of curvature). Here the sandstone masonry ends, giving way to brickwork that continues up to the summit of the two shells (the bricks are of different sizes, the two most frequently used being approximately 17 × 34 × 5 cm and 22 × 44 × 5 cm). The pattern of the brickwork gradually changes. This different organisation, though some scholars argue that it is not well-defined or systematically used,[2] is apparent enough, so much so that it was also observed on the extrados of the outer shell when the external covering of large terracotta tiles was removed and partially replaced. This pattern is known as *corda blanda* or *branda*, meaning 'slack line' (literally, rope), because the bricklaying beds have a concave arrangement as they rise towards the summit of the Cupola. In particular, in each segment the mortar beds binding each course of bricks to the one above it (from here on, simply 'mortar beds') are laid on ruled surfaces generated by a segment perpendicular to the surfaces of the shells gliding along a curved directrix. Indeed the latter, instead of being a horizontal straight line as in the segment—and as was the case for the stone courses (see above)—, curves slightly downwards (the concavity facing upwards). The degree of curvature is such that, at any given elevation, the mortar beds of the eight segments taken together belong very nearly to a

a

b

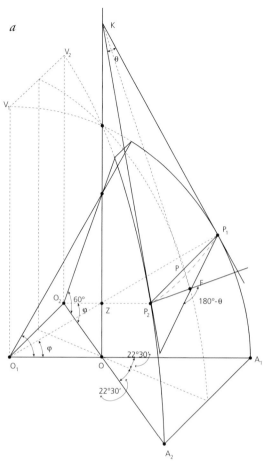

1.5.1a–b. Geometric reference scheme for the 'slack-line' course of the brickwork.

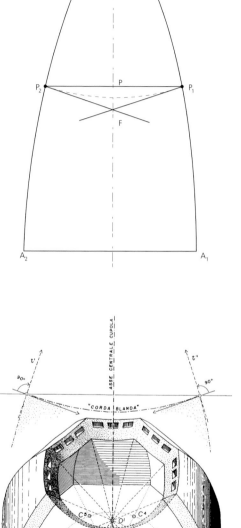

1.5.2. Perspective view of the 'slack-line' bricklaying surfaces (Ippolito–Peroni, 1997).

common conical surface; the cone's vertical axis coincides with the central Cupola axis and the vertex points downwards. It follows that at each inter-segment edge the traces of the brick courses visible on the intrados and extrados of two adjacent segments appear to form an obtuse angle opening downwards, and present a perceptible inclination with respect to the horizontal.[3]

In order to complete the description of the brickwork, it is necessary to add that above the level of the second walkway the brick courses are interrupted, at nearly regular intervals, by oblique bands of bricks laid out on radial planes with their long sides vertical. These bricks are of variable size, the most frequently used being $22 \times 22 \times 5$ cm, corresponding to a mass of 25–30 Florentine pounds each—see the 1426 alterations to the original programme. The bands are spaced on average about 1.20 m apart and their midlines are inclined about 40° to the horizontal, thanks to a regular offset in elevation from one brick of each band to the next. These offsets amount to about one third of a brick's height, so that there is an ample overlap between consecutive bricks. The arrangement of the inclined bands gives the brickwork a characteristic her-

ringbone appearance, which is clearly visible not only from the inter-shell space (both on the extrados of the inner shell and on the intrados of the outer shell), but also in limited sections of the inner shell's intrados, where the frescoed plaster fell off. This feature of the Cupola's brickwork was, and still is, known as *spinapesce* ('herringbone': → Figs. 1.5.3–5).

These 'slack-line' and herringbone arrangements were adopted starting from elevations where the inward inclination of the mortar beds became significant—namely about 10° to the horizontal for the beginning of the 'slack line' and about 20° for the herringbone. It will be shown (→ § 1.6) that both these arrangements perform essential structural functions in Brunelleschi's design.

Lastly, it is interesting to note that the thickness of the mortar beds gradually increases from the interior to the exterior of the structure. This can be observed on the few visible transverse surfaces and is a natural consequence of the convergence of the layers towards the centre of curvature of each segment. The variations between minimum and maximum thickness are of the order of one centimetre or more, so that the joint

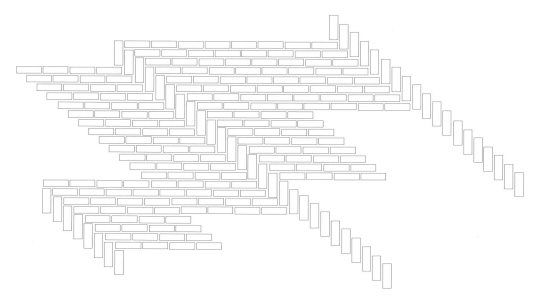

1.5.3. The herringbone pattern of the brickwork.

1.5.4–5. The herringbone brickwork along the edge between the north and north-east segments, respectively 27 and 15 m from the third walkway, uncovered during restoration work on the vault.

thickness across the same mortar bed, already rather large on average, can vary from 1–1.5 cm to 2–2.5 cm (and in some instances up to 3–4 cm). By contrast, the joints between the bricks are quite thin on the surfaces of the inter-shell space, as a result of a more carefully finished surface layer of brick; the latter, however, accurately reproduces the sub-surface texture of both the 'slack-line' and herringbone brickwork.

Standard bricks (*quadroni*) were used for the mass masonry while, according to most scholars, at the segment edges and other particular points Brunelleschi used specially shaped and manufactured bricks to ensure the utmost continuity of the masonry texture. Further on (→ Fig. 2.1.2) more will be said about the role of these special bricks (angle moulds, etc.) in the structural behaviour of the Cupola.[4]

1.6. The Raising Methods

The decision to build the Cupola without centring was only taken after lengthy and heated debate, and not without reservation. Indeed, the 1420 programme stated that the masonry was to be raised without centring up to a height of 17.5 m. Only then would a final decision be taken as to how to build from there on.

The strategy of building without centring helps explain the division of the worksite into eight sections, one for each segment; this organisation meant that the eight segments grew at the same pace, so that each successive octagonal ring, once the mortar had set, was immediately self-sustaining.

In modern parlance one might say that, in order to speed up the raising of the Cupola, Brunelleschi took pains to identify the critical path—namely, those activities that cannot be carried out in parallel, but only in succession, and which therefore affect the total duration of work. For instance, successive rings necessarily had to be laid one after the other, but at any given level work could proceed on all eight segments at the same time, thereby optimising

progress. The rate of progress was established by three 'critical' operations: on the exterior, the tracing of the profile and the raising of the work platforms; and on the inside, the laying of the herringbone brickwork.

The 'slack-line' and the herringbone brickwork, the two fundamental building solutions adopted by Brunelleschi, will now be examined in greater detail.

The 'slack-line' arrangement of the brick courses, which has already been described in geometric terms, fulfils the function of creating mortar-bed surfaces devoid of any discontinuity in their tangent planes at the junction of two adjacent segments. The systematic adoption of this arrangement, together with the use of angle moulds at the edges, ensured an unbroken course along each ring. This was important in order to avoid creating weak zones at the corner spurs, which even then were felt to play a fundamental role in ensuring the Cupola's stability. Indeed, any damage or weakening of these spurs was perceived as a serious structural threat.[5]

First of all, the herringbone pattern played a fundamental role in the *building* process, in view of the fact that the vertical planes to which the herringbone courses of the different segments belong converge towards the central Cupola axis. In fact, each pair of these was ideally suited to containing the horizontal courses of bricks just laid on the fresh mortar beds, in places where the inward slope of these beds could have caused the bricks to slide. (It is, however, probable that containing wooden planks were also temporarily positioned on the inner face of the masonry, and then removed as soon as the mortar had set.) Thus, the herringbone pattern was essential for, or at least greatly facilitated, the raising of the Cupola without permanent centring. However, the herringbone probably also had a *structural* significance, which will be discussed further on (→ § 2.2).

It should be noted that *the herringbone pattern appears singularly appropriate in raising a big pointed dome without centring.* Indeed, in a round dome the convergence of the herringbone courses would be very limited near the dome's summit (on the axis, it would in fact be nil), and the containing action of two consecutive herringbones on the freshly laid horizontal courses between them would thus become ineffectual. By contrast, in a pointed dome this convergence still has a finite magnitude even near the top (in addition, the proximity of the summit brick courses to the Cupola axis is limited by the width of the lantern opening). In fact, in Brunelleschi's Cupola the maximum inward slope of the horizontal brick courses is only about 60°, while in a round dome springing from the same base and having the same lantern opening the maximum slope would be about 80°. Correspondingly, in the pointed dome the vertex of the virtual cone to which the surfaces of the mortar beds belong moves gradually upwards as the bricklaying proceeds in height, so that the half-aperture of the highest cone would be about 30°, while in the round dome this vertex would remain fixed in

the centre of the base octagon (the half-aperture of the narrowest cone would be only about 10° in this case).

The pointed-fifth profile of the Cupola, the 'slack line' and the herringbone seem, in the light of knowledge acquired since then (→ § 2.2), to form a coherent whole that obeys a very precise structural conception. Of course, in the absence of explicit documents to this effect, it is not possible to ascertain beyond all doubt that what appears to us today to be a unified and carefully organised whole is not the fortuitous product of a chain of unrelated decisions. However, it can quite reasonably be affirmed that the structural insight that unquestionably guided Brunelleschi's thinking and modus operandi seems to have led to solutions revealing, a posteriori, an astonishing degree of synergy.

As regards the *tracing* of the Cupola's profile, there is no certain information about the methods used. Rowland J. Mainstone has attempted to interpret the *gualandrino con tre corde* method

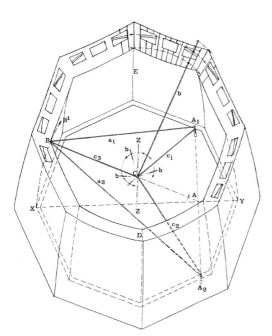

1.6.1. System for control of the radial disposition of the masonry and its inclination towards the opposite pointed-fifth centre (*gualandrino con tre corde*: Mainstone, 1977).

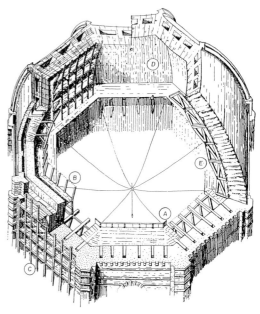

1.6.2. Another possible method of tracing the intrados of the inner shell and relative arrangement of the work platforms (Ippolito–Peroni, 1997).

mentioned in some documents. He assumes that the tracing of each intrados edge was effected with a system of three ropes or wires (laid out as in Figure 1.6.1)[6] to form an isosceles triangle which could be made to rotate around its horizontal base. The latter passed through the edge's centre of curvature and was perpendicular to the vertical plane containing the edge; the end points of the base were established on its intersections with the intrados of the vault, where the lower ends of the other two ropes were fastened. In this way the vertex of the triangle would move along the intrados of the edge to be traced. Moreover, it has been ascertained that from 1420 onwards wooden templates, protected against wear by iron sheets and periodically replaced, were fastened along the edges to guide the bricklaying. Each template, about 2.65 m long and 0.58 m thick, was probably held fast by wires attached to the iron hooks jutting out from the masonry until the corresponding portion of the two adjacent segments had been laid. The template was then moved up to perform the same function on the next layer. Once the edges were traced, the surfaces of the segments, each formed by horizontal lines spanning two adjacent edges, could be easily traced by means of levels and simple optical sights. However, it is unclear how the 'slack-line' curves were traced.

It remains to be added that Manetti and later (during the 16th century) Giovanni Battista Gelli claim that various parts of the Cupola were drawn out in full scale on the bank of the Arno, where Brunelleschi had had a wide flat stretch of ground prepared for this purpose. The drawings thus obtained were possibly used to make the templates and whatever else was needed.[7]

1.7. The Models

Between 1418 and 1420 the Opera held various competitions which called for the construction of models of the Cupola; among the participants were Lorenzo Ghiberti and Filippo Brunelleschi. Ghiberti's model was made from small, unbaked bricks, while Brunelleschi used normal-sized, common building bricks. Extant documents in the Opera archives attest that Brunelleschi's model was completed in ninety days—without the aid of centring—by four masons, who needed forty-nine carts of quicklime. The scale of the model is not recorded, and there has been a good deal of conjecture about this among scholars; according to Prager, it may have been 1:12,[8] while Saalman estimates it as 1:8.[9] The latter seems more in accordance with the time it took to build it as well as with the workforce used, if a direct proportion is assumed between the respective volumes and the man-days required (the actual raising of the Cupola occupied an average of fifty workers for twelve years), and supposing the man-hour productivity to be the same in both cases. The model, built without centring expressly in order to show that this technique could also be adopted for the real Cupola, served as the basis for the drawing up of the 1420 building programme. Underwritten also by Ghiberti, the programme proposed to avoid using centring, at least up to a certain elevation, deferring a final decision as to how to proceed higher up.

Beside this model, Brunelleschi provided further demonstrations of the feasibility of building without centring, a signal example being the Ridolfi chapel in the church of San Jacopo Sopr'Arno, destroyed in 1709. This—and probably other minor Brunelleschi domes as well—could be loosely interpreted as 'models' of the Cupola of Santa Maria del Fiore. Moreover, the ancient octagonal dome of the Baptistery, with its pyramidal, eight-segment roof connected to the dome by walls perpendicular to the segments, may have inspired the double shell of the Cupola and acted as a model (the scale between the two buildings being about 1:1.7), even though it is not geometrically similar. These existing structures reassured contemporaries about the feasibility of the 1420 programme and, as they showed no visible sign of damage, inspired confidence about the structural soundness of the design. It will be shown further on (→ § 2.1) that although fully compatible with the architectural and engineering culture of the times, the extrapolation from smaller sizes to the unprecedented scale of the Cupola was unjustified. At the time it was held that the crucial element responsible for the *firmitas* of a building were the proportions between constituent parts, irrespective of size. In the light of subsequent knowledge, it is now clear that similarity of geometric shape, building materials and raising methods is no guarantee that a structure will not crack from excessive stress. On the other hand, the above-cited examples—apart from the Baptistery—could rightly be adduced as 'proof' of the feasibility of the *method* of raising without centring.

In raising the Cupola, Brunelleschi also used models in the way that was most usual at the time, namely as models reproducing just the geometric features of the object concerned. A fine example is the full-size model of the oculus ring he built and raised to the summit of the Cupola to verify its geometric compatibility with the already-existing parts.[10]

1.8. The Equipment and the Organisation of Work on Site

It can be assumed that the organisation of the building site was thought out and prepared well in advance. Indeed, there is no evidence that work got off to a slow, problem-ridden start, as might well be expected if the complex interplay of different activities had taken shape in a haphazard way as needs arose. It is of course only right to point out that the preceding phases in the raising of the Cathedral had effectively tested and improved the organisation of the site and the workforce; in this respect, Brunelleschi could draw on the invaluable experience of the master builders (*capomaestri*). But it is also evident that the raising of the Cupola posed completely new problems that called for a radical rethinking of the complex 'machine' of the building site. This section will attempt to offer a succinct outline of the main features of what was

an essential aspect of Brunelleschi's endeavour; this covered a whole range of working practices required to maintain strict control of every phase of the work.

In order to gain access to the level where masonry was being laid, a huge wooden platform was built. Temporary wooden floors were constructed on the inside at different heights for the various phases of the work. The highest floor, which was periodically raised by erecting new supports, was used by masons engaged in laying the brickwork of the segments. The intermediate floors were sustained by inclined props supported by the drum gallery at the springing of the Cupola. The lowest floor was probably supported by stout beams (60 × 60 cm) driven into putlog holes; there were six of these for each segment, and they crossed the full thickness of the drum. Fresh points of support could always be found for the new floors, which were built as required, by connecting the wooden horizontal beams carrying the planks to firm iron 'eyes' welded to iron chains deeply embedded in the masonry; these eyes, which still exist, are clearly visible at regular intervals along the inner edges of the Cupola.

The workmen could reach the lowest platform via the spiral staircases leading to the top of the drum and its gallery. However, the huge quantities of building materials—such as bricks, stone blocks, iron pieces, wooden beams—required for the construction could not be brought up in the same way. The problem of raising, day after day, considerable weights from the Cathedral floor to the various working levels therefore had to be solved by other means. As the options existing at the times were clearly inadequate to the magnitude of the task, Brunelleschi had to devise new solutions. Once again, his ingenuity proved decisive.

* * *

The machines built to Brunelleschi's designs and used in the building of the Cupola—in particular the *hoisting and positioning equipment*—were, in large measure, important innovations well in advance of what was then available. These machines captured the imagination of his contemporaries[11] and inspired other Renaissance engineers, including Leonardo da Vinci. However, they stopped being used after the raising of the Cupola, mainly as a consequence of humanistic trends and a return to ancient authorities such as Vitruvius.

Contemporary illustrations, such as those contained in Bonaccorso Ghiberti's *Zibaldone*, show winches and cranes operating at ground level or on already-built masonry (these machines were adequate for raising material over short heights: → Figs. 1.8.1–2), as well as examples of ground-based hoists, with a carrying capacity of a few hundred kilograms. A vertical shaft (made to rotate by radial levers moved by muscular force) carried a toothed gear, the vertical teeth of which meshed with radial rollers carried by a vertical gear mounted on a horizontal shaft; the latter was fixed to the hoist's drum, on which the ropes were wound.

But the main load-raising installation used by Brunelleschi was a ground-based hoist on which it was possible to wind and unwind a rope, the latter going up to a pulley suspended at a great height on the work platform. This is the most remarkable, innovative machine whose invention can be reliably attributed to Brunelleschi: the great reversible hoist built and installed on the Cathedral floor, under the main platform, in order to raise heavy loads (→ Figs. 1.8.3–4). One notable feature was the possibility of reversing the direction of the load (rising or descending loads) without having to invert the direction in which the animals powering the machine were moving. This avoided the dead time that would have been required to unyoke and yoke the animals, speeding up operations considerably. Besides, the machine could be run at three different raising speeds (→ Inset 1), which made for

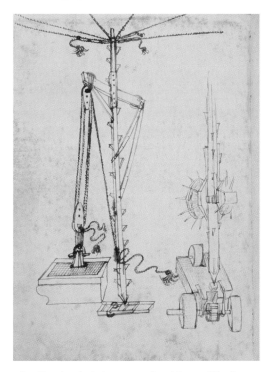

1.8.1. Drawing depicting a high-elevation hoist in place on the masonry (BNCF, MS BR 228, fol. 94r).

1.8.2. Drawing depicting a crane for raising small loads (BNCF, MS BR 228, fol. 95v).

added flexibility. Indeed, the three speeds made it possible to raise a wide range of load weights (from a few dozen kilograms to several tons) employing practically the same amount of physical power. These widely variable weights could thus be raised without altering the number of animals or splitting heavier loads.

Besides the hoists and winches for bringing the loads from the Cathedral floor up to the main platform, several cranes and load-positioning devices were used to transfer the loads to the work stations; these lighter machines were installed either on the platform itself or on parts of masonry that had already been built.

Straddle cranes, quite similar to the previously described machines, were used to position heavy loads with great precision—for instance, the elements of the longitudinal and transverse stone chains; these were prepared on the ground with interlocking dovetails and had to be placed in the lattice with the utmost accuracy. These machines were provided with a horizontal shaft along which a bronze block moved, driven by a horizontal screw, while a vertical screw engaging a female thread in the block positioned the load at the required height. The horizontal shaft could be rotated, because it was mounted on a vertical shaft which could be turned by means of a rudder. The load was fastened to the suspending rope by means of a system of turnbuckles (usually three: → Figs. 1.8.6 and 1.8.8): this allowed the suspended piece to be held level and be positioned as required. These machines were also installed either on the work platforms or directly on the masonry, and could be provided with winches to raise the loads by rope or pulleys attached to the horizontal arm (→ Fig. 1.8.7).

The largest of these revolving cranes, mounted on a rotating pedestal and probably used to close the oculus of the Cupola and to position the block forming the base of the lantern, was about 20 m high. (→ Fig. 1.8.6). It carried a horizontal shaft along which a stout block was made to move by means of a horizontal screw; a vertical screw engaging a female thread in the block raised or lowered the load. Along a second hor-

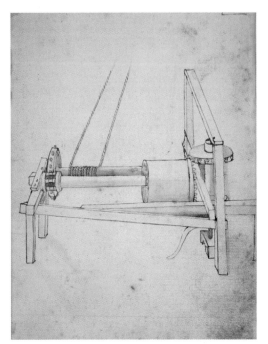 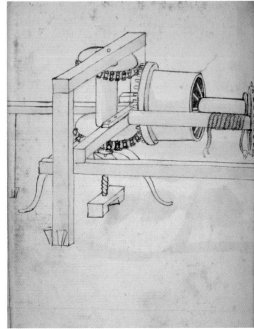

1.8.3–4. Two views of Brunelleschi's three-speed reversible hoist (BNCF, MS BR 228, fols. 102r and 103v).

1. The Great Reversible Hoist

Figures 1.8.3 and 1.8.4 show a great reversible hoist and are probably a faithful representation of the machine built in 1420 according to Brunelleschi's instructions and used for the raising of the Cupola. Documents from the Opera archives mention features that can be seen in the figures; moreover, the hoist is described by Mariano di Jacopo known as Taccola (1381–1458?), and in the 16th century by Bartolomeo Neroni known as Riccio (c. 1500–71). There are records of two carpenters having worked on it for more than two months, and that the cost was 135 florins, plus Brunelleschi's fee, which amounted to 100 florins.

From the drawings one can clearly see the various parts of the machine and understand how it operated. A massive wooden frame "as big as a house" (Prager)—about 7.30 m high, and with an overall shaft length of about 4.95 m (Saalman)—absorbed the forces transmitted by three rotating cylindrical shafts, one of them vertical and the remaining two horizontal. Attached to the bottom end of the vertical shaft were the beams to which the oxen or horses driving the hoist were yoked, and a worm-screw mechanism which raised or lowered a pair of 24-cog horizontal gears rotating together with the vertical shaft. These two horizontal gears were about 1.75 m apart, so that the distance between them was slightly greater than the diameter of the large vertical gear (about 1.45 m in diameter) attached to and rotating with the first horizontal shaft, which was about 5 m long. On the rim of the vertical gear there was a set of twenty-four teeth or rollers, which engaged the cogs of the upper or the lower horizontal gear, the vertical position of which was controlled by the worm-screw mechanism. In this way the large drum attached to the end of the horizontal shaft (1.55 m in diameter) could be made to rotate in both directions, and therefore could be used for both raising and lowering loads; with this system it was no longer necessary to unyoke and reyoke the oxen so they faced the opposite direction, and this saved a great deal of time. At the other end of the first horizontal shaft there was another, smaller drum (0.50 m in diameter) with a small 'lantern' gear (0.75 m in diameter)—a cylindrical cage with ten pins or rollers parallel to the horizontal shaft. This gear engaged the thirty teeth of a large vertical gear (2.10 m in diameter) keyed to a second horizontal shaft, parallel to and as long as the first one, which had a small drum 0.50 m in diameter. The rope running up to the high pulley could thus either wind or unwind on any one of these three drums. A safety device prevented the vertical shaft from rotating in the reverse direction. The hoist was basically a speed-reduction and force-multiplication device for use with heavy loads: indeed, with the vertical shaft rotating at the same given speed, it was possible to obtain three different raising speeds depending on which one of the three drums the rope was wound around. Expressed in terms of the force output required of the oxen to raise the load (or to brake it during descent), the different drums were in a ratio of 4, 12 and 36, force being in inverse ratio to the distance moved. This calculation does not take account of friction losses, which must have been quite high; Brunelleschi tried to reduce these losses by using gears equipped with anti-friction rollers instead of teeth or pins.*

Various specific parts of the great reversible hoist are mentioned in the Opera documents. The hoist remained in operation for more than a decade, and required very little repair work and no major modifications. A pulley was attached high up on the main work platform on the inside of the vault. Through this ran the thick rope (*canapo*) wound or unwound by the hoist: this rope weighed 1425 Florentine pounds.** The load was attached to one end of the rope, while a counterweight could be hung on the other. In this way the loads could easily be raised up to platform level, where they could be manoeuvred as required by means of cranes or other load-positioning devices. Small winches or composite pulleys operated by muscular force could then be employed for the final placement.

* For a detailed description, see Saalman, *Filippo Brunelleschi. The Cupola*, 154–8.
** P. Sanpaolesi, *La cupola di Santa Maria del Fiore: il progetto, la costruzione*, photographic reprint of the original edition, Rome 1941, with a new preface by the author (Florence: Edam, 1977).

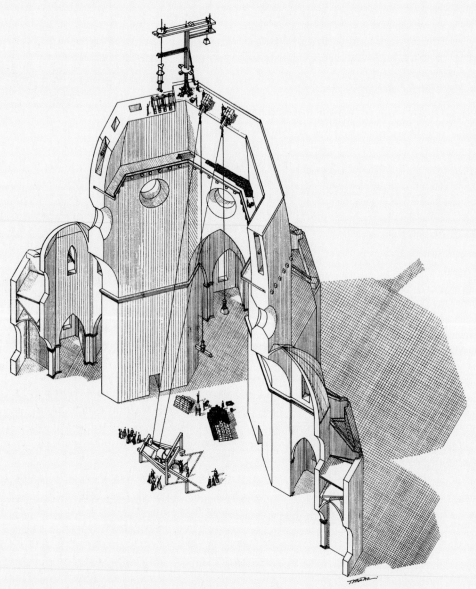

1.8.5. Reconstruction of the loading platform in place and the 'great hoist' and 'great crane' in operation at the level of the second walkway (Saalman, 1980).

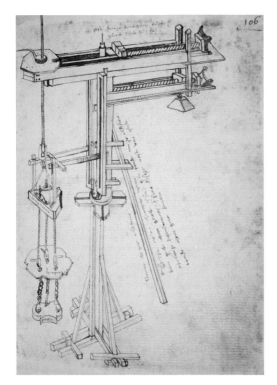
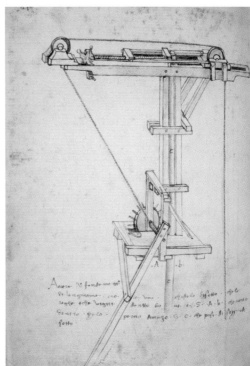

1.8.6–7. Revolving cranes with load-positioning devices (BNCF, MS BR 228, fols. 106r and 107v).

izontal shaft, parallel to the first one, another horizontal screw shifted a counterweight in the opposite direction to the movement of the load, in order to avoid the machine being overturned by the load. Four teams of workmen were required to operate this crane: "one to rotate the crane, two to turn the screws for the radial displacement of the load and counterweight, and one to operate the vertical screw"[12] which positioned the load at the right height.

Documents make a particular mention of a crane built in 1423, to which a second revolving crane was added in 1432, which was better suited for use on the increasingly high work plat-

forms (to transfer the loads, raised to the main platform by the great hoist, up to their final destination) or within the lantern opening during the construction of the oculus ring. Other revolving cranes were used in the building of the lantern (→ Figs. 1.8.8–9). On the other hand, external scaffolding was used to repair lightning damage to the lantern in 1601 (→ Fig. 1.8.11).

Many more machines (light hoists, revolving elevators and so on) which were used during the raising of the Cupola have been variously attributed to Brunelleschi.

Some parts of these machines are housed today in one of the apsidioles.[13]

199

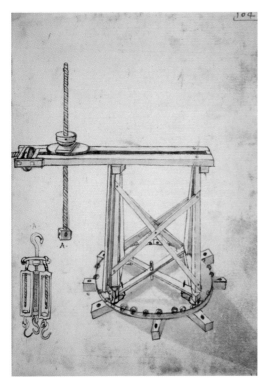
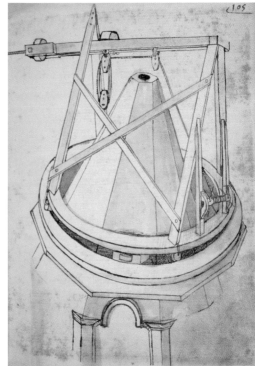

1.8.8–9. Revolving crane on a rotating platform and crane with load-positioning device, employed during the construction of the lantern (BNCF, MS BR 228, fols. 104r and 105r).

1.8.10. Equipment used in the construction of the Cupola: iron pincers, hangers and pulleys.

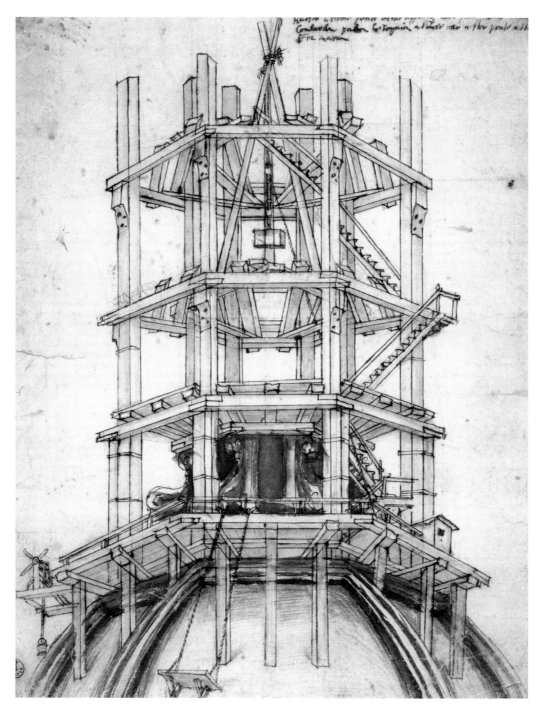

1.8.11. Hoisting equipment and platforms used in 1601 to repair lightning damage to the lantern, in a drawing attributed to Gherardo Mechini (Florence, GDSU, 248 A).

AN INTERPRETATION OF THE STATIC BEHAVIOUR OF THE CUPOLA

2.1. The Static Behaviour of the Cupola in the Context of the Development of the Science of Structures and Materials

As far as we know, the builders of Brunelleschi's times thought of structures in elementary, empirical terms of loads transferred by vertical or inclined supports (piers, buttresses) to the horizontal members (architraves, flat arches, trusses, chains) or curved ones (arches), as well as to the foundations (plinths). It was not until two centuries later, with Galileo Galilei, that a scientific approach to the static behaviour of structures and the strength of materials was initiated, with the application of the quantitative methods of mathematics to these fields and to mechanical sciences in general.[1]

In order to understand how the structural problems posed by the Cupola were perceived by Brunelleschi in the design and executive phases and by those who down to the present day have been responsible for diagnostic studies, maintenance and repair work, it is advisable to build up a historical overview of the development of the science of structural analysis, as new conceptual and mathematical tools became available.

In his treatise entitled *Discorsi e dimostrazioni matematiche intorno a due nuove scienze attenenti alla mecanica et i movimenti locali* ('Discourses and mathematical demonstrations concerning two new sciences pertaining to mechanics and local motions'), Galileo cast into sharp historical perspective the contrast between the practice of early architects (amongst whom one must obviously include Brunelleschi himself, his signal innovative genius notwithstanding) and the new ideas, borne out by the practical experience of the master builders, about the crucial *influence of size on the resistance of geometrically similar structures* (→ Inset 2).

It has been noted that "the science of building can be divided into two great historical periods. In the first one there was no precise conception of stress and deformation, and it was believed that the *firmitas* of a structure could be achieved through the mutual arrangement of its parts, so as to avoid the possibility of relative motion. The shape of an arch, of a vault, of profiled masonry courses were the variables the builder could play with in order to create self-balanced systems of active and reactive forces. In other words, the *firmitas* was believed to be determined by the relative proportions between the parts, quite irrespective of size. In the second period, on the other hand, once a given structural shape is chosen, the builder investigates the resistance properties of the material in order to avoid fracturing, and defines the size of the different members so that stresses are kept within admissible limits".[2] And, it may be added, given the shape, the material and the constraints there follows necessarily an *extreme admissible size* beyond which, as Galileo clearly saw, the *dead weight* alone compromises the structural equilibrium. Galileo studied structures of different size loaded by their own weight: he took natural creatures as an example (in his eyes they were perfect and therefore could be used as a paradigm for artificial structures), observing that the bones of large-size animals are thicker and stouter than those of smaller beasts (→ Fig. 2.1.1).

In two geometrically similar structures of the same material, the respective weights are in the ratio of their linear dimensions raised to the power of three, while the resistance of the cross-sections carrying those weights is proportional to their areas, i.e. to the square of their dimensions. Therefore, the stresses acting on a similarly located unit surface of the two structures—to

2. The Lesson of Galileo

It is true, says Sagredo to Salviati, the advocate for new ideas, that it is often useful to question those who have acquired experience and competence in their field of work. Sometimes, however, what is perceived by the senses may be unacceptable to reason: "Notwithstanding the fact that what the old man told us a little while ago is proverbial and commonly accepted, yet it seemed to me altogether false, like many another saying which is current among the ignorant; for I think they introduce these expressions in order to give the appearance of knowing something about matters which they do not understand."

The "old man" whom Sagredo had encountered at the Arsenale in Venice maintained that structures grow weaker as their dimensions increase, "because many devices which succeed on a small scale do not work on a large scale"; the geometrically minded Sagredo could not accept this thesis, and in fact he countered: "Since mechanics has its foundation in geometry, where mere size cuts no figure, I do not see that the properties of circles, triangles, cylinders, cones and other solid figures will change with their size. If, therefore, a large machine be constructed in such a way that its parts bear to one another the same ratio as in a smaller one, and if the smaller is sufficiently strong for the purpose for which it was designed, I do not see why the larger also should not be able to withstand any severe and destructive tests to which it may be subjected."

But Salviati retorts with an opposing argument: "The common opinion is here absolutely wrong. Indeed, it is so far wrong that precisely the opposite is true, namely, that many machines can be constructed even more perfectly on a large scale than on a small; thus, for instance, a clock which indicates and strikes the hour, can be made more accurate on a large scale than on a small. [...] Here I trust you will not charge me with arrogance if I say that imperfections in the material, even those which are great enough to invalidate the clearest mathematical proof, are not sufficient to explain the deviations observed between machines in the concrete and in the abstract. Yet I shall say it and will affirm that, even if the imperfections did not exist and matter were absolutely perfect, unalterable and free from all accidental variations, still the mere fact that it is matter makes the larger machine, built of the same material and in the same proportion as the smaller, correspond with exactness to the smaller in every respect except that it will not be so strong or so resistant against violent treatment; the larger the machine, the greater its weakness. Since I assume matter to be unchangeable and always the same, it is clear that we are no less able to treat this constant and invariable property in a rigid manner than if it belonged to simple and pure mathematics. Therefore, Sagredo, you would do well to change the opinion which you, and perhaps also many other students of mechanics, have entertained concerning the ability of machines and structures to resist external disturbances, thinking that when they are built of the same material and maintain the same ratio between parts, they are able equally, or rather proportionally, to resist or yield to such external disturbances and blows. For we can demonstrate by geometry that the large machine is not proportionately stronger than the small. Finally, we may say that, for every machine and structure, whether artificial or natural, there is set a necessary limit beyond which neither art nor nature can pass; it is here understood, of course, that the material is the same and the proportion preserved."*

* Galileo Galilei, *Dialogues Concerning Two New Sciences*, translated by H. Crew and A. de Salvio, with an introduction by A. Favaro, unabridged and unaltered republication of the 1914 edition published by Macmillan (New York: Dover, 1954), 1–3.

be compared with the admissible stress limit for the given material—stand in the same ratio as the quotients of the cube and the square of their linear dimensions, namely in direct proportion to their size. As the latter increases, sooner or later—depending on the shape and on the constraints—the stress limit of the material will be exceeded. This interplay of size and resistance is common knowledge today, thanks also to the general framework provided by dimensional analysis and by the principles of mechanical similitude.[3]

Another important consequence of this modern conceptual knowledge is that in order to faithfully reproduce the behaviour of the actual structure in a reduced-scale model it is necessary to artificially increase the specific gravity of the material in the model (if it is the same as that of the structure) or the ratio between specific gravity and material strength (if a different material is used in the model). The factor of increase is the ratio between the actual size and the model's size; in the current practice of physical modelling of big structures (for instance dams), such an increase is effected in an approximate way by means of a dense array of vertical tendons, fixed to points distributed in the interior of the model and loaded by appropriately proportioned external weights.[4]

The transition from the first to the second period could not have taken place before a clear acceptance, on the part of the prevailing scientific and technical culture, of the concepts so compellingly expounded by Galileo in his *Discourses* two centuries after the raising of the Cupola. The building knowledge and practice of Brunelleschi's times fall squarely in the first of the two mentioned periods.

It is, therefore, quite reasonable to presume that the success in raising smaller domes more or less similar to the Cupola in design, and also the Baptistery itself (about 60% of the size of the Cupola and with no apparent structural problems), led Brunelleschi and his contemporaries to feel confident on two counts. On one hand,

the feasibility of the method of building without scaffold-supported centring had been proven; on the other hand, the successful experiments with the models were grounds for presuming that the actual project would be successful as well, its vastly increased proportions notwithstanding. In other words, Brunelleschi—and those called upon to assess the validity of his plans—might have inferred from the successful completion of the models, not only that the building method was practicable, but also that the load-bearing capacity of the full-size structure would be adequate. Alas, such a conclusion should not have been drawn without due consideration of the resistance properties (in relation to compressive and above all to tensile stresses) of the masonry of the Cupola.

This does not mean that the intuitive conclusions of Brunelleschi were *necessarily* faulty; but there can be no doubt that he was venturing, without being fully aware of it, far beyond what could be learned from existing buildings. Within this uncharted territory his paradigms, based on the sole parameters of *similarity of shape* and *use of the same materials and building techniques*, were not *sufficient* to yield the certainties he probably thought he had reached.

Some residual doubts about the wisdom of applying the experience gained on smaller structures to the much more large-scale project of the Cupola did seem to linger in the minds of Brunelleschi's contemporaries, as can be seen in the following comment by Manetti: "after this experience [the building of the Ridolfi chapel], his [Brunelleschi's] words began to gain some credit, but not entirely, because this was a small thing and the other a huge one".[5]

* * *

What has been said thus far still does not take into account the *deformation* of the structure, as an intuitive understanding of the relevant concepts only requires a simple analysis of the *equilibrium* between external actions and internal reactions (→ Inset 3). After Galileo, an increasing need was felt to analyse redundant structures, i.e. structures with more constraints than are necessary to prevent rigid-body motion. An investigation of the internal stress distribution in these structures cannot be carried out without analysing strain distribution; therefore the rigid-body model had to be superseded. This need led in due course to the development of the Mechanics of Deformable Bodies, which requires the postulation of an analytic law (known as the 'constitutive law') governing local stresses and strains. Initially, and for a considerable time thereafter, the simplest assumption was accepted, namely that a proportional, or linear, relationship existed between internal stresses and local strains.[6] New mathematical tools such as the infinitesimal calculus developed by Newton and Huygens in the 17th century—which later evolved into modern differential and integral calculus—prepared the ground for the Theory of Elasticity (thanks to the likes of Lamé, Cauchy, Airy and others), and for the more technical offshoots of modern Structural Analysis and Strength of Materials (Mariotte, Bernoulli, Euler, Coulomb, Navier and so on).[7]

The most recent studies of the Cupola were carried out in the 1980s and 1990s (→ § 3.2) and used modern computerised methods of numer-

ical analysis (the Finite Element Method). These methods make it possible to obtain approximate solutions to the linear differential equations of the Theory of Elasticity—once a mathematical model has been set up to include (in a form suitable to the numerical approach) the structure's geometry, the acting forces, the properties of materials and the constraints. The results, which lie within a tolerable margin of approximation, offer a detailed description of the stress distribution in the structure assuming a linear constitutive law for the stress-strain relationship. It thus becomes possible to pinpoint the lines, surfaces or volumes of the continuum where the numerical model yields high stress values (particularly tensile ones), thereby enabling identification of the regions of the structure where local fractures or non-elastic deformation are likely to occur in the actual material. In order to determine whether these disorders can find a new equilibrium or will, on the contrary, increase and extend to other zones, theories and analytical tools of a different nature are required.

Amongst these one should mention Fracture Mechanics, the development of which started in relatively recent times (Griffith, 1920). Based on theoretical knowledge of the molecular structure of solid materials, Fracture Mechanics investigates the behaviour and resistance conditions around specific points (for instance reentrant corners) where the theoretical solutions of the linear Theory of Elasticity equations would yield infinitely large stress values. In physical reality, these conditions would produce a crack, which, depending on local conditions, could either propagate or stabilise.[8] An important achievement of Fracture Mechanics is the theoretical and experimental finding that crack formation and propagation is a scale-sensitive process, in the sense that a large-size structure is more 'brittle', namely more prone to cracking and to sudden structural failure, than a geometrically similar but smaller structure. From this viewpoint as well, therefore, any attempt to extrapolate from experience acquired either on reduced-

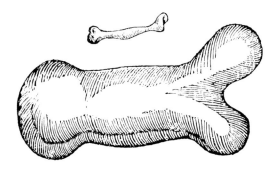

2.1.1. Bone structure of different-sized animals (from Galileo's *Discorsi e dimostrazioni matematiche intorno a due nuove scienze attenenti alla mecanica et i movimenti locali*).

scale models or on smaller structures and to apply it to larger structures should be approached with the utmost caution and investigated with appropriate tools.

This knowledge was obviously not available when the Cupola was built; nevertheless, there is some indication that Brunelleschi paid keen attention towards details of building technique that would nowadays fall within the sphere of fracture susceptibility. (Evidently his approach was based purely on intuition, probably corroborated by frequent and careful observation of ancient monuments in varying states of repair.) The 'slack-line' arrangement of the brickwork, for instance, testifies to his constant care to avoid as much as possible any angular discontinuity along the corner spurs, where the bricklaying beds of two adjacent segments intersect. Indeed, at the intersection of two segments, their intrados surfaces make a reentrant solid angle which, starting from 135° at the springing of the Cupola, opens gradually with increasing elevation, tending to about 157° near the oculus ring. Stemming inevitably from the octagonal geometry of the Cupola, this reentrant angle would by itself be potentially conducive to dangerous levels of stress concentration even in a homogeneous solid. To this should be added the effect of the inherent heterogeneity of the masonry, which would have been further accentuated had the mortar beds of the two segments followed *plane* surfaces perpendicular to the segments themselves and parallel to the straight generatrices of the extrados and intrados surfaces; the bricklaying beds of the two adjacent segments would then have met along the common edge under another solid angle (the edge of which is perpendicular to the edge of the angle at the intersection of the two segments). This second reentrant solid angle—which is flat (180°) at the springing of the Cupola and progressively closes 'bookwise' as the elevation increases, down to a value not too far from 135° at the oculus ring—would have made it impossible to maintain a regular, continuous masonry tex-

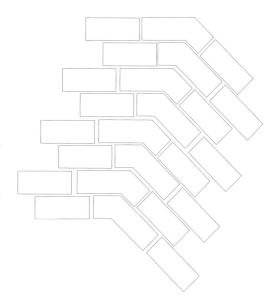

2.1.2. Layout of the masonry texture along the corner spurs: the angular bricks have sides of uneven length.

ture along the corners of the Cupola, and would have multiplied the stress concentration due to the presence of the first reentrant angle. The technique of laying the brickwork in 'slack-line' fashion—that is, along curved rather than plane surfaces—together with the adoption of angular bricks with uneven-length sides and with an inclined profile, alternating along the edge (→ Fig. 2.1.2), made it possible to minimise this secondary effect of stress concentration. Indeed, in this way the masonry texture retains, at least in principle, the regularity of a straight wall, where heterogeneity is induced solely by the mortar joints between the bricks.

The cause that triggered the main cracks, however, lay—as will be seen shortly—not so much in the stress concentration along the corners as in the configuration of the octagonal drum, whose sides, loaded by the immense weight of the Cupola, rest alternately on the four massive piers and on the four great pointed arches. The complex flexural behaviour of this huge three-dimensional deep beam sustaining the Cupola on eight sides and supported by the piers on only four sides could not have been ascertained

3. The Equilibrium Between External Forces and Internal Reactions in a Rotationally Symmetric Membrane and in an Octagonal Dome

In a rotationally symmetric *membrane* (a thin shell the thickness of which is negligible compared to its size; → Fig. 2.1.3) loaded by rotationally symmetric forces, local and global *equilibrium* conditions alone are sufficient to determine the stress regime along the meridian and parallel lines, these stresses being of a purely compressive or tensile nature. In a rotationally symmetric *dome of finite thickness* joined to other structures there arise, beside the membrane stresses, boundary-condition-induced disturbances consisting of bending moments and shear forces acting on the meridians. These flexural stresses cannot be accounted for merely by considering equilibrium conditions, but require the introduction of the appropriate boundary conditions (constraints at the lower edge and loads on the upper edge) and resort to the mechanics of deformable bodies. Such stresses propagate along the meridians, diminishing more or less progressively as the distance from the edges increases, and produce appreciable effects over a varying area extending from the edges themselves, depending on the ratio between thickness and the radii of curvature of the parallels. The latter remain under purely axial stress, which in the case of a dome loaded by its own dead weight are compressive in the upper and tensile in the lower parts, provided the curvature of the meridians is uniformly concave towards the interior.

In an *octagonal dome* the static regime is more complex, since there are bending moments and shear forces along the parallels as well (→ § 2.2). In Brunelleschi's Cupola the situation is rendered even more complicated, since in addition to its octagonal shape, one must consider the interplay between the two shells. Only a three-dimensional mathematical model that takes into account the actual geometry and constraint conditions can provide an accurate picture of the stress distribution, both for an undamaged and a cracked structure. Such a model was developed during the 1980s and 1990s (→ § 3.2). Accepting some approximations, one can however conduct a simpler analysis, which is perhaps even more illuminating from the point of view of 'structural intuition' (→ § 2.2 and § 3.4).

It seems unlikely that builders in Brunelleschi's time were equipped with conceptual models of the kind briefly outlined above, not even the simplest one of the rotationally symmetric membrane; they lacked fundamental concepts and abstractions such as the notions of *internal stress* (in

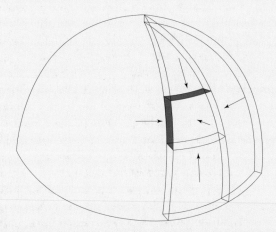

2.1.3. Diagram showing the equilibrium of forces in a rotationally symmetric membrane.

its various components) and *local equilibrium*; static analysis of arches, vaults and domes only got under way in the 17th century.* During the 19th century, when it had become clear that what was needed was an analysis not only of equilibrium but also of deformations, the problem received systematic treatment, at least of a linear elastic nature. The formal advances made in this period have survived more or less intact to the present day and are still taught in engineering schools.

Considering the long, arduous process that led to an *analytic* understanding of the structural behaviour of domes, the *synthetic* genius of Brunelleschi is all the more remarkable, given that he was able to conceive and successfully realise this extraordinarily bold project relying only on structural intuition and experience.

* Amongst the most significant contributions produced during the 18th century one should mention: Charles-Augustin de Coulomb's "Essai sur une application des règles de maximis et minimis à quelques problèmes de statique, relatifs à l'Architecture" (*Mémoires de mathématique et de physique présentés à l'Académie royale des sciences*, 1776), in which he studies arches and flat arches; Lorenzo Mascheroni's important *Nuove ricerche sull'equilibrio delle volte* (Bergamo 1785), which deals, amongst other things, with polygonal domes; and Leonardo Salimbeni's six-volume *Degli archi e delle volte* (Verona 1787), which also contains an examination of formwork-related problems.

4. The Analysis by Giovanni Poleni

Of all the analyses of the behaviour of the Cupola conducted in the five centuries that have elapsed since Brunelleschi's day, the work of Giovanni Poleni, *Memorie istoriche della Gran Cupola del Tempio Vaticano* ('Historical Account of the Great Dome of the Vatican Temple', Padua 1748), is particularly noteworthy. Poleni not only examined the dome of St Peter's in Rome, but also the Cupola of Florence, which he had visited in order to study its cracks. He was a precursor of an experimental procedure not unlike the one employed in the 1930s by Antoni Gaudí to define the shape of the structural members of the Sagrada Familia in Barcelona. In order to interpret the shape of the Cupola in a simple way, Poleni considered the curve assumed by a freely hanging piece of string fixed at both ends on the same horizontal level and loaded with weights proportional per unit length to their distance from a central symmetry axis (a conceptual model that had already been studied by James Stirling in 1717). It can be shown that this equilibrium curve, when reversed, can also be seen as the meridian equilibrium configuration of a thin segment of a rotationally symmetric membrane of uniform thickness under the action of the dead weight *where the stiffness of the parallels is neglected*. In likening the three-dimensional behaviour of a *dome* to that of a *two-dimensional arch*, Poleni argued that the shape assigned to a meridian section of the Cupola, strikingly close to one of the theoretical 'catenary' configurations of his string ($\rightarrow$ Fig. 2.1.4), was capable of achieving a membrane equilibrium, namely an equilibrium without bending moments. Poleni implicitly applied this conclusion to the Cupola in its original, undamaged state; in this state, however, the stiffness of the parallels is such that, owing to the interaction of meridians and parallels, a condition of membrane equilibrium can also be achieved with meridian curves very different from the string-generated catenaries. But his conceptual model *can* be likened to the behaviour of the Cupola *when assumed to be damaged by numerous, circumferentially distributed meridian cracks extending from the springing line to the summit* ($\rightarrow$ § 3.4); in this case, the parallels would no longer contribute to the equilibrium along the entire length of the meridians. It would

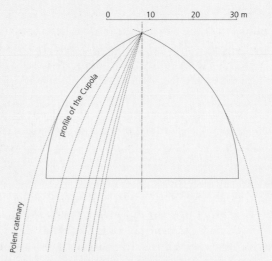

0   10   20   30 m

profile of the Cupola

Poleni catenary

2.1.4. Comparison between one of Poleni's catenaries and the section of the intrados of the inner shell with a vertical plane passing through two diametrically opposite edges.

seem, then, that Poleni's model suggests *the possibility for the Cupola to achieve a stable equilibrium*, under the action of its dead weight, *even after the development of extensive vertical cracking right to the top of the structure*. Strictly speaking, this conclusion only really applies if one disregards the disturbances caused by boundary conditions, which alter the membrane regime; besides, in reality there is not a closely distributed pattern of cracks, but essentially just four full-thickness ones, so that the four resulting 'segments' into which the Cupola is divided are very substantial, and unlike the string which is endowed only with axial stiffness, they also have a meridian bending stiffness. Finally, at both extremities Poleni's catenary is inclined to the vertical and not tangent to it as are the meridian curves of the Cupola (→ Fig. 2.1.4), suggesting that the lower rim of the Cupola can never be free from radial thrusts and bending moments. However, the close resemblance between the two curves allows one to surmise that the bending moments generated along the meridians of the Cupola after the development of the main cracks were limited (→ § 3.4).*

* On the other hand, the theoretical possibility of reaching an equilibrium that is almost exempt from bending moments even after cracking, thanks to the Cupola's meridian shape, is not entirely reassuring. Poleni's findings only apply (approximately) when dead weight is the sole load considered. Under different loading conditions, for instance in the event of an earthquake, the meridian equilibrium of the cracked structure would necessarily call into play bending moments, which are quite dangerous for the masonry. By contrast, an undamaged dome could deal with these additional loads through a redistribution of the stresses among meridians and parallels, without generating bending moments (or at least only very limited ones).

at the time of raising. Even on a purely intuitive and qualitative level, an understanding of this behaviour would have required the availability of concepts—and of an elaborate formal language—suitable to describe, at least phenomenologically, the statics of deformable bodies. Not even the most basic notion of such tools existed in those times.

*   *   *

Even after the enormous development of analytical tools in the 20th century and the beginning of systematic quantitative measurements, the commission appointed in 1934 still expressed strong doubts about the possibility of successfully applying the methods of structural analysis to interpret the Cupola's static behaviour.[9] This was allegedly in view of the difficulties of introducing into a mathematical model all the details of the building, the external actions (amongst which great importance was attributed to thermal loads) and the constraints. While the commission's scepticism was dictated by observations which can partially be shared, it was certainly overly pessimistic. Apart from the more recent numerical analyses carried out with Finite Element numerical models in the 1980s and 1990s (→ § 3.2), which enabled remarkable advances in the detailed comprehension of the structure's static behaviour, even the traditional methods of structural analysis—well-known to engineers since the end of the 19th century and thus available to the commission—could have yielded useful insights regarding the interplay of internal reactions (→ § 2.2).

*   *   *

Although certainly not exhaustive, the above historical outline probably suffices to delineate the evolution of the conceptual models successively employed to interpret the static equilibrium of the Cupola and to chart and explain the changes that have occurred over the intervening centuries. These topics will be examined in more detail further on (→ §§ 2.2–3, 3.1–2, 3.4), partic-

ularly with regard to current interpretations of the cracking phenomena and to the conclusions about the present state of the damage and possible future scenarios.

2.2. Interpretation of the Static Behaviour of the Cupola Both in the Undamaged and in the Cracked State

First of all, the static behaviour of the Cupola in the undamaged state shall be described in the simplest possible terms according to the conceptual models of structural analysis. The same conceptual tools will then be used to illustrate the radically different behaviour of the Cupola after the formation of the main cracks—the four vertical fissures traversing the whole thickness of the two shells in the four segments resting directly above the piers, i.e. the ones facing northeast, south-east, south-west and north-west.

The description of the static regime of the damaged Cupola will not include consideration of the *origin* and *development* of the cracks themselves, which will be tackled later on (→ § 3.2) in the light of the results of sophisticated numerical investigation. For the sake of simplicity, in what follows reference will be made to a single shell rather than to the twin shells bound together by radial spurs. The perturbations caused at the top by the load of the lantern and at the bottom by the constraint of the drum and surrounding structures (apses, nave) will also be neglected; considerations of *equilibrium* alone shall suffice to carry out the analysis as an extension to polygonal domes of the theory for rotationally symmetric shells. The regime of the completed Cupola will be analysed, introducing where suitable a few considerations about the equilibrium conditions during raising.

*   *   *

The interpretation of the behaviour of the undamaged Cupola constantly ran up against the difficulties posed by a *polygonal* rather than a *circular* plan.

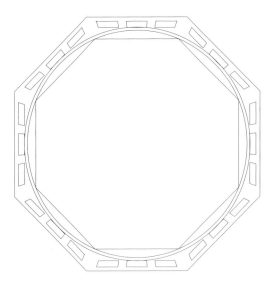

2.2.1. Diagram showing a circular ring inscribed within the thickness of the inner shell.

A few of the early scholars who studied the problem (Leon Battista Alberti), and some of the modern ones (Rowland J. Mainstone), tried to get round it by falling back on the well-known and relatively unproblematic case of rotationally symmetric 'membranes' or domes. They substituted the octagonal Cupola with a virtually 'equivalent', rotationally symmetric dome, to which they assigned a geometry as close as possible to the real one, namely containing most of the masonry of the Cupola. Other scholars (once again including Alberti) proposed an interesting, intuitive conceptual model.[10] They observe that inside the thickness of the inner shell it is possible to inscribe at any given elevation an uninterrupted circular ring which can behave as the circular 'parallel' of a rotationally symmetric shell, with compressive hoop stress in the higher part of the Cupola and a tensile one in the lower part. However, the problem is that in such a model the rings end up being quite thin near the springing of the Cupola (→ Fig. 2.2.1) and increasingly thick with growing elevation; this should be something of an embarrassment to exponents of this model, since the need for substantial hoop re-

sistance is greater in the lower parallels, subject to tensile stresses, than in the higher ones. They implicitly assume, without however providing any proof, that the inscribed rings are stressed uniformly across their thickness as in a circularly symmetric membrane. Trusting in the self-sustaining capacity of each ring, they maintain that the octagonal Cupola can be thought of as behaving almost like a circular one. They also claim that Brunelleschi had envisaged the possibility of this structural behaviour, and that his intention was therefore to have his Cupola behave as a circular shell, its polygonal geometry notwithstanding.[11]

In actual fact the concept of the circular rings inscribed within the thickness of the polygonal ones is both misleading and unnecessary for a correct interpretation of the behaviour of the octagonal parallels. Indeed, it is quite easy to show that in the upper part of the Cupola the octagonal parallels are subjected to combined compressive and bending stresses, in a static regime similar to that of a *flat arch*. Moreover, this analysis results in an interesting interpretation of the vital *structural* functions played by *building* techniques such as the 'slack line' and the herringbone. Ingrained in the texture of the masonry itself and variously described and interpreted by scholars, these techniques appear, from this point of view, to be closely correlated and to play complementary roles in ensuring optimal stress transmission across the mortar bed joints between brick layers. It is improbable that all of this could have been clear to Brunelleschi at the time; with the benefit of hindsight it might even remind one of Pier Luigi Nervi's conception of the arrangement of structural members along the 'isostatic lines' of a structure. Nevertheless, thanks to his profound grasp of the underlying unity of *form* and *function*, it is not inconceivable that he understood all this at an intuitive level. The *considerations of geometry and symmetry* that feature prominently in the following analysis would certainly have been familiar to Brunelleschi, the inventor of geometric perspective and a friend and pupil of the mathematician Paolo dal Pozzo Toscanelli.

The following analysis of the Cupola takes its octagonal geometry into account and is therefore a necessary introduction to the subsequent description of the static regime of the cracked Cupola, which could not be fully understood by referring to a circularly symmetric geometry.

a. Analysis of the Static Regime
of an Undamaged Octagonal Shell

Let us consider,[12] at an intermediate elevation (say at an inclination greater than 30° from the horizontal), a pair of planes close to each other, normal to the intrados and extrados surfaces of a segment and containing its horizontal generatrices. The intersections of these planes with the inner and outer surfaces of the segment are four parallel, horizontal straight lines (→ Fig. 2.2.2). Starting from the intersections of these four lines with the planes of the segment corners, similar lines can be drawn on the two adjacent segments. Repeating the procedure for each successive segment, an octagonal ring with a nearly rec-

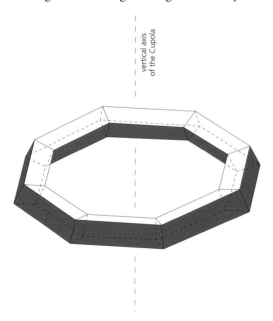

vertical axis of the Cupola

2.2.2. Complete octagonal ring, the equilibrium of which is analysed here (axonometric view).

tangular cross-section is defined. (The cross-section is actually slightly trapezoidal because of the convergence of the section planes caused by the curvature of the segments.)

Consider now the equilibrium of this octagonal ring under the dead weight of the segment; without going into the details of the analysis,[13] the following important results emerge:

• compressive stresses act all along what, for the sake of simplicity, may be called meridian lines; these stresses increase from the summit down, their resultant offsetting with its vertical component the weight of the overlying parts in any given section. Compressive internal forces (*meridian thrusts*) directed tangentially to the meridians can therefore be found on the two sections of the octagonal ring normal to the meridians; their intensity, known from the above-mentioned global equilibrium condition, is greater in the lower surface of the ring—for simplicity these thrusts are assumed to be uniformly distributed along each of the sixteen sections lying on the above-defined planes normal to the meridians;

• the internal actions transmitted within the octagonal ring across the vertical sections of the ring lying on the edge planes between two segments must consist, *for reasons of symmetry*, of axial stresses normal to the sections themselves. The line of action of the resultant of these internal stresses will be more or less eccentric with respect to the centroid of the shell's thickness (see further on), but equally so for all eight corners of the ring, again for reasons of symmetry. The eight lines of action (one for each corner of the ring) are therefore contained in a single horizontal plane, parallel to the plane that contains the octagonal axis of the ring.

Now let us consider the equilibrium of one of the eight sides of the ring (→ Fig. 2.2.3a–b), first in the direction normal to the local meridians ('radial equilibrium'), then along the meridians themselves ('tangent equilibrium'). Symmetry ensures that what is found for one side holds for all eight of them.

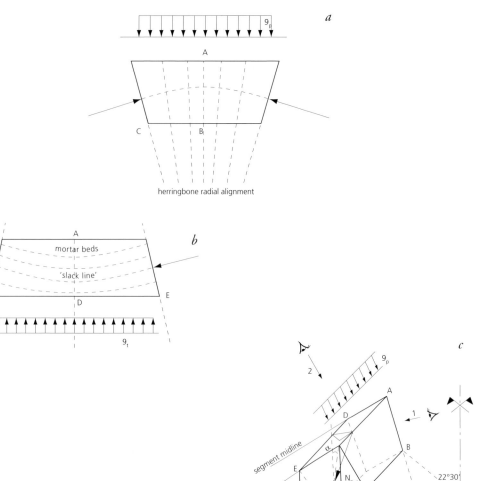

2.2.3. Radial (*a*) and tangential (*b*) equilibrium of the side of an octagonal ring subjected to compression and bending in the upper part of the Cupola.
a. line of view 1, normal to the mortar beds: flat-arch mode of functioning.
b. line of view 2, normal to the extrados surface of the shell.
c. one eighth of the octagonal ring, perspective view.

In the *radial direction*, there must be equilibrium between the following forces: (1) the component of the weight of the side normal to the meridian; (2) the radial component of the resultant of the two meridian thrusts acting on the lower and upper section of the side (see above: the thrusts can be determined from the conditions of vertical equilibrium); (3) the two projections on the radial plane of the internal corner forces the *direction* of which was determined above, these projections being directed towards the exterior of the ring, namely upwards. This *global* equilibrium of the side of the ring makes it possible to establish the *magnitude* of the corner forces, the direction and intensity of which are now known. Yet, in addition to this global equilibrium, there must also be *local* equilibrium in all points along the side itself. Once again *symmetry* can be invoked to define the constraint conditions of the side at both ends. Indeed, assuming that the masonry does not break anywhere, no rotations (either relative or absolute) can take place at the corners in the ring plane without violating the symmetrical behaviour of the sides of the ring.

It can thus be shown (→ Fig. 2.2.4), once again ignoring the finer details, that each of the ring sides is subjected to *combined compressive and bending stresses*, under conditions very much like those of a *flat arch* with fixed ends. This unambiguously defines also the *eccentricity* of the internal corner forces transmitted through the ends of the side with respect to the middle surface of the shell. In this way the internal 'parallel' stress at the corners, and thus along the whole side, is completely determined—in the plane of the ring—in each of its components: axial stress, bending moment and shear. The deformed shape assumed by the ring sides is shown in Figure 2.2.5, where the arrows represent the displacements from the undeformed to the deformed position; note that the displacements take place on radial planes, hence on a different plane for each side of the ring.

In particular, the following could happen:

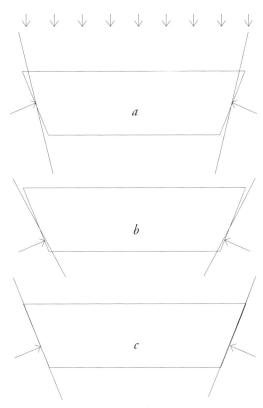

2.2.4. Deformation of the side of an octagonal ring subjected to pressure and bending in the upper part of the Cupola: the condition of zero end-rotation obtains only for a well-defined value of eccentricity.
a. eccentricity < ⅙ h: rotation producing a decrease of the angle formed by the two end-faces (constraint weaker than the perfect fixed-end condition)
b. eccentricity > ⅙ h: rotation producing an increase of the angle formed by the two end-faces (constraint stronger than the perfect fixed-end condition)
c. eccentricity = ⅙ h: zero rotation of the two end-faces (perfect fixed-end condition)

(1) that as a consequence of this global equilibrium the internal forces transmitted across the ring corners are *tensile* instead of compressive (this occurs in the parts of the Cupola between the springing line and an elevation of about 16 m above it, corresponding to an inclination to the centre of 27°); the rings in this part of the Cupola are subjected to *combined tension and bending*—their deformation, confirmed also by the more accurate Finite Element analyses (→ Fig. 3.2.7b–c), is depicted in Figure 2.2.6. At

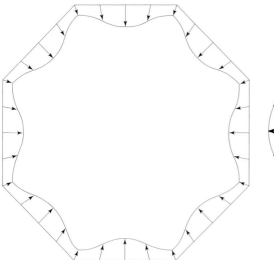

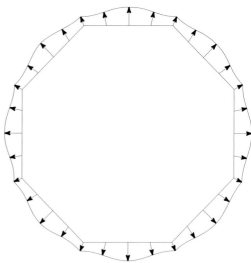

2.2.5. Deformation (greatly exaggerated) of the axis of an octagonal ring subjected to combined compression and bending in the upper part of the Cupola.

2.2.6. Deformation (greatly exaggerated) of the axis of an octagonal ring subjected to combined tension and bending in the lower part of the Cupola.

the base of the Cupola the highest horizontal tensile stresses occurring along the intrados of the inner shell near the corners can be estimated (discounting disturbances owing to boundary conditions) at about 7.5 kgf/cm², which is certainly greater than the tensile strength of the brick masonry; cracks across the whole thickness are to be expected in these low rings;

(2) that, though the internal forces transmitted across the ring corners are *compressive* (this occurs in the parts of the Cupola over 16 m above the springing line), the eccentricity of the line of action of these forces with respect to the middle surface of the shell is greater than one sixth of the shell's thickness. This is more likely to happen for the widest of these rings—and with greater probability at the corners, where the eccentricity is twice that of the midline of the segment; in this case horizontal tensile stresses will occur on the extrados of the shell. Indeed, at intermediate elevations fine vertical cracks can be observed, from the inter-shell cavity, in some of the corner spurs: these cracks, however, do not penetrate the whole thickness, because the rings in question are subjected to combined compres-

sion and bending, while in the lower parts—where there are stresses of a tensile and bending nature—the cracks run right through the shell. *The fact that in this higher part of the Cupola any given side of the ring behaves as a flat arch is consistent with the converging radial alignments of the planes along which the brick courses of the herringbone are oriented* (→ Fig. 2.2.3a). It is worth noting that Brunelleschi was very familiar with the structural device of the flat arch, which he also used to bridge wide spans—for instance, the great one in the Sacrestia dei Canonici (Canons' Sacristy) in Santa Maria del Fiore[14] (→ Fig. 2.2.8), the proportions of which are remarkably similar to those of the segments' sections. The application of the herringbone technique to circular domes, well-known in Brunelleschi's times, relied on the circular segments between two successive herringbones acting as segments of a circular arch; sliding towards the centre, these locked together progressively in mutual contrast. But Brunelleschi had to make the structure of the segments conform to the octagonal geometry of the drum, and therefore could not build circular rings. It is not unreasonable, then, to

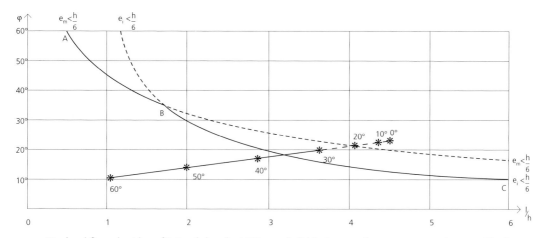

2.2.7a. Fixed-end flat arch without friction: below the ABC curve (solid line) no tensile stresses occur under normal load on the upper side.

The asterisks denote points corresponding to horizontal sections of the Cupola's segments; the values shown correspond to the sloping of the mortar beds towards the Cupola's axis. Note, however, that between 0° and about 30° the rings are subjected to tension and bending because the load p is negative.

2.2.8. The flat arch of the Canons' Sacristy (also known as the Old Sacristy) inside the Cathedral of Santa Maria del Fiore.

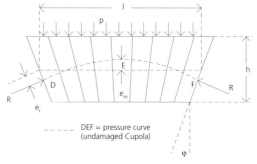

2.2.7b. Diagram showing one side of the octagonal ring when interpreted as a flat arch.

imagine that the idea of making the sides of the octagonal rings function as flat arches might well have occurred to him.[15]

It is important to note that the radial equilibrium of an octagonal ring is more delicate during bricklaying, even after the mortar has set. In these conditions there is no masonry above the ring, and below it the meridian thrust is very nearly zero, as there is only the ring's own weight to balance; hence the resultant of the meridian thrusts on the ring obviously lacks a radial component. The radial components of the ring's weight must be offset solely by the self-tightening of the ring and by the radial shear forces—

between the new ring and the underlying masonry—acting through the fresh mortar bed laid on the 'slack-line' surface. This static regime is therefore very different from the membrane regime previously described.

It is also evident that during this phase, and until the masonry had appreciably progressed above the ring, the support provided by two converging, adjacent herringbones to the brickwork in between was indispensable. But since the horizontal tensile stresses appear to be crucial to the structural integrity of the Cupola, it should be pointed out that the points where these stresses are most critical are across the herringbone bands themselves. The distinctive geometry of this arrangement causes the mortar bed joints inside a band to have greater continuity along the vertical than along the horizontal. This fact is at the root of the different behaviour of the herringbone bands with respect to brick detach-

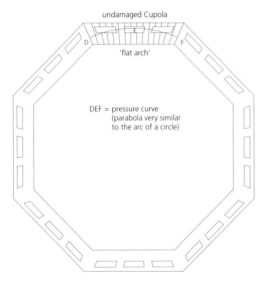

DEF = pressure curve
(parabola very similar
to the arc of a circle)

undamaged Cupola

'flat arch'

2.2.9. The claim by some experts that Brunelleschi intended his Cupola to function as a rotationally symmetric structure despite its octagonal shape can only be accepted in a very narrow sense: the pressure curve is very close to the arc of a circle in the compressed parallels (above an elevation of about 17 m from the springing of the Cupola), but the 'flat-arch' surfaces created by the herringbone arrangement of the brickwork are subjected to combined compression and bending rather than to compression alone, as would be the case in the arc of a circle.

ment along vertical surfaces. Suffice it to consider that in the masonry outside the herringbone bands a vertical crack must either break some bricks or, given the usual offset of bricks between adjacent courses, 'pull out' some bricks; the long, compressed horizontal mortar joints of the bricks with the underlying and overlying courses are broken in shear, and only the short, vertical joints with the adjacent bricks of the same course in tension. Inside a herringbone, on the other hand, a crack can break in tension the relatively long vertical mortar joints between a brick and the adjacent ones and in shear the short, compressed horizontal mortar joints with underlying and overlying bricks. Since the shear resistance of the compressed horizontal mortar joints and the brick tensile resistance are certainly much greater than the tensile strength of the vertical joints, it follows that the cracks along vertical surfaces are more likely to occur inside herringbone bands. Indeed, appreciable stretches of the vertical cracks can be seen in the form of brick detachments along the mortar joints of the herringbone (→ Figs. 2.2.10–1). Thus the herringbone brickwork, although it offered a brilliant solution to the problem of raising the Cupola without centring and enabled the sides of the octagonal rings to behave as flat arches, ultimately introduced into an otherwise compact masonry texture surfaces of lesser resistance to horizontal tensile stresses.

* * *

Let us consider next the equilibrium of one side of the octagonal ring *in the direction of the local tangent to the meridian*: it can be shown that, in the upper section of the Cupola, the tangential component of the meridian thrusts and the tangential component of the dead weight have a resultant that is directed towards the segment's summit. (This result seemingly runs counter to intuition, but is in fact a necessary consequence of the segment's geometry, of the global vertical equilibrium and of the magnitude and orientation of the internal forces in the corners of the ring.) On the other hand, the projections on this plane of the internal forces in the corners of the ring are directed towards the base of the segment. As a consequence, *the 'slack-line' arrangement of the brickwork, besides avoiding any angular discontinuity between the brick beds of two adjacent segments, achieves the result of orienting the mortar bed joints lying on planes normal to the 'slack-line' surfaces in a direction perpendicular to the parallel thrusts all along the side of the octagonal ring* (→ Fig. 2.2.3b).

If one were to interpret the two *building* techniques of the herringbone and the 'slack line' in contemporary terms, it would be possible to attribute to them the *structural* function of allowing the mortar joints to follow surfaces that are normal to the 'isostatic lines' (i.e. the lines that are everywhere tangent to the principal stress directions inside the shell). This means that shear stresses are largely avoided along the mortar joints, thus creating the best joint resistance conditions *provided the stresses transmitted across*

2.2.10. Top, view of the frescoed vault of the Cupola: the masonry texture can be seen where the frescoed plaster has become detached along the oblique line of the herringbone brickwork.
2.2.11. Bottom, a fissure in one of the segments as seen from the first walkway.

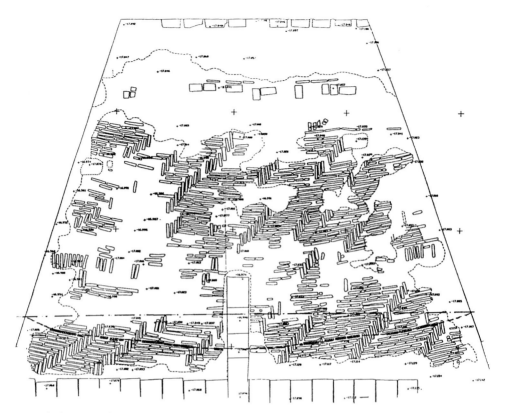

2.2.12. Detail of a section of the masonry texture of the outer shell, from the photogrammetric survey commissioned by the Opera di Santa Maria del Fiore: the 'slack-line' and herringbone arrangement of the brickwork can both be clearly seen.

2.2.13. Reconstruction of various sections of the structure while building work was under way (Rossi, 1977).

the joints are compressive. While this remarkable state of affairs might, of course, have been entirely accidental, the endless discussions about the real origin and function of these building solutions only go to show that there is little concrete knowledge about Brunelleschi's actual insight and intentions. What is certain is that inside the masonry of each segment the internal stress flow along the parallels traces very shallow inverted arches that follow the 'slack-line' surfaces without ever crossing the external surface of the segments. In the planes normal to this surface it is not possible to follow the internal stress flow with 'internal arches' without crossing external surfaces, but it *is* possible, as the next best thing, to realise, by means of the herringbone, flat arches accommodating the stress flow (provided the ring sides are compressed).

b. Analysis of the Static Regime of an Octagonal Shell Riven by Vertical Full-Thickness Cracks Along the Midlines of Four Segments Alternating with Four Undamaged Segments

In this model the structure no longer has complete octagonal symmetry, where each side of a ring (see above) behaves identically. Here a dual symmetry is postulated with respect to a pair of perpendicular vertical planes, each containing the Cupola's axis and the midlines of the undamaged segments, which are opposite each other; one of these planes is oriented from north to south and the other from east to west. In order to simplify the analysis, the full-thickness cracks are assumed to be perfectly vertical (when in fact they follow a somewhat erratic, zigzag path), and to lie exactly on the vertical planes crossing the midline of the damaged segments. According to this new symmetry, each quarter of the ring, formed by a central undamaged segment and by two adjacent half-segments terminating at the cracks, behaves like the three remaining quarters; the conditions of the central segment, however, differ from those of the two half-segments. The width of the full-thickness cracks (amounting to some centimetres at the

level of maximum aperture) is such that no internal stresses can be transmitted from one half-segment to the other across the gap. It is clear, moreover, that in the cracked rings—namely in the 'parallels' belonging to the lower two thirds of the Cupola—the internal axial forces must drop to zero.[16]

Although less complete, this new dual symmetry—together with the global equilibrium conditions in the vertical direction—still ensures that the 'meridian' axial thrusts do not differ appreciably from those acting on the undamaged shell. Now, however, there are bending moments along the meridians (→ § 3.4), and the radial equilibrium of each quarter of the octagonal ring—a middle segment and two half-segments—is ensured entirely by internal forces that consist of bending moments and possibly also of torsional moments. Indeed, the mutual forces at the corners between the sides of the ring have now disappeared completely, because there are no longer any axial thrusts along the ring. Note that the forces that need to be balanced by the new internal actions in the radial planes of the sides of the ring are basically the same as before cracking, with the addition of the resultants of the two distributions of meridian bending moments transmitted to the quarter ring across the two sections cutting off the ring from the rest of the shell.

It is possible to show—using calculations that for ease of description have been omitted—that there are bending moments in each quarter ring (in the radial plane of each side), the distribution of which is symmetrical with respect to the vertical symmetry plane of the undamaged middle segment. These moments grow from zero at the crack face to a maximum on the above-mentioned symmetry plane, and are oriented in such a way that they tend to 'open' the quarter ring, stretching the intrados fibres and compressing the extrados ones (→ Fig. 2.2.14). A deformed configuration of this kind is clearly shown by the results of more accurate Finite Element analysis (→ Fig. 3.2.9b–c).

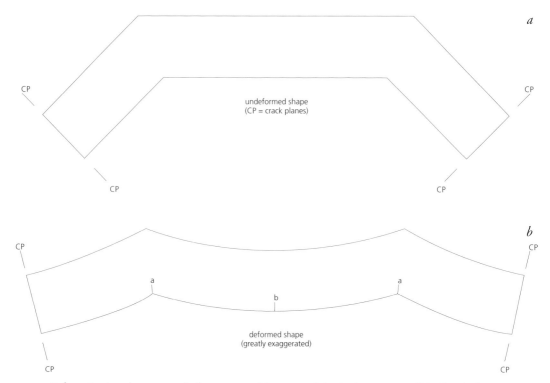

2.2.14. Deformation (greatly exaggerated) of one quarter of the octagonal ring in the upper part of the Cupola after the appearance of the four main cracks.
a. cracking caused by stress concentration as a consequence of the reentrant angle
b. cracking caused by the peak of the bending moment

At the intrados corners of the quarter ring horizontal tensile stresses caused by the bending moment are intensified by way of the local singularity caused by the reentrant angle (the Theory of Elasticity shows that in such a case the tensile stress tends to infinity as the angle vertex is approached). Vertical intrados cracks are then to be expected along the corner edges (see the *a*-points in Fig. 2.2.14), tapering out to nought inside the shell thickness as the extrados is compressed. These cracks can actually be seen on the intrados of the Cupola, and were called *peli* or *screpoli angolari*, that is hair-thin corner cracks, by those who first observed them. Clearly they appeared well before the execution of the frescoes, at which time they must have been visible even from ground level. Indeed, in the section frescoed by Zuccari it is possible to observe, in the lower parts of the corners between two seg-

ments, figures damned to eternal suffering ripping open their chest or belly along the crack lines, the aim clearly being to mask these fissures. It is also possible to observe other intrados flexural cracks along the midline of the undamaged segments (see the *b*-points in Fig. 2.2.14), where the bending moments reach their maximum value. Along these lines the bending moments in question are greater by about one order of magnitude than those in the corners, and it comes as no surprise that the tensile intrados stresses generated by these bending moments should have produced cracking even in the absence of stress-intensifying local singularities.

It must be emphasised that these secondary flexural cracks, generally not extending through the whole thickness of the shell, are much smaller and less dangerous for the static regime of the Cupola than the four main full-thickness cracks.

They are worth mentioning none the less, since they can be interpreted in the framework of an elementary analysis; the fact that the estimates of analytical forecasting are in agreement with *in situ* observation of these secondary lesions also supports other theoretical findings about how the static regime of the Cupola has changed as a consequence of the four full-thickness cracks.

The new stress distribution that took shape after the formation of these main cracks, as well as its possible evolution in the future, will be described in greater detail in §§ 3.2 and 3.4.[17]

2.3. A Brief History of the Structural Disorders of the Cupola: Investigations, Hypotheses and Proposals

The complex vicissitudes of the Cupola's structural disorders span several centuries and have been marked by doubt, incomplete knowledge and fierce controversy. Natural events such as earthquakes and lightning strikes[18] have dramatically punctuated the periodic flaring of concern and the hurried adoption of stopgap and often bungled remedial measures. Until very recently there has been a notable lack of any in-depth analysis or a comprehensive, far-sighted strategy for rationally monitoring and conserving the structure. Despite substantial advances in our knowledge of the causes and evolution of the damage, and in the available methods for analysis and monitoring, it is only fair to say that the problem has not as yet been tackled with the necessary determination, which, one might add, is indispensable for a clear assessment of potential hazards and any measures that may need to be taken in order to safeguard the Cupola.

Until just a few years ago the structure had not even been subjected to any really comprehensive and accurate static analysis. Occasional comments and qualitative evaluations can be found in the works of Mainstone, Saalman, Sanpaolesi, Di Pasquale and others; but quantitative knowledge of the stress distribution inside the masonry was not available until the 1980s and

1990s, when the national electricity board's centre for hydraulic and structural research (CRIS–ENEL), in cooperation with Florence University's Department of Civil Engineering, carried out extensive Finite Element numerical analyses. The main results of these studies will be illustrated in § 3.2.

*   *   *

No documented information is available about the first appearance of the cracks. Although it is likely that they began to form shortly after completion of the Cupola, the cracks are not mentioned until two centuries later, in 1639, when Gherardo Silvani, the architect of the Opera di Santa Maria del Fiore, judged them to be of little importance and recommended small-scale repair work (plaster filling, metal clamps).

In 1691 another architect of the Opera, Bernardo Possi, noted that the cracks had widened. Evidently there was growing concern about the problem, as in 1695 Grand Duke Cosimo III appointed a committee to investigate the matter. This consisted of the grand-ducal architect Giovan Battista Foggini, the architect Giovanni Filippo Sengher, the physicist and mathematician Vincenzo Viviani (a pupil of Galileo), Giovan Battista Nelli and Father Giovanni Guerrino Guerrini. Available evidence suggests that the commission contacted Carlo Fontana, the author of a book on the cracks in the dome of St Peter's; the commission's conclusions may also have been influenced by suggestions regarding the installation of iron chains made by Filippo Baldinucci in his work on the life of Bernini. The commission submitted its written report in the same year (1695), recommending that the drum should be hooped with four large iron chains. Sengher executed the drawings for these chains, which began to be manufactured in the grand-ducal iron works. But the architect Alessandro Cecchini fiercely criticised and opposed this solution; his criticisms, together with those of others, were published in 1753 by Giovan Battista Clemente Nelli, son of Giovan Battista Nelli.

Cecchini ascribed the origin of the cracks to foundation instability, maintaining that they had appeared shortly after construction. He argued that installing chains would prove inadequate and could even have adverse effects, citing the example of the double dome of San Lorenzo which cracked despite having been hooped. (He was mistaken on this count, because the chains were only installed after the cracks formed.) In the meantime swallow-tail-shaped test pieces in marble, which had been installed in the cracks in order to reveal any further widening, showed no sign of movement, so worries were allayed. In 1696–7 both Nelli and Viviani disassociated themselves from the chain proposal, which continued to be advocated by Fontana but to no avail. The fact that a minor earthquake in 1697 did not cause any further widening of the cracks seemed to give further credibility to those who were against the hooping scheme. In his unpublished work *Considerazioni sopra la stabilità della Gran Cupola del Duomo di Firenze esposte in un breve discorso apologetico in risposta alle contrarie opposizioni* ('Reflections on the stability of the Great Cupola of Florence Cathedral, expounded in a brief apology answering opposing views'), Nelli again discussed Cecchini's theories and suggested that the wooden chain had only been useful in an initial period.

Around 1720 two unpublished papers by Bartolomeo Vanni, an engineer of the 'Capitani di Parte' (the Grand Duke's public works office) reported the testimony of old people still living at the end of the 17th century, according to whom the cracks dated from ancient times. Vanni went on to argue that, since the cracks had caused no major damage over the course of three centuries, they were stable and posed no danger—hence, the hooping was unnecessary.[19] He attributed the cracks to earthquakes.

Later, in 1743, the Florentine scholar Domenico Maria Manni sent information about the cracks to Marquis Giovanni Poleni, a mathematician and engineer in Padua who had been appointed by Pope Benedict XIV to study the cracks in the dome of St Peter's. Poleni inspected the Cupola on his return from Rome, and in his *Memorie istoriche della Gran Cupola del Tempio Vaticano* ('Historical Account of the Great Dome of the Vatican Temple'), published in 1748, he reported his observations and conclusions (Book II, Chapter XVIII: "On the Defects of the Cupola of Florence Cathedral"). He ruled out foundation subsidence as the cause of the cracks, which he attributed, quite correctly, to the action of dead weight. He also declared himself an advocate of hooping (the chains for hooping the dome of St Peter's were manufactured to Vanvitelli's specifications around 1740) and refuted Cecchini's contention that the use of chains in San Lorenzo had caused any damage, claiming instead that it had been beneficial in preventing the spreading of the cracks.

In the 18th century the Jesuit astronomer Leonardo Ximenes studied the cracks in order to determine whether possible deformations of the vault might be affecting the accuracy of observations of the sun's passage across the local meridian at the summer solstice. (These observations were carried out by means of the gnomon installed by Paolo dal Pozzo Toscanelli: see *Del vecchio e nuovo gnomone Fiorentino*, Florence 1757.) He made careful measurements and listed thirteen cracks; he ascribed these to differential settling of the piers, having detected a slight deviation from the vertical of both the Cathedral and the Campanile, which according to him lean towards the river Arno. From Ximenes' work it is clear that of the four main full-thickness cracks that exist today only two were visible in 1757, namely those along the midlines of the northeast and south-east segments (→ Fig. 3.1.4).

Almost two centuries were to pass till, in 1934, the board of the Opera di Santa Maria del Fiore decided to appoint a new commission, which was presided over by Rodolfo Sabatini and included the famous architect and engineer Pier Luigi Nervi. Its task was to establish whether the structure had found a new stable equilibrium after the onset of cracking or whether, assuming that the *primary causes* still existed, its static conditions were bound to progressively deteriorate. Curiously enough, the identification of such primary causes was not explicitly included in the commission's brief; however, the terms of reference included the search for *other causes*—mention is made of vibrations and thermal variations—that might have contributed to the structural disorders, and for the means of neutralising them; finally, the commission was asked to indicate possible measures to *reinforce* the Cupola, should this be required. At long last measuring devices were permanently installed in order to detect and record variations in the cracks, and the results of these observations were analysed, even though a full account of this analysis was never published. The variations observed were fundamentally non-progressive in nature, revealing instead a cyclic behaviour clearly connected to daily and seasonal thermal changes. The possible influence of vibrations caused by traffic around the Cathedral (especially trams) was also considered; this was not judged to be dangerous, but it was recommended that efforts be made to reduce it. In the commission's report, published in 1939, the probable cause of the cracks was ascribed to thermal variations, and foundation subsidence was discounted; however, the overall stability of the Cupola was not considered to be at risk, even though the need for close monitoring was stressed.

After the Second World War, this recommendation was taken up by a new commission, appointed in 1950; chaired by Aristide Giannelli, it once again included Pier Luigi Nervi. The work of this new commission is summarised in a series of minutes dating from 1950 to 1953.

In 1970 Rowland J. Mainstone analysed the situation, describing three major cracks instead of four; the crack affecting the south-west segment is in fact less well-defined than the other three. Mainstone supported the theory that the cracks were caused by thermal variations, accompanied by minor exacerbating factors, such as masonry deterioration in the external shell

(due to water infiltration) and swelling of the iron clamps holding together the pieces of the stone chains. In his view, the resulting cracks had propagated in the course of time until the Cupola found a new structural equilibrium. Indeed, as the tensile stresses in the lower parallels had been nullified by the onset of the cracks, containment of the Cupola's outwards thrusts falls entirely upon the surrounding structures, which in order to react have to yield in some measure, thus resulting in a certain bulging of the dome. Mainstone was puzzled (mistakenly, as will soon become apparent) by the fact that the full-thickness cracks had developed on the 'strong' sides of the structure, namely those directly supported by the piers, rather than on the 'weak' ones, namely those resting on the sides of the drum supported by the four large pointed arches. On the other hand, he correctly recognised the role played by the great round windows of the drum in exacerbating local tensile stresses in the horizontal direction.

In 1971 an accurate photogrammetric survey of the Cupola was carried out.[20]

In 1975 the then Minister of the Cultural Heritage, Giovanni Spadolini, appointed a new commission whose most prominent member was Salvatore Di Pasquale. In 1976 Di Pasquale reported that, in the light of observations made since 1950, there was a worrying increase in both the width and length of the cracks. He supported the view that vibrations caused by motor traffic were having negative effects, and succeeded in having restrictions placed on traffic around the Cathedral.

In 1976 the hydrologist Lino Borga, who had studied the underground water table of Florence, claimed that an underground stream flowing from the river Mugnone in a south–south-westerly direction along Via de' Servi ran under the Cathedral and into the Arno after passing under Via dell'Oriuolo. According to Borga, this could be linked to effluent seepage problems that had arisen in 1384 during excavation work for the south-west pier, ultimately solved by draining.

Borga also made a connection with the slight tilt of the structure mentioned by Ximenes: the presence of water could have resulted in the piers settling irregularly, and this in turn could have caused the cracks.

In 1977, on the occasion of the celebrations marking the sixth centennial of Brunelleschi's birth, many studies were published concerning the history of the Cupola, the organisation of the worksite, the geometry and tracing of the structure. In the same year a tender was issued for the construction of suspended metal scaffolding for use in restoring the fresco cycle by Vasari and Zuccari. The scaffolding, which was built in 1980 and remained in place until the restoration was completed in 1995, permitted close-up examination of the masonry texture.

From 1984 to 1986 a detailed survey charted the various types of cracks in the Cupola and in the rest of the Cathedral. This survey, published by the Ministry of the Cultural and Environmental Heritage under the title *Catalogo dei plessi fessurativi della Cattedrale di Santa Maria del Fiore in Firenze*, is a milestone document depicting the status quo at the date of publication.

The latest commission to date was set up in 1975, under the presidency of Guglielmo De Angelis d'Ossat. Following renewed worries reported by the local media, it was re-appointed in 1983 and 1984 by three successive deliberations of the Ministry. Throughout the 1980s, and in close cooperation with the commission (particularly the structural committee, chaired by Carlo Cestelli Guidi), in-depth structural analysis financed by ENEL was conducted jointly by CRIS–ENEL (Milan) and by Florence University's Department of Civil Engineering (Andrea Chiarugi); this analysis was done with the help of Finite Element numerical models. In the same period, ISMES (Bergamo) designed a comprehensive permanent installation for monitoring the Cupola, with automatic data recording, and planned a one-off *in situ* survey of the mechanical properties and stress conditions of the masonry; both the installation of the monitoring

and recording system and the *in situ* survey (→ § 3.3) were carried out between the end of the 1980s and the beginning of the 1990s. The numerical models allowed, at long last, a clear and consistent interpretation of the crack distribution—not only of the four main, full-thickness cracks, but also of the family of secondary cracks (generally not crossing the full thickness of the shell) on the intrados of the inner shell, at the corners of the segments and along the midlines of the four segments not affected by the main cracks. The numerical models also provided an understanding of the origin of a number of full-thickness cracks under the great round windows of the drum near the vertex of each of the four big pointed arches, as well as of some shear dislocations located at the junction between the domes of the apsidioles and the drum or at the junction between the drum and the nave. These dislocations were due both to lateral thrusts of the Cupola and the more pronounced vertical settling of the piers (under the huge weight of the dome) with respect to the foundations of the remaining parts of the Cathedral.

The main conclusions of the numerical analyses, confirmed by evidence deriving from visual and instrumental observations, were included in the commission's 1985 report. They basically attributed the origin and development of the four main cracks to localised horizontal tensile stresses exceeding the strength of the masonry. These tensile stresses—caused by the action of the Cupola's dead weight on the structures of the octagonal drum, supported only on every other side by a pier—were intensified locally by the presence of the great round windows. The models also showed that once the main full-thickness cracks had developed, the secondary lesions observed were a necessary consequence of the changed static regime. The influence of differential vertical settling of the piers was ruled out (while, as already said, the settling of the octagon itself differed from that of the apsidioles and the nave, a fact that caused the shear dislocations at the junction between these structures). *Seasonal* thermal variations[21] were a possible concurrent factor facilitating the progressive extension of the cracks; earthquakes of significant intensity and lightning-induced shocks may have caused sudden exacerbation of the lesions. The width of the main cracks now appears to be stable, or at least to be growing much more slowly than the former average rate of about 7 mm per century (→ Fig. 3.1.5). The long-term static stability of the Cupola is not at risk (→ § 3.4), but the issue of its safety in the event of a major earthquake remains open and will require further in-depth evaluation.

Further analyses and investigations had already been planned, the aim being to clarify a number of unresolved issues—the exact role of the horizontal arches, the stress distribution caused by thermal variations, the seismic hazard and—last but not least—the usefulness and feasibility of actively hooping the Cupola with tensioned steel cables, which would be invisible from the exterior since they could be installed in the space between the two shells (→ § 3.5). Unfortunately, after 1993 such investigations were suspended when the funding, formerly provided by ENEL, was terminated. However, if there were the necessary political will and financial resources, the knowledge gained thus far could be used as a basis for completing the task. This in turn would provide the necessary framework for developing different monitoring and conservation strategies; the options would then be presented to the pertinent authorities for a final decision (→ §§ 3.5–6).

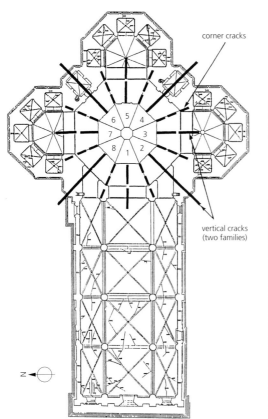

corner cracks

6 5 4
7   3
8 1 2

vertical cracks
(two families)

N

3.1.1. Plan showing the three families of systematic cracks
in the Cupola.

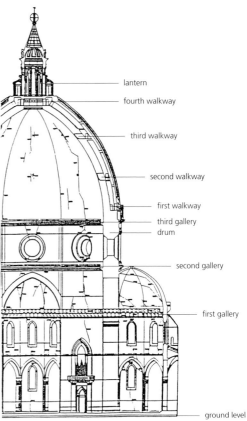

lantern
fourth walkway
third walkway
second walkway
first walkway
third gallery
drum
second gallery
first gallery
ground level

3.1.2. Cross-section of the Cupola and surrounding
structures showing the course of the main cracks.

THE CUPOLA TODAY: NUMERICAL ANALYSES, MONITORING AND TESTING, CONSERVATION MEASURES

3.1. The Cracks

The nature and pattern of the cracks that for centuries have affected the masonry texture of the Cupola, growing progressively longer and wider, have already been mentioned elsewhere, together with the worries expressed by scholars and those responsible for its safety. This section deals in greater detail with the main features of the different families of cracks, description of which is limited to the Cupola itself and its immediately adjoining structures. Only the clearly organised families of cracks will be considered here, disregarding the countless minor lesions (from hairline cracks to superficial discontinuities just a few millimetres wide) that have no clear pattern and are therefore hard to interpret. The accompanying diagrams provide an overall picture of the cracks and illustrate the situation as seen by the experts who have attempted, with varying degrees of success, to offer an interpretation of this phenomenon.

Figures 3.1.1–3 show the three main families of cracks that have been the main focus of attention in recent studies.

For ease of reference, the segments are numbered from 1 to 8 in a counterclockwise direction; number 1 is the segment whose midline is aligned with the axis of the nave, i.e. the one facing west; number 2 is thus the one facing southwest, number 3 faces south, number 4 southeast, number 5 east, number 6 north-east, number 7 north and number 8 north-west.

The first—and most damaging—family of cracks includes the four extended, subvertical full-thickness cracks, the maximum width of which amounts to some centimetres, affecting the midlines of segments number 2, 4, 6 and 8. These cracks run in a line directly above the four piers, extending upwards to at least two thirds of the height of the Cupola and downwards to well below the great round windows of the drum. The maximum width of the cracks is just above

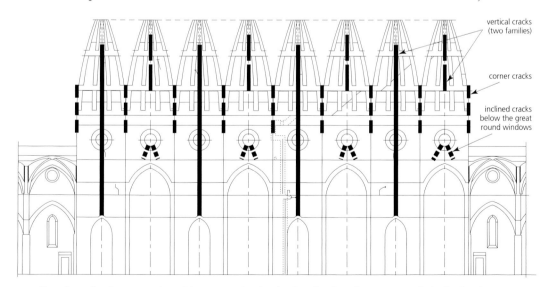

3.1.3. Two-dimensional representation of the octagon showing the three families of systematic cracks in the Cupola.

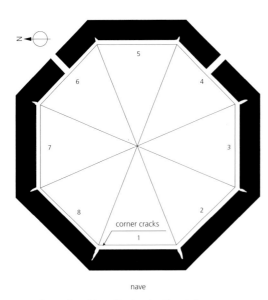

nave

3.1.4. State of cracking affecting the Cupola in 1757, according to Leonardo Ximenes.

these windows, and is 2–3 cm in segments 2 and 8 (the ones nearest the nave) and 5–6 cm in segments 4 and 6 (the ones nearest the apse). As has already been said, the cracks in segments 4 and 6 seem to have developed earlier than those in segments 2 and 8 (→ Fig. 3.1.4). Historical evidence, albeit scanty, has permitted a conjectural reconstruction of the growth of the crack in segment 4 over time (→ Fig. 3.1.5). The four main cracks affect both the inner and the outer shell of the Cupola.[1]

The second family consists of eight cracks located along the edges where the segments intersect, in the lower section (roughly the lower third) of the Cupola. These cracks probably extend through the full thickness in the area near the drum, with a maximum width of a few millimetres, while further up they affect only the intrados of the inner shell, where the width gradually decreases towards the summit.

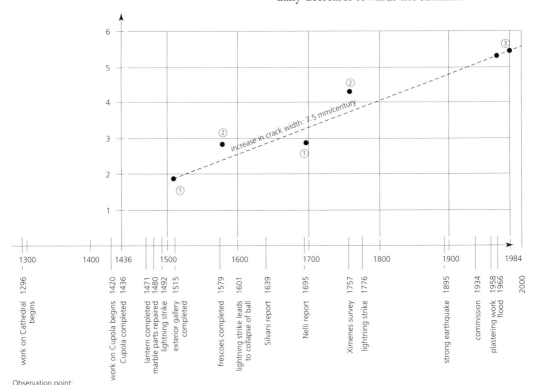

Observation point:
1: exterior gallery built by Baccio d'Agnolo; 2: third gallery; 3: inner frame of the great round windows of the drum.

3.1.5. Reconstruction of the development of the subvertical crack in segment 4.

The third family comprises four subvertical cracks in the mid and upper sections of the Cupola. These extend only through the innermost part of the inner shell and run along the midlines of segments 1, 3, 5 and 7, i.e. those directly above the four big pointed arches of the octagonal presbytery. The cracks are only a few millimetres wide.

One additional family of minor systematic cracks should also be mentioned. These consist of fractures inclined at about 60° to the horizontal, to the right and left of the great round windows of the drum. More pronounced under the windows than above them, they too affect segments 1, 3, 5 and 7 (→ Figs. 3.1.2–3).

As expounded in other sections of this book, the position, pattern and features of the sixteen major cracks just mentioned are satisfactorily explained by Finite Element numerical models. The concordance between models and observation is not only qualitative, but for the most part also quantitative, with the exception of the width of the cracks and the asymmetry of the 'first-family' crack in segment 2 (→ note 1).

Besides the lesions in the Cupola itself, systematic families of inclined cracks are to be found in the three small domes of the apses where they adjoin the drum, and in the walls and vaults of the nave in proximity to the octagonal section of the presbytery area. On the basis of the results obtained by the numerical models the cracks can justifiably and satisfactorily be interpreted as having been caused by the interaction between these lateral structures and the Cupola and drum.

3.2. Modern Interpretations of the Origin of the Cracks: Mathematical Models and Material Evidence

A range of modern methods and tools are available today for the diagnosis and conservation of ancient monumental structures, the validity of which have been amply tested in the analysis and monitoring of large-scale civil engineering works. Brunelleschi's Cupola is an exemplary case of the application of such methods and tools, resulting in a flurry of investigations over the years, though not all the possibilities have been fully exploited. Modern computer hardware and software have been used for structural analyses, representation of the results and data storage. State-of-the-art instrumentation has also been installed for real-time monitoring of the structure (→ § 3.3).

The structural damage to the unit comprising the Cupola, drum and relative supports, illustrated in detail in other sections of this book, consists essentially in the gradual development of an extensive series of structurally significant cracks. The average rate of increase in the width of the four main full-thickness cracks is about 7 millimetres per century.

The dearth of scientifically accurate and up-to-date analyses, combined with the fact that eminent scholars have at various times expressed contradictory opinions regarding the causes of the cracks and possible remedial measures, led to an attempt to reassess the problem. This became possible in the wake of the recent systematic survey of the different families of cracks carried out by the Soprintendenza per i Beni Ambientali e Architettonici, which provided solid evidence against which to test the worth of the new analytical tools. A procedure involving successive stages of approximation was adopted to analyse the Cupola in both its pristine, undamaged state and its current cracked state. These studies were carried out by means of a computer code based on the Finite Element technique (→ Inset 5); this required the setting up of a series of ever more accurate geometrical models of the Cupola.

*   *   *

The Finite Element analyses of the Cupola started with a very simplified model consisting only of an octagonal, double-shell dome built for the most part in brick masonry. When the numerical results were examined, however, it became

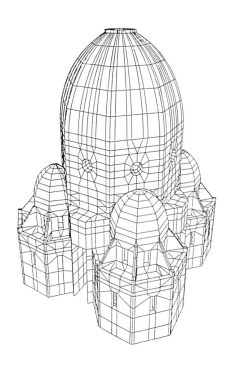

3.2.1–2. Finite Element mesh used for the structural analysis of the Cupola.

clear that the model had to be extended, and several more parts were therefore added in succession: first the octagonal drum of stone masonry, then the four massive piers (also in stone), and finally the surrounding structures. The latter included the apses on the north, east and south sides of the Cupola.

Instead of adding the nave on the west side, which would have called for an exceedingly large and complex model, a fourth apse identical to the other three was inserted in its place. Even though the geometry of the lantern was not modelled in detail, its weight—the most important factor in relation to the overall static regime of the structure—was applied to the oculus ring at the summit of the dome. The geometric representation of all the different structures successively added to the model proved to be remarkably faithful to the real ones, thanks to very thorough preparatory work in generating the Finite Element mesh (→ Figs. 3.2.1–2).

The final version of the numerical model thus included (→ Figs. 3.2.3–4):
• the two shells of the Cupola with their connecting corner and intermediate spurs;
• the drum with its eight great round windows and the four large pointed arches carrying the weight of the odd-numbered segments down to the piers (while the even-numbered ones are supported directly by them);
• the four piers, the section of which varies with height—the springing of the piers (rigidly fixed in the mathematical model) was taken to be five metres lower than the Cathedral floor, so as to account in an empirical way for the settling of the foundations; moreover, in the model the north-west and south-west piers were assumed to be identical respectively to the north-east and south-east ones;
• the three apses (the east apse and those at the end of the transept arms); on the west side, the model included a fourth apse identical to the

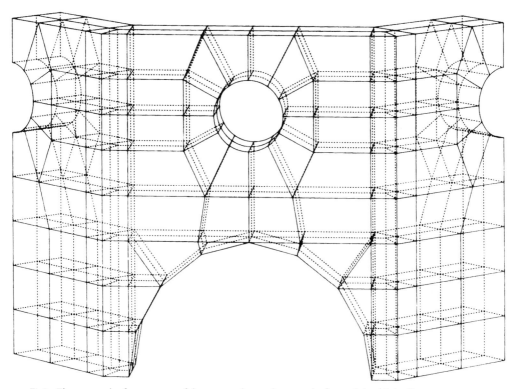

3.2.3a. Finite Element mesh of one quarter of the structural parts, between the first and the third gallery.

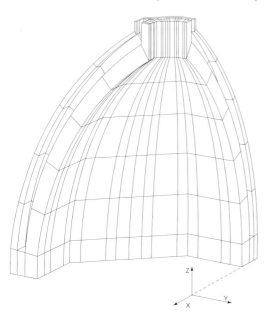

3.2.3b. Finite Element mesh of one quarter of the Cupola (showing the two shells, the spurs and the oculus ring).

other three, which obviated the need to shape the complicated structure of the nave while at the same time providing a certain constraint on this side as well.

The mathematical model therefore has a fourfold mirror symmetry with respect to the vertical north–south, east–west, north-west–south-east and north-east–south-west planes, and in this respect differs from the actual structure. This was done in order to simplify the computations.

With regard to the forces and external actions acting on the structure, the model takes into account the dead weight of the structure itself and an extremely simplified, azimuthally symmetric distribution of thermal variations.

The assumed constitutive law is the stress-strain relationship of the linear Theory of Elasticity; the model was later modified in order to take account of the strength of materials in the masonry, or rather of the masonry's resistance to brittle fracture.

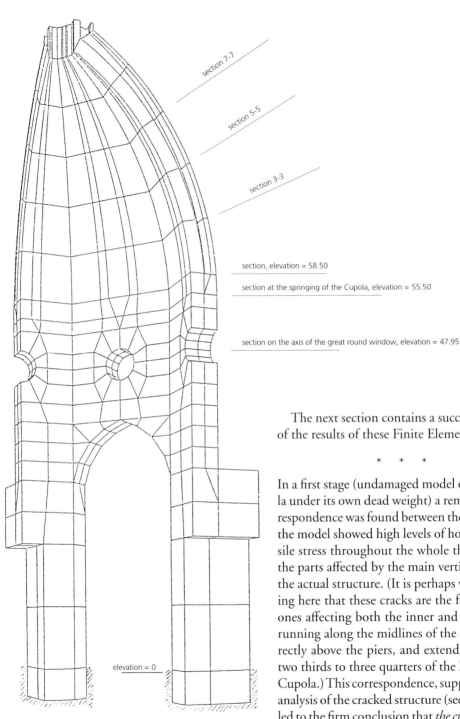

section 7-7

section 5-5

section 3-3

section, elevation = 58.50

section at the springing of the Cupola, elevation = 55.50

section on the axis of the great round window, elevation = 47.95

elevation = 0

3.2.4. Finite Element mesh used for the structural analysis of the Cupola: merging of the meshes of one quarter of the Cupola, the drum and the piers.

The next section contains a succinct account of the results of these Finite Element analyses.

* * *

In a first stage (undamaged model of the Cupola under its own dead weight) a remarkable correspondence was found between the parts where the model showed high levels of horizontal tensile stress throughout the whole thickness and the parts affected by the main vertical cracks in the actual structure. (It is perhaps worth recalling here that these cracks are the full-thickness ones affecting both the inner and outer shells, running along the midlines of the segments directly above the piers, and extending to about two thirds to three quarters of the height of the Cupola.) This correspondence, supported by the analysis of the cracked structure (see further on), led to the firm conclusion that *the cracking is primarily the result of stress distribution caused by the dead weight*. The action of the latter is par-

5. Brief Introduction to the Finite Element Method of Structural Analysis

The Finite Element method belongs to the vast category of so-called interpolation methods for the approximate solution of systems of differential equations accompanied by the appropriate boundary conditions. The method is based on a very simple, intuitive idea.

The geometric domain where the phenomenon to be studied takes place is subdivided into a large number of small, simple shapes called *finite elements* that form a *mesh*. Within each element the (unknown) problem variables (for instance the displacement of material points as the result of acting forces) vary from point to point, also in an unknown way. But provided the element is small enough, such variations can be approximated with a fair degree of accuracy by using adequate functions to interpolate the displacements (also unknown) of a few points (*nodes*), generally border points, with respect to their co-ordinates. The analytic form of the interpolation functions is defined a priori; the simplest case is that of linear interpolation. (Intuition suggests that this assumption is acceptable if the finite elements are small enough and do not contain singularities that might cause sharp variations in the variables.) In this way the unknowns are reduced from an infinite to a finite number, namely the ones at the nodes.

The physical properties of each finite element and its connection conditions with other elements and constraints are assigned. The method then draws on powerful *minimum* principles (for instance, the principle which states that at equilibrium the total potential energy of the system must reach a minimum) which are *globally* equivalent (though less constraining *locally*) to the local conditions expressed by the differential equations of equilibrium. Applying these principles to the Finite Element system with the reduced number of unknowns, the problem can be reduced from a differential problem to a much more readily solvable algebraic one. In practice, instead of having to solve a system of partial differential equations, which can only be done in particular cases and with very simple shapes, the task becomes one of solving a large system of algebraic equations whose unknowns are the variables in the nodes of the Finite Element mesh.

When applied to problems of structural analysis, the resulting algebraic equations are linear in the nodes' unknowns, if the linear Theory of Elasticity is used. The computation of equation coefficients and the subsequent solution of the system of equations present no problem thanks to the availability of appropriate hardware and software, for instance computer-aided design (CAD) programmes. Large structures may require the solving of systems with many thousands of unknowns. Using the space derivatives of the interpolation functions it is then possible to evaluate other quantities of interest, such as stress distribution in the case of structural analysis. Finally, computer graphics is used to translate the numerical results into visually effective diagrams which permit the rapid, synthetic appraisal of the solution.

The results of such analyses can be considered reliable provided the following conditions are fulfilled:
- the problem must be well formulated and the input data (for instance the shape of the structure and the mechanical properties of the materials) must be reliable and accurately checked;
- the software must be error-free and thoroughly tested;
- the numerical model should not merely be used as a 'black box'—competence, experience and a critically minded approach are required;
- the Finite Element mesh should not be too coarse—the higher the number of elements, the more accurate the numerical solutions of the differential equations taken as a model of the structure's behaviour.

If the results of the numerical model results are to be a significant indication of the behaviour of the actual structure, it is crucial that the analytical model chosen (for instance the equations of the Theory of Elasticity) respect the actual properties of the materials. Verification of the fulfilment of this condition and the devising of means of dealing with any local violation that may arise (such as modification of the initial model or the introduction of local discontinuities) require great skill and extensive experience.

6. The Structural Behaviour of the Drum

If we open up the eight sides of the octagonal drum so they lie on a common vertical plane, the drum appears to be an unbroken, variable-section deep beam loaded on its upper edge by the forces transmitted by the Cupola, which in approximate terms may be regarded as a uniform vertical load. The four spans corresponding to the even-numbered segments and directly supported by the piers constitute a very stiff fixed-end constraint for the other four spans above the big pointed arches (→ Fig. 3.2.5). Near the centre of the spans above the piers, fixed-end bending moments cause full-thickness horizontal tensile stresses along the *upper* fibres (near the edge where the drum meets the Cupola). Near the centre of the spans above the arches, on the other hand, bending moments of opposite sign cause full-thickness horizontal tensile stresses along the *lower* fibres (right on top of the arch and under the corresponding great round window). The presence of the great round windows in the areas subjected to tensile stresses exacerbates them locally; besides, the outward radial thrusts along the parallels in the lower parts of the Cupola tend to propagate to the upper parts of the drum, causing an increase in the horizontal tensile stresses along the upper edge of the even-numbered sides and along the lower edge of the odd-numbered sides.

The total tensile stresses deriving from the sum of these concurring effects (→ Figs. 3.2.6–7) exceed the tensile strength of the masonry. Therefore it was inevitable that cracks would open, along tendentially vertical lines, near the springing of the Cupola along the midlines of the even-numbered sides (where the fixed-end moments are at a maximum); and along lines about 30° to the vertical, between the summit of the pointed arches and the great round windows along the midlines of the other four sides. Once formed, the four cracks on the pier-sides had to propagate upwards along the midlines of the corresponding segments. When vertical cracks were introduced into the numerical model, the results showed that horizontal, full-thickness tensile stresses persisted at their upper apex, causing the cracks to propagate further; this continued up to an elevation of a little less than three quarters of the height of the Cupola, beyond which the compressive forces were such that no further crack propagation occurred.

This step-by-step analysis clears up an issue that had long perplexed scholars—why, that is, the main cracks formed on the 'strong' sides of the drum rather than on the 'weak' sides. The answer is that the stiffer 'strong' sides were subjected to greater loads than the strength of the masonry could withstand. There is no need, then, to assume the existence of iron chains inside the masonry of the 'weak' sides in order to explain the absence of cracks above the corresponding great round windows.

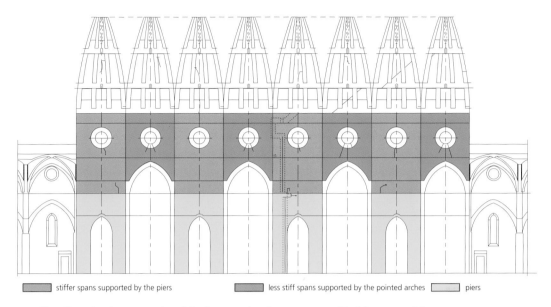

| | stiffer spans supported by the piers | | less stiff spans supported by the pointed arches | | piers |

3.2.5. Two-dimensional representation of the drum as a deep-beam structure with eight spans and four supports: the four stiffer spans are supported directly by the piers while the others are supported by the pointed arches.

ticularly critical on the octagonal drum, which is loaded along its upper rim by the distributed vertical forces transmitted on all eight sides by the Cupola, but is supported by the four piers only on every other side (→ Inset 6).

The constraint conditions of the initial model (undamaged Cupola) were modified in successive stages to simulate the progressive extension upwards of the four main full-thickness cracks. At each stage of the procedure the analysis results indicated whether or not horizontal tensile stresses were acting immediately above the apex of the crack; when they were, a further extension upwards of the cracks was simulated. A final stage was thus reached in which, the cracks having been extended up to an elevation corresponding to between two thirds and three quarters of the height of the Cupola, the horizontal stresses at the apex became nil or weakly compressive, and it was therefore reasonable to postulate that crack propagation had stopped. This was then taken as an approximate numerical model of the Cupola in its present condition.

The results of the analyses carried out on this final model will now be expounded.

With the four full-thickness cracks extending up to above-mentioned limit, numerical analysis reveals that under the action of dead weight *secondary areas of tensile stress* in the horizontal direction arise on the intrados of the inner shell; these occur both along the midlines of the odd-numbered segments (those supported by the big pointed arches) and at the corners where two adjacent segments meet. Tensile stresses in the vertical direction also appear in the outer shell about halfway up the segments (→ Figs. 3.2.8–9). The secondary horizontal tensile stresses affect only one section of the segments (the other being compressed) and their location corresponds strikingly to the family of secondary vertical cracks (open only on the intrados of the Cupola) that can be observed in the actual structure.[2]

The deformed shape of the relative horizontal sections at different elevations (→ Fig. 3.2.9) matches the results of the qualitative analysis examined in § 2.2 (→ Fig. 2.2.13). In the model the stresses yielded by the postulated thermal loads appear to be of secondary importance in that, although they may favour crack propagation due to the tendency to cause periodic ex-

237

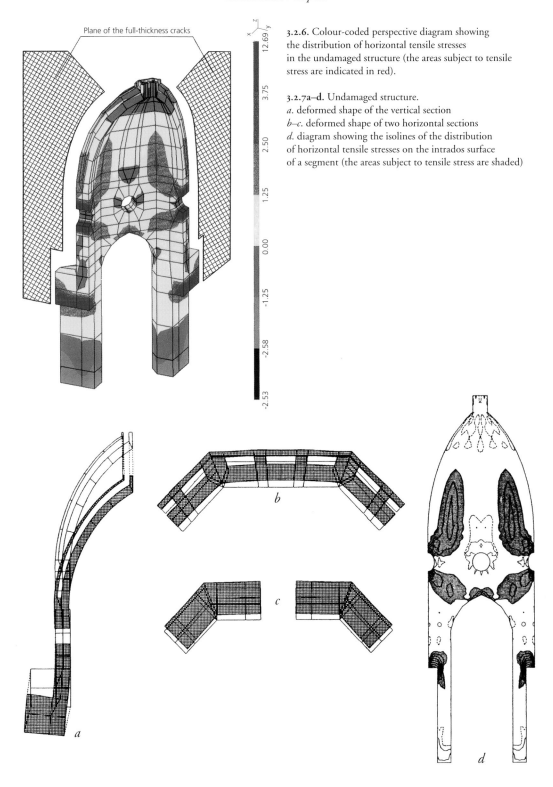

Plane of the full-thickness cracks

3.2.6. Colour-coded perspective diagram showing the distribution of horizontal tensile stresses in the undamaged structure (the areas subject to tensile stress are indicated in red).

3.2.7a–d. Undamaged structure.
a. deformed shape of the vertical section
b–c. deformed shape of two horizontal sections
d. diagram showing the isolines of the distribution of horizontal tensile stresses on the intrados surface of a segment (the areas subject to tensile stress are shaded)

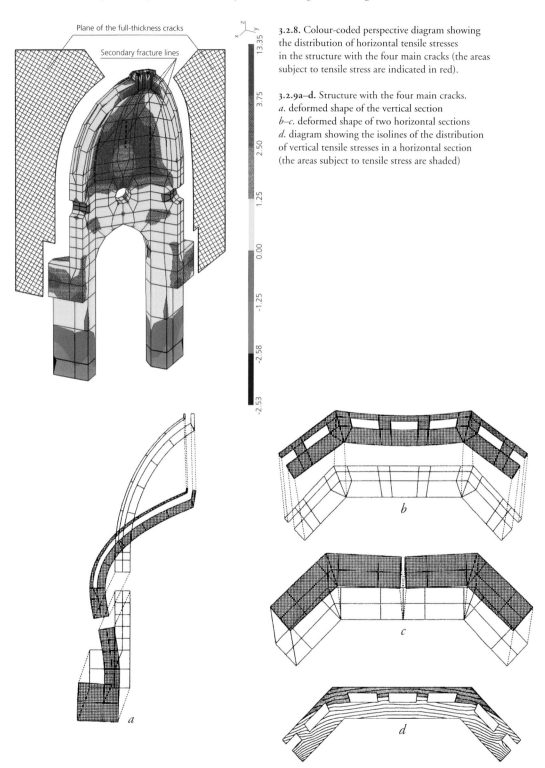

Plane of the full-thickness cracks

Secondary fracture lines

3.2.8. Colour-coded perspective diagram showing the distribution of horizontal tensile stresses in the structure with the four main cracks (the areas subject to tensile stress are indicated in red).

3.2.9a–d. Structure with the four main cracks.
a. deformed shape of the vertical section
b–c. deformed shape of two horizontal sections
d. diagram showing the isolines of the distribution of vertical tensile stresses in a horizontal section (the areas subject to tensile stress are shaded)

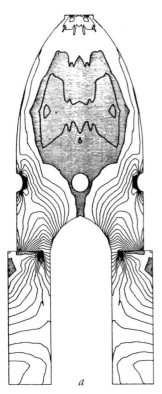
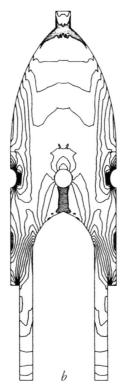
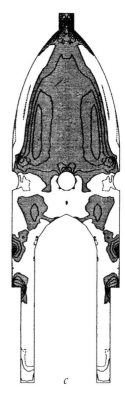

3.2.10a–b. Structure with the four main cracks. Diagram showing the isolines of the distribution of vertical tensile stresses on the extrados (*a*) and intrados (*b*) surface of a segment (the areas subject to tensile stress are shaded).
3.2.10c. Diagram showing the isolines of the distribution of horizontal tensile stresses on the intrados surface of a segment (the areas subject to tensile stress are shaded).

pansion and contraction of the cracks, they do not account for their formation, which appears to be sufficiently and convincingly explained by the effects of dead weight alone.[3]

Vertical stress distribution is shown in Figure 3.2.10a–b by isolines, and in Figures 3.2.11–4 by colour-coded diagrams of horizontal planes at various elevations and the vertical plane bisecting the angle at a corner. These illustrations evidence a substantial and to some extent worrying evolution from the static regime of the undamaged Cupola. Indeed, along the 'meridians' there is a change from a regime where the vertical stresses are entirely compressive to one of appreciable bending, where vertical tensile stresses appear in the outer shell. Such significant change can be readily appreciated in visual terms by comparing the profiles of the meridian before

and after deformation (→ Figs. 3.2.7a, 3.2.9a, 3.2.15a–b). These findings were confirmed by investigations to measure the vertical stresses, carried out using flat jacks in the space between the two shells (→ § 3.3). The tests revealed, at elevations shown by the analysis to be the site of maximum bending, regions where the vertical stresses drop to zero on the intrados of the outer shell and even in limited areas of the extrados of the inner shell. Taking into account that flat jacks can only measure compressive stresses (and that masonry cannot sustain tensile stresses for very long, but gives way with either localised or distributed cracking, which eliminates the stress in a direction normal to the plane of the crack), this is a strong clue that near the measuring points tensile stresses might have developed that were greater than the strength of the masonry.

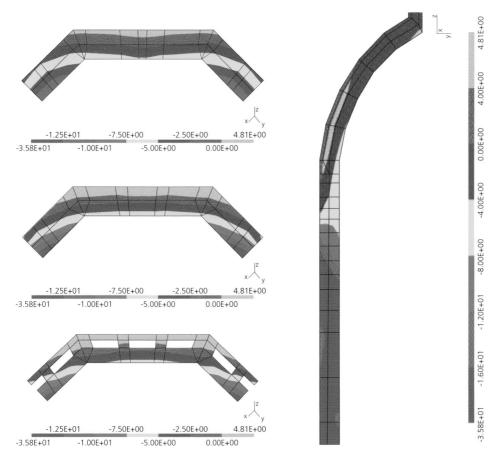

3.2.11–3. Colour-coded diagrams showing the distribution of vertical tensile stresses in different horizontal sections of the structure with the four main cracks (the areas subject to tensile stress are indicated in pink).

3.2.14. Colour-coded diagram showing the distribution of vertical tensile stresses in the vertical section at the corner of the structure with the four main cracks (the areas subject to tensile stress are indicated in pink).

Looking now at the lesions that are located at the points of junction between the drum and the small domes of the apses, the mathematical model reveals that intense shear and tensile deformations (and the corresponding stresses) are at play in these areas. These can be attributed both to the outward thrusts exerted by the Cupola and to the more pronounced settling of the Cupola itself, the drum and the piers in comparison with the surrounding structures. The inclined fracture lines observed in the actual structure are therefore explained once again by the mathematical model in terms of the effects of dead weight (→ Fig. 3.1.2).

Although in the model the nave was not represented as such (being replaced instead by an apse identical to the other three), it can be reasonably assumed that similar conditions occurred at the junction between the nave and the drum; in fact, inclined fracture lines can also be found in the vaults of the nave closest to the presbytery area, showing that tensile and shear stresses greater than the masonry strength must have occurred there in the past.

On the other hand, it stands to reason that the nave constitutes a much stiffer structure than the apses with regard to horizontal outward displacement, which may explain why the cracks in

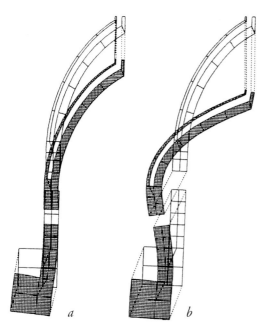

a   *b*

3.2.15a–b. Comparison between the deformed shapes of the vertical section at the corner under the action of the dead weight in the undamaged (*a*) and cracked (*b*) Cupola.

the north-west and south-west segments have an appreciably smaller width than those in the north-east and south-east segments.

* * *

Summing up, the almost exact correspondence[4] between the results of the numerical analyses and the objective evidence gathered during investigation of the cracks justifies the following conclusions:

• the primary cause of the four main full-thickness cracks is the action of the dead weight on the complex formed by the Cupola, drum and piers; *it is therefore probable that the cracks developed shortly after the Cupola was raised*;

• other possible causes of deterioration, such as thermal variations and earthquakes, may have *contributed*—in a respectively gradual or punctual way—to the evolution of the cracks, but do not explain their origin;

• the main families of secondary cracks, most of which are not full-thickness ones, were triggered as a result of the change in the static regime

of the Cupola caused by the opening of the four main full-thickness cracks;

• the numerical model generated and used in the analysis has time and again proved remarkably reliable and convincing in reproducing the observational data;

• this model, possibly further refined with the addition of the nave factor, could therefore confidently be used for predictive purposes, not only to integrate actions that have not yet been considered (such as asymmetrical thermal variations and seismic loads), but also to evaluate the possible steps that might be taken to consolidate the structure;

• once all the physical parameters (Young's moduli, thermal dilatation coefficient, etc.) of the numerical model have been effectively calibrated, it could be used, in conjunction with the data provided by the equipment already in place, for the on-going monitoring of the behaviour of the Cupola, as is done routinely in the case of other large civil engineering structures (→ Inset 7).

3.3. The Permanent Monitoring System and One-off Investigations

a. The Permanent Monitoring System
The commission appointed in 1983 by the Ministry of the Cultural and Environmental Heritage deemed it necessary, in view of the problematics involved, to conduct constant monitoring, over a considerable period of time, of all the data that most significantly reflect the structural behaviour of the Cupola. In 1986 the Soprintendenza per i Beni Ambientali e Architettonici commissioned ISMES to supply and install an adequate monitoring system, including various kinds of measurement sensors and the hardware and software required for data acquisition, processing and storage. The system was due to be up and running by September 1987.

* * *

There were two main goals to be achieved by installing the monitoring system:

• to continually monitor the evolution of deformation processes in the Cupola by measuring variations in the width of the main cracks and other structural displacements, so as to provide a warning in the event of pre-established thresholds being exceeded; in this respect, the monitoring system constitutes the first and immediate means of safeguarding the whole Cathedral complex from structural deterioration;

• to obtain a sufficient quantity of qualitatively reliable primary data that are essential for identifying the correlations between the forces involved in the deformation process (the observable effects) and its possible causes (thermal variations, differential settling of the foundations, etc.); such correlations are of invaluable assistance in interpreting the present state of the Cupola, and facilitate the task of generating and calibrating the mathematical models for simulating the structure's behaviour.

* * *

The technical specifications of the monitoring system were defined in relation to the nature of the structural problems involved and the functional requirements of the system itself. The guidelines adopted in designing the system can be summarised as follows.

(1) The type, number and location of the sensors were dictated by the need to observe the variations with a sufficient degree of detail, while containing the number of sensors, and therefore the overall cost of the system, within acceptable limits. These choices were made on the basis of a preliminary analysis of the state of deformation at the time and the results of a qualitative model of the structural behaviour.

(2) Decisions regarding the sensitivity, precision and long-term reliability of the sensors, as well as the extension and density of the various data-acquisition networks, were taken on the basis of the estimated variations in the phenomena to be monitored.

(3) The various procedures involved in data acquisition, processing and storage had to be completely automated, so as to streamline the periodic gathering of the data and their transfer to a computerised storage system without the need for external intervention; in other words, the system had to be designed in such a way as to be capable of operating autonomously for many months at a time.

(4) The monitoring system had to be highly flexible and expandable, so as to allow—should the need arise in the light of the initial, running-in phase—any necessary additions or alterations to the sensor network and/or the data acquisition, processing and storage systems.

(5) Particular care had to be devoted to making the system reliable and modular, with the aim of facilitating maintenance and minimising the risk of malfunctioning; these important requirements obviously conditioned decisions regarding the selection of the components to be adopted in the system.

* * *

The cracks that were judged to be of the greatest structural significance, and which therefore needed to be monitored closely, were schematised. (These cracks have already been illustrated in Figure 3.1.1. For ease of reference the segments of the Cupola were numbered from 1 to 8 in a counterclockwise direction, starting with the one facing the nave.)

The cracks that undoubtedly required the greatest attention were the four full-thickness ones running along the midlines of the even-numbered segments and extending from the piers up to almost two thirds of the segments' height. It was considered important to monitor the *opening and closing movements* of these cracks in the circumferential direction at five different elevations; the much less pronounced radial movements, on the other hand, were not considered worthy of measurement.

On the odd-numbered segments it was decided to monitor the opening and closing move-

7. The Monitoring of Large Structures

Of all large civil engineering structures, dams are perhaps the most carefully studied and monitored—and with good reason, considering the huge destructive potential of reservoir waters in the event, albeit unlikely, of sudden structural failure. Since the 1960s effective methods for the constant monitoring of their structural behaviour have been developed; the currently available technology is well tried and tested, and has already been installed on a number of major dams. As this could be applied without difficulty to a structure like the Cupola, the main principles of these methods will be outlined below.

We shall suppose that the geometrical and mechanical properties of the structure to be monitored, as well as its constraints, are known, or can at any rate be ascertained by one-off investigations carried out directly or indirectly by means of *in situ* surveys (the sought-after properties can then be deduced using the mathematical procedures of identification). The structure is subject to a number of external actions from the environment. Some, for instance the dead weight, are constant, while others, including thermal variations and, in the case of dams, the hydrostatic load (dependent on the water level in the reservoir), are variable. All these actions make up the external input, and can be constantly monitored by means of suitable equipment installed on and in the structure.

Variations in the external input produce variable effects in the structural behaviour (such as local displacements), and these too can be measured by sensors permanently installed on the structure. Minor variations in these effects—which may however be significant in the long term—can also be caused by constant actions, as a consequence of the rheological properties of the materials employed and how they respond over time. (Creep phenomena are one example of this, but note, however, that effects of this kind are not always directly measurable, in particular stress variations.)

The next thing to do is to set up a mathematical model of the structure's behaviour, the reliability of which must have been previously ascertained by separate tests. The model must be capable of simulating the structure's response, in normal conditions, to variations in the external input. Also, it must be capable of operating in real time, feeding in data regarding the external actions as it becomes available. At any given moment, the model will predict the structure's theoretical response, which can then be compared with the actual response as measured by the sensors installed on the structure. This comparison may result in one of two outcomes: either the predicted and the measured response coincide (allowing for the inherent approximation of the model and limits to the precision of the measurements), or they differ significantly. In the first case it is safe to assume that the structure is behaving as predicted by the model, that is 'normally', while in the second case the actual behaviour must be departing from the normal one for some significant reason. The behaviour of the structure will then have to be examined with greater attention in order to determine the causes of such a discrepancy, a necessary preliminary for any corrective action that may need to be taken.

In order to implement the method briefly described above, it is necessary to use appropriate hardware and software, which is now available at an acceptable cost. The vast body of experience that has been built up in this field makes it possible to affirm that this type of control can be used with considerable confidence for the safety management of important structures.

ments across the inclined cracks located below the great round windows; likewise, it was decided to monitor the opening and closing movements of the eight vertical cracks at the corners of the octagon, a little above the great round windows.

Figure 3.3.1 shows the position of the thirty-six displacement transducers (or deformeters) installed across the cracks on the intrados of the inner shell.[5] This type of sensor has a precision of ±0.02 mm, and can also be used to measure the radial shift between the edges of the crack. Shifts of this kind were observed with regard to the cracks on segments 4 and 6, confirming the lack of symmetry in the structural behaviour of the Cupola with respect to the vertical north–south plane. (As we have already seen, this asymmetry is caused by the fact that the nave constitutes a stiffer constraint against the east-to-west displacement of segment 1 than the constraint provided by the east apse against the west-to-east displacement of segment 5.)

As concerns the *horizontal displacements* of some key points of the structure, eight plumb lines, each about 50 m long, were installed near the corners of the octagon; they were suspended

from points near the third interior gallery, at the springing of the Cupola. For each plumb line, three telecoordinometers were fixed to the piers at three different elevations: ground level, 28 m (the level of the first gallery) and 39.5 m (above the keystone of the big pointed arches). These instruments measure—along two perpendicular axes—the horizontal components of the relative displacements between the suspension point of each plumb line and the point of the pier to which the telecoordinometer was attached (→ Fig. 3.3.2).

As concerns possible *vertical displacements*, a hydrostatic levelling system composed of eight measurement stations was also installed (→ Fig. 3.3.3). A station was located near the centre of each of the eight segments at an elevation of 39.5 m (the level of the second gallery). This system was designed to detect two different kinds of settling displacement: differential vertical movements of the four piers, leading to a rigid rotation of the Cupola, and vertical displacements along the centreline of the huge, variable-section deep beam constituting the drum. These levelling instruments have a precision of about ±0.04 mm.[6]

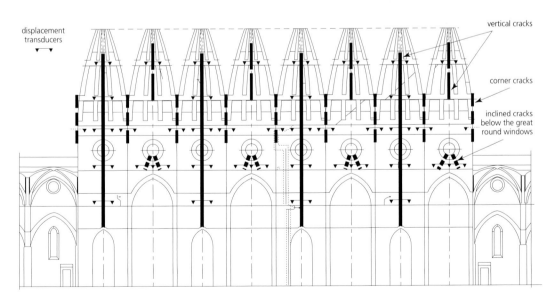

displacement transducers

vertical cracks

corner cracks

inclined cracks below the great round windows

3.3.1. Position of the displacement transducers used to measure variations in the opening width of the cracks.

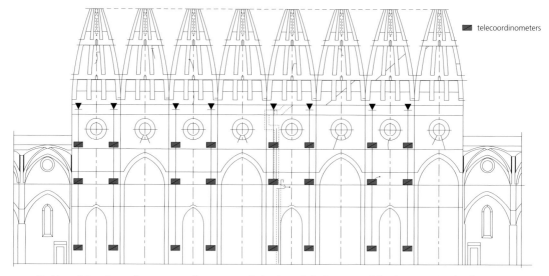

telecoordinometers

3.3.2. Position of the telecoordinometers used to measure the horizontal displacement of the piers at various heights.

hydrostatic levelling instruments

3.3.3. Position of the levelling instruments used to measure the vertical displacement of the summit of the piers and arches.

Finally, a piezometer was installed near the foundation of the south-east pier in order to observe variations in the level of the water table.

*   *   *

In order to interpret variations regarding the periodic opening and closing movements of the cracks, it is essential to have adequate *temperature* measurement data. For this purpose, a network of sixty thermal sensors was installed all along the octagonal perimeter at the level of the second gallery (39.50 m) and along two meridians of the Cupola aligned to the north and to the south-west, these planes corresponding respec-

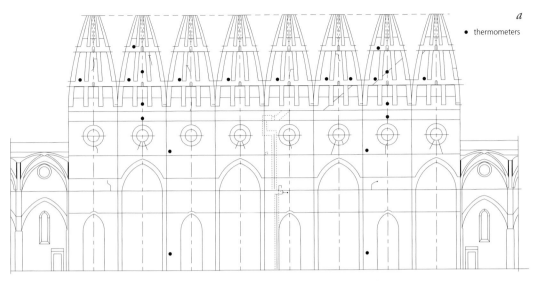

a

• thermometers

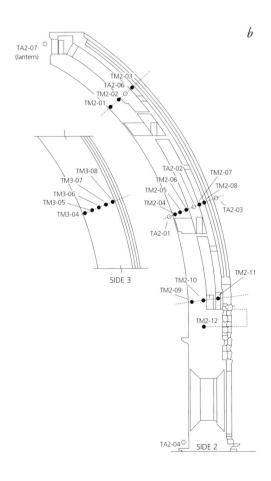

b

3.3.4a–b. Position of the thermometers used to measure thermal variations at various heights.

tively to minimum and maximum sunlight exposure (→ Fig. 3.3.4). At each of these measurement points readings are taken of the air temperature in the space between the two shells, on the extrados of the inner shell, on the intrados of the outer shell, and on the innermost and outermost surfaces of the Cupola. Several thermal sensors were also inserted into the thickness of the two shells at various depths and in a radial pattern. These sensors are of the resistor type and have a sensitive platinum element; their precision is about ±0.1°C.

The installation of the permanent monitoring system was completed in 1987, and has been operational since 1988. In its final configuration, it comprises 165 measuring instruments. Measurements are taken and automatically recorded four times a day.

The initial published results of the processed data[7] indicated that temperature variation causes two different kinds of effects: a reversible one (related to periodic seasonal and daily thermal changes) and an irreversible one. In the analysed period (from 1987 to 1993), the latter proved to be negligible, thus indicating that at present the cracks are stable.

247

8. The Use of Flat Jacks for *In Situ* Measurement of Stress and Elastic Properties

The flat-jack testing technique for *in situ measurement of the local stress state* in a given structure involves the following steps. First, two points are chosen on the surface of the structure, and the distance between them is measured. Then, at equal distance from the two points, a cut 20 to 30 cm deep and about as much wide is made perpendicularly to the surface and to the presumed direction of one of the principal stresses (in the case of masonry, presumably a compressive stress). The stress in that part of the surface is thereby removed, since it can no longer be transmitted across the cut, and as a result the distance between the two points decreases. A flat jack (a steel casing built from two dishes welded together) is then inserted into the cut and injected with a fluid (e.g. mineral oil) that puts it under increasing pressure. At a certain point the pressure will be such that the distance between the two points returns to its original value: provided the stiffness of the flat jack's dishes is negligible (i.e. all the pressure is in fact transmitted to the surface), this pressure value must be equal to the stress value transmitted across the surface prior to the cut (→ Fig. 3.3.5).

The flat-jack testing technique for *in situ measurement of the local elastic properties* (through the determination of the Young's modulus) is based on the same principle. Once again, two points are chosen on the structure's surface, and their relative distance is measured. *Two* parallel cuts similar to the one described above are then made in the surface so that the two reference points lie between them. Once the cuts have been made, the masonry in between becomes unstressed, and the distance between the two points increases. Two flat jacks are then inserted into the cuts and equally pressurised with the progressive injection of mineral oil. As the pressure increases, the masonry in between is compressed in such a way as to draw the two points closer, until they finally return to their original position. The relationship between the pressure value applied and the decrease in the distance between the two points yields the value of the Young's modulus.

a. Pre-test condition. The compression σ acts on the surface. The distance between the two marks (l) is measured.

b. The cut is performed. The compression σ no longer acts on the surface. The distance between the two marks (now $l-a$) is measured.

c. Pressure (p) is applied to the cut, and increased until the distance between the two marks returns to l, at which point $p = \sigma$.

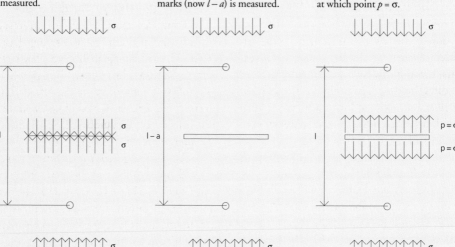

3.3.5. Diagrams showing the various steps of the flat-jack testing technique for *in situ* stress measurement.

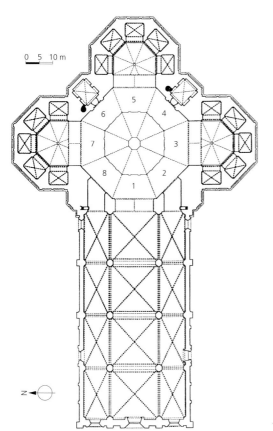

0 5 10 m

3.3.6. General plan of the Cathedral used as a framework for the one-off investigations.

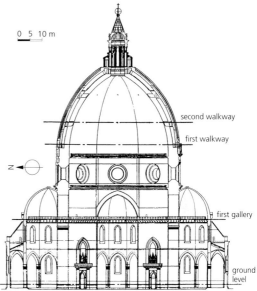

0 5 10 m

second walkway

first walkway

first gallery

ground level

3.3.7. Vertical section of the Cupola used as a framework for the one-off investigations.

b. One-off Investigations Using Flat Jacks and Camera Probes

In addition to the regular monitoring, it was also decided to carry out a series of one-off investigations, the aim of which was to determine in a more direct way the stress state of the masonry, as well as its petrographic and mineralogical composition. These *in situ* measurements were carried out by ISMES (Bergamo) at the request of CRIS–ENEL (Milan) and in collaboration with the Soprintendenza per i Beni Ambientali e Architettonici (Florence).

The *in situ* survey of the stress state of the masonry in the segments (caused by a vertical stress component) was carried out using *flat jacks* (→ Inset 8) applied at various points up to the level of the second walkway. Particular attention was devoted to segments 4 and 8. In order to ascertain the internal composition and stress state of the masonry in the piers underlying these segments, boreholes were drilled and flat jacks inserted at various elevations. The internal composition of the masonry was ascertained by examining the cores extracted from the boreholes and by using camera probes. Several small core samples (diameter <56 mm) recovered from the boreholes were tested in the laboratory in order to build up a picture of the petrographic and mineralogical composition of both the mortar and the aggregates. Direct measurement of the vertical stress component in the masonry was supplemented by *in situ* determination of local elasticity (Young's moduli), once again employing flat jacks.

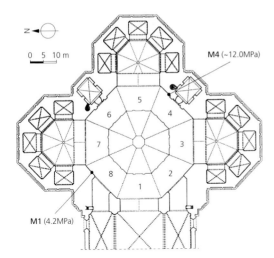

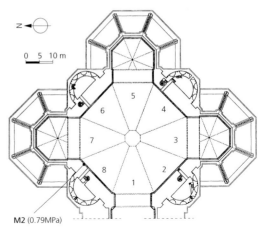

3.3.8. Flat-jack test results: stress measures in the piers at ground level.

3.3.9. Flat-jack test results: stress measures in the pier beneath segment 8 at the level of the first gallery.

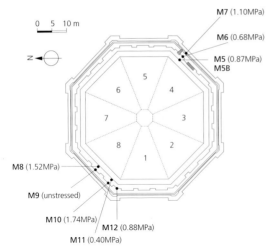

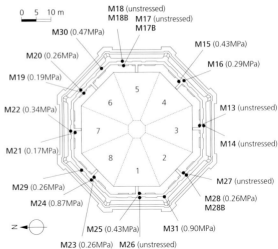

3.3.10. Flat-jack test results: stress measures at the level of the first walkway.

3.3.11. Flat-jack test results: stress measures at the level of the second walkway.

Figures 3.3.8–11 illustrate the positions where the vertical stress measurements were taken, as well as the results obtained. Figures 3.3.12–3 show the location of the boreholes drilled into the piers for inspection by camera probes.

Thirty tests were conducted in thirty different points of the masonry of the Cupola and piers for direct stress measurement. In the segments, the measurements carried out on the stone ma-

sonry at the level of the first internal walkway yielded vertical stress values ranging from about 4 to about 17 kgf/cm²; the masonry was found to be unstressed in just one point of segment 8, on the intrados of the outer shell. In the brick masonry of the segments at the elevation of the second internal walkway the vertical stress values varied considerably, ranging from a maximum of about 9 kgf/cm² to values at which the ma-

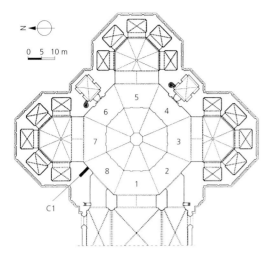

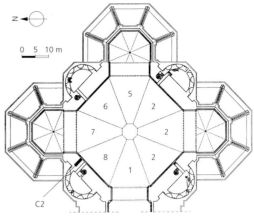

3.3.12. Position of the boreholes drilled into the piers: ground level.

3.3.13. Position of the boreholes drilled into the piers: first gallery level.

sonry can be considered to be unstressed; these minimum values were found both on the intrados of the outer shell and on the extrados of the inner shell.

In the piers at ground level (→ Fig. 3.3.8) the vertical stresses were found to vary between values of about 42 kgf/cm² (in the pier underlying segment 4) and about 120 kgf/cm² (in the pier underlying segment 8). The first of these values does not differ greatly from the theoretical value generated by the numerical analyses, while the second one is probably best interpreted as a local stress concentration relating to the particular type of masonry used. *Inspection with camera probes* conducted inside the boreholes drilled into the piers (→ Figs. 3.3.12–3) revealed that, behind strong and carefully cut stone facings, the pier consisted of rubble masonry bound together with dense mortar. Now, it is a well-known fact that, since the stone of the facing is stiffer than the internal rubble masonry, local peaks of compression usually develop in the former; such peaks are not necessarily dangerous, provided the internal conglomerate is, as is the case here, of good quality and firmly bonded to the facing. The value of the compressive vertical stress was much lower (about 8 kgf/cm²) in the pier un-

derlying segment 8 at the level of the first gallery (about 28 m from ground level).

As regards the direct measurements taken in order to calculate the Young's moduli, the values obtained for the stone masonry ranged between about 33,500 and 45,500 kgf/cm², while in the brick masonry they varied from about 17,000 to 43,500 kgf/cm². Such values should only be seen as an indication of the short-term behaviour of the materials, and are not applicable in relation to long periods of sustained load.

On the whole, it can be stated that the average value of the compressive stresses measured in the masonry is consistent with the estimates of the numerical analyses, while the appreciable scatter reflects heterogeneities both in the masonry texture and in the stress flow. These heterogeneities can safely be ascribed, at least in part, to the current state of the cracking, characterised by a substantial number of irregularly distributed lesions.

It is worth noting that, in addition to supplying valuable data, these one-off investigations also provide an accurate picture of the status quo at a given date; it will also be possible to use them as a reference point when evaluating data gathered by any future surveys.

3.4. Static Behaviour and Structural Hazard: Possible Scenarios[8]

The analyses carried out with Finite Element numerical models (→ § 3.2) concerned both the undamaged structure and the Cupola as affected by the four main cracks, extended to such an elevation as to cause the disappearance of the tensile stresses which the analyses had shown to be acting at the apex of the cracks. This condition was pinpointed through successive stages of approximation (with the progressive extension upwards of the four main full-thickness cracks) and was found to represent quite accurately the present condition of the Cupola.

*   *   *

The analyses and observations yielded the following results:

• the four main full-thickness cracks—wider at the base and closing progressively with increasing elevation—affect segments 2, 4, 6 and 8 (the segments resting directly above the four piers), extending upwards to about 10 m below the springing line of the lantern (i.e. almost two thirds of the overall height of the Cupola), and downwards at least to the upper rim of the great round windows of the drum;

• the extension and opening width of these cracks have increased steadily over the centuries (at an average rate of about 7 mm per century), and still show a constant, if very slow, rate of progression;

• the four piers are not solid wholes, but are pierced (and hence weakened) by various cavities near the octagonal symmetry planes where the four main cracks are located;

• the current maximum opening width of the cracks amounts to several centimetres (about 6 cm in the north-east and south-east segments and about 3 cm in the north-west and south-west segments).

This evidence suggested the possibility of setting up a theoretical *limit state* as a means of studying the possible evolution of the equilibrium condition in the Cupola.

Let us assume that the cracks affect *the whole height* of the Cupola, extending from the base of the piers up to the oculus ring. The structure would then be divided into four sectors or sub-structures subjected to their own dead weight and to the purely compressive actions they exert at the summit, where they mutually constrain each other by leaning on the oculus ring; at this elevation it would be reasonable to assume that the opening width of the cracks dwindles to nought (provided of course that the junction between the Cupola and the oculus ring is fully intact). The behaviour of such a structure under the action of dead weight differs substantially from that of an undamaged octagonal Cupola—and also, albeit to a lesser degree, from that of the Cupola in its present condition—in that the four substructures described above can no longer exchange mutual actions across the parallels, either of a tensile (as is the case for the lower parallels of the undamaged Cupola) or of a compressive nature (as is the case at present for the upper parallels of the actual structure; → §§ 2.2 and 3.2).

In order to make a preliminary, synthetic assessment of the static conditions in which this particular limit state operates without resorting to complex and expensive Finite Element numerical models, the four substructures defined above were assimilated—in a first approximation—to huge variable-section cantilevers with a subvertical axis. Disregarding for the moment some finer points that will be dealt with later on, we may say that each of these cantilevers has a vertical symmetry plane that bisects both the undamaged segment and the underlying pointed arch; the four symmetry planes are oriented to the north, east, south and west. To be on the safe side, we shall postulate an abstract condition in which the buttressing action exerted by the surrounding structures (the apses and the nave) is completely neglected.[9]

The dead weights of the various parts of each cantilever are not uniformly centred with respect to the centroids of the underlying sections;

moreover, the 'parallel' continuity that characterised the undamaged structure is no longer in place, since mutual actions cannot be transmitted through the cracked surfaces. The four cantilevers would therefore bend towards the central axis of the Cupola. At the summit, however, the cantilevers come into contact with the oculus ring, and further radial displacement is impeded by their mutual constraint. The internal actions arising from this constraint can be broken up into a horizontal force acting in each cantilever's symmetry plane and a torque (also contained in this symmetry plane). The intensity of these actions can be determined by applying compatibility conditions: at the summit of each cantilever the centripetal component of the displacement must be nil, while the local rotation in the symmetry plane must be compatible with the torsional stiffness of the oculus ring.

Once the values of the actions at the summit have been calculated, it will be easy to determine the deformed shape of the four cantilevers—in particular, the horizontal displacements at all points of the cantilevers' height. From this it is possible to derive the width of a crack along its entire length, as well as the stress state in any horizontal section of the cantilever. This final step is necessary in order to ascertain whether, in the limit state considered here, the cantilevers might be in danger of collapsing due to their inability to withstand the bending moments acting in their horizontal sections (which, incidentally, are also compressed by the above weights). These calculations were carried out on the assumption of linear elastic behaviour—an assumption which subsequently proved to be justifiable (see further on).

To better illustrate the static conditions just described, an axonometric view of the apsidal (east) cantilever is shown in Figure 3.4.1 (some of the quantitative results of the actual analysis are also given).

The main results of this analysis are given below; the procedure employed is outlined briefly in Inset 9.

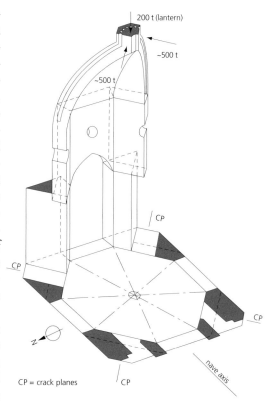

3.4.1. Axonometric view of the apsidal 'cantilever' as used in the limit-state analysis of the theoretical structure, with the four main cracks extending from the base of the piers up to the oculus ring.

*   *   *

As regards the vertical stresses acting in the four horizontal sections considered (p.b. = pier base; p.s. = pier summit; d.b. = drum base; c.b. = Cupola base), the simplified analysis generally shows (→ Table I) compression values no higher than 34 kgf/cm², and a moderate tensile stress value of about 1.4 kgf/cm² on the external rim of the horizontal section at the springing line of the Cupola (note that 'external' and 'internal' are used here with reference to the space enclosed by the overall structure formed by joining the four cantilevers together).

The study therefore indicates that even in the assumed limit state (i.e. an extreme condition in which *open cracks extend up to the oculus ring* and

9. Outline of the Procedure Adopted in the Analysis of Limit States

Before we describe the method adopted in the present analysis and some of its results, it should be emphasised that, although the assumed structural model undoubtedly constitutes the most probable extrapolation of the trend shown so far by the Cupola, it is but *one* amongst the many possible *limit states* of the structure, and has therefore nothing to say about the existence and characteristics of *other, different limit states*. For all its drawbacks, however, this approach has yielded results of the greatest interest regarding the maximum opening width of the cracks and where those maximum values are to be found (see further on).

Figure 3.4.2 shows a vertical section of the apsidal 'cantilever' as seen along the vertical symmetry plane. Figure 3.4.3 shows the horizontal sections of the base of the Cupola (c.b.), drum (d.b.) and piers (p.b.), as well as the moments of inertia of these sections, the values of which are essential for the computations. These are carried out under the so-called Coulomb assumption (more

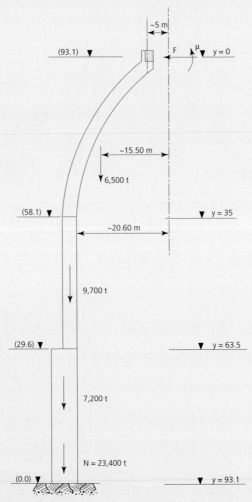

3.4.2. Vertical section of the apsidal 'cantilever' along the midline of the undamaged segment, with the values of the dead weights acting on the cantilever itself.

commonly known as the Navier assumption and widely adopted in engineering studies), according to which the sections remain plane during bending deformation. It is furthermore assumed that the cantilever is subjected to 'straight bending' in its vertical symmetry plane. The kite-shaped sections of the two half-piers supporting the drum and Cupola quarters, though not directly connected, behave as a single symmetrical section. These two half-piers are connected at their summit, at their point of junction with the drum and Cupola, and the stiffness of this connection constrains them to bend almost as one. Now, since neither of the two 'principal planes' of inertia of each half-pier coincides with the bending plane (the symmetry plane) of the cantilever, each half-pier will be subjected to 'skew bending' in a plane parallel to the cantilever's symmetry plane. It follows that the bending moments transmitted by the drum to the half-piers lie in planes containing the diameters of the respective ellipses of inertia conjugated with respect to the normal to the symmetry plane. And it is interesting to note (→ Fig. 3.4.3, line c–c) that these conjugate diameters—and thus *the planes of the moments exchanged between the Cupola and drum and the half-piers—are very nearly parallel to the two corner spurs included in the quarter*: the corner spurs are therefore subjected to straight compression and bending (without harmful torsional effects). This fact once again highlights the *fundamental importance of the corner spurs* in the static behaviour of the Cupola, as well as the perception shown by Brunelleschi (and his predecessors) in arranging and proportioning the sections and masses of the various members.

In turn, the equal and opposite bending moments transmitted by the two half-piers to the upper part of the cantilever tend to push the overlying pointed arch and Cupola quarter towards the symmetry plane, so that in this particular limit state it seems unlikely that the cracking will progress any further, at least as far as the effects of the dead weight are concerned.

The constraint actions at the summit of the cantilever were evaluated with the usual methods of modern structural analysis. Some level of approximation had to be accepted, which however

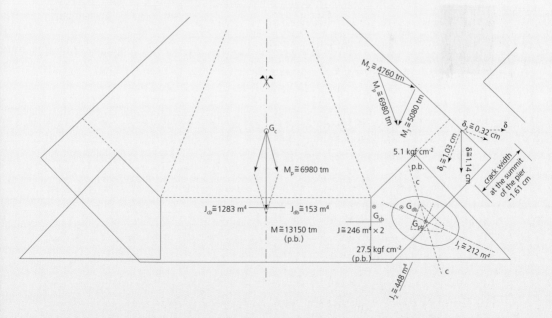

3.4.3. Plan view of a 'cantilever' showing the bending moments acting on the summit of the piers and the 'skew bending' of a half-pier.

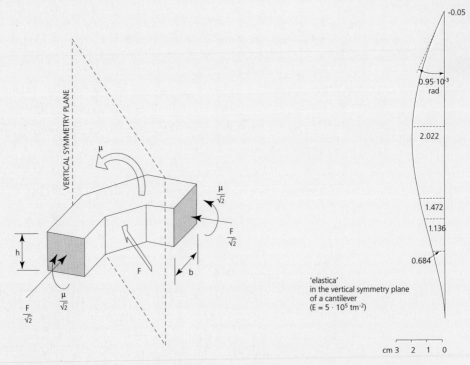

VERTICAL SYMMETRY PLANE

μ

$\frac{\mu}{\sqrt{2}}$

$\frac{F}{\sqrt{2}}$

h

F

b

$\frac{F}{\sqrt{2}}$

$\frac{\mu}{\sqrt{2}}$

$\frac{F}{\sqrt{2}}$

$\frac{\mu}{\sqrt{2}}$

-0.05

0.95·10⁻³
rad

2.022

1.472

1.136

0.684

'elastica'
in the vertical symmetry plane
of a cantilever
($E = 5 \cdot 10^5$ tm⁻²)

cm 3   2   1   0

3.4.4. Diagram showing the internal actions at play in a quarter of the oculus ring in the assumed limit state.

3.4.5. 'Elastica' (horizontal displacements) in the vertical symmetry plane of a cantilever in the assumed limit state.

does not seem to affect the calculations in any appreciable way. The details of such calculations would be of interest only to a limited number of readers, and are therefore omitted. Only the final results are given here.

Figure 3.4.4 shows a schematic view of the oculus ring, with the internal actions transmitted at that level to the cantilever in question by the adjacent ones. The values obtained for the two horizontal forces acting in mutually perpendicular planes amount to about 500 t; their resultant, amounting to about 700 t, lies in the symmetry plane of the cantilever. The value of the two torques is about 150–200 t per metre; they too lie in mutually perpendicular planes, and have a resultant of about 200–300 t per metre, also acting in the symmetry plane of the cantilever. This system of internal actions is compatible with both the deformability and the resistance of the oculus ring.

Finally, Figure 3.4.5 shows the 'elastica' (namely the deformed shape of the cantilever's axis after deformation, defined in terms of outward horizontal displacements in the cantilever's vertical symmetry plane), computed assuming a uniform Young's modulus of 50,000 kgf/cm², which is probably overestimated for the brick masonry and underestimated for the stone masonry.

Figure 3.4.6 illustrates the estimated variation in the opening width of the cracks with elevation, under the assumption that the four cantilevers behave identically (which, as noted above, is not the case). Under this assumption the opening width of the cracks is obtained simply by multiplying the above-mentioned horizontal displacements by $\sqrt{2}$. It is interesting to note that the maximum values thus obtained—about 3 cm—are located near the upper rim of the great round windows of the drum, precisely the point revealed by the analysis of the undamaged structure to be the location of the full-thickness tensile stress concentrations that probably triggered the main cracks.

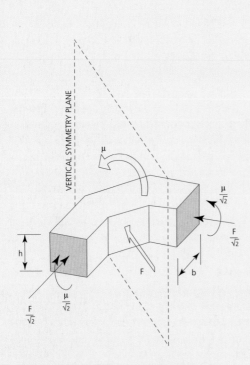

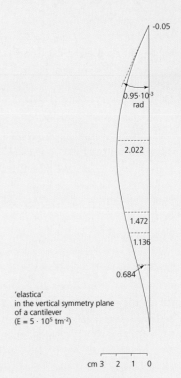

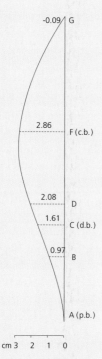

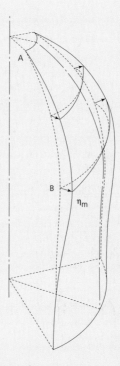

3.4.6. Variations according to elevation in the opening width of one of the four main cracks in the assumed limit state.

3.4.7. Secondary deformation mechanism leading to an increase in the opening width of the four main cracks in the assumed limit state.

Figure 3.4.7 shows a secondary deformation mechanism in the cantilever, leading to an increase of about 1 cm in the maximum opening width of the cracks, which would therefore reach a value of about 4 cm.

The maximum width value of the cracks obtained by the present study is somewhat inferior to the value observed in the actual structure (averaged over the four cracks), while one might have reasonably expected a larger one, given that in the limit state which has been assumed the extension of the cracks is greater than is actually the case. This apparent contradiction, however, is not surprising for at least two reasons: on the one hand, in the deformations that have taken place over the centuries there was undoubtedly a significant 'creep' component which, approximately speaking, must have at least doubled the elastic component that is the sole object of the present study; on the other hand, the value of the Young's modulus adopted here, namely 50,000 kgf/cm^2, is certainly overestimated for the brick masonry inside which such maximum values occur.

no containment is provided by the surrounding structures) the bending moments pose no real danger to any of the horizontal sections of the structure.

In view of all this, one cannot but marvel at the depth of structural intuition displayed by Brunelleschi (and by his predecessors, since all the above considerations apply to the piers and drum as well). It is, of course, impossible to claim that Brunelleschi had made provision for such an extreme condition; but, guided by his natural insight, he may have 'felt' on a purely intuitive, synthetic level that his creation was endowed with enough redundancies to be reasonably safe from collapse even in the face of serious structural disorders.

The fact that the four cantilevers are not identical, and that two of them are not symmetrical, suggests a number of qualitative considerations. Their implications cannot be dealt with here in detail, so we shall limit ourselves to two important results: first, the opening width of the two cracks between the north, west and south cantilevers (namely in segments 2 and 8) should be inferior to that of the other two cracks; second, the big pointed arch on the west side should be more susceptible to splaying with respect to the other three. These conclusions are confirmed by observation of the actual structure.

Before we move on, it is worth pointing out that this study was limited to analysis of the effects of dead weight alone. Favourable conclusions regarding the safety of the Cupola therefore only hold good for this type of load. The conclusions might be different if other actions were added, first and foremost—in terms of hazard and scale—the horizontal and vertical inertial forces generated by intense seismic activity. Indeed, an in-depth seismic analysis of the Cupola has yet to be carried out and should be regarded as a priority ($\rightarrow$ § 3.6), not only to obtain a more complete understanding of its structural behaviour, but also to refine our ability to predict future developments and, should the need arise, to suggest ways of strengthening the structure. The necessary mathematical tools for carrying out such an analysis already exist, and are known to yield reliable results. The real problem lies in defining what kind of earthquake could be taken as a credible benchmark, given the significant number of variables involved (seismological characteristics of the site, probability of occurrence, magnitude, etc.).

There is a need, then, for close cooperation between seismologists and civil engineers specialising in structural analysis, so that the work carried out so far may be completed, paving the way for effective conservation guidelines.

section	radial displacement / crack width (cm)	σ_1 (kgf/cm²)	σ_2 (kgf/cm²)
A (p.b.)	0 / 0	27.5	5.1
C (p.s.)	1.1 / 1.6	9.4	20.8
C (d.b.)	1.1 / 1.6	33.6	10.3
F (c.b.)	2.0 / 2.9	−1.4	11.4

Table I. σ_1 = stress at the outer rim of the section; σ_2 = stress at the inner rim of the section; + = compression, − = tensile stress. (The stress values are given in kgf/cm², displacements and crack widths in cm.)

3.5. Possible Measures for Ensuring the Long-Term Safety of the Cupola

The analyses that have been examined indicate that the permanent loads (dead weight, thermal actions) do not pose serious threats to the safety of the Cupola. Unfortunately, such confidence cannot be extended to the possible effects of dynamic actions, particularly those that might be caused by earthquakes of a certain magnitude, a possibility which cannot be discounted in Tuscany (→ § 3.6). Indeed, preliminary evaluations suggest that the margin of safety has been significantly reduced by the existing cracks.

On the other hand, attempts to repair the existing masonry and restore it to something like its original state would ultimately be quite ineffective, as they would fail to address the root cause of the problem, namely that the masonry strength is not sufficient to withstand the tensile stresses across the meridian planes. This kind of solution, which has been sporadically attempted in the past, would actually accentuate the problem, as the filler material would form a wedge at the apex of the cracks when they contract at certain times of the year, ultimately favouring their further extension. It is therefore necessary to devise and evaluate other options.

Di Pasquale proposed filling the cracks with a highly deformable and adhesive plastic material in order to prevent masonry fragments from detaching and falling into the cracks. Indeed, in periods in which thermal variations tend to reduce the width of the cracks, these fragments could end up acting as local 'wedges', thereby favouring the upward progression of the cracks. Although this proposal is undoubtedly a sensible solution with regard to problems arising from the normal static behaviour of the Cupola, it does nothing to address the issue of seismic hazard.

In the light of the numerical analyses carried out by CRIS–ENEL, Chiarugi proposed *actively* hooping the inner shell with tensioned steel cables laid out in the space between the two shells at the springing of the Cupola. These ca-bles would be suitably anchored to the extrados of the inner shell at the corners where the segments intersect; at these points, the shell would receive, in the form of radial thrusts, the resultant of the tensions of the cables lying along two adjacent sides. The function of this supplementary static system (→ Fig. 3.5.1a–b) would basically be similar to that of a hoop; but while previous hooping schemes envisaged the use of *passive* iron rings, which would not begin to exert any radial action until such time as there was further outward splaying of the Cupola, with the *active* hooping the tensioned cables would immediately give back to the masonry the internal energy lost as a result of the formation of the cracks. This would essentially restore the structure to an ideally undamaged state, artificially compensating for the inadequate tensile strength of the masonry.

From this point of view the proposed solution might be regarded as a more advanced version of the ideas once advocated by Viviani and Nelli, whose passive hooping scheme was fundamentally correct, at least in qualitative terms. It was, however, quantitatively insufficient, and would also have been difficult to implement, since the *octagonal* geometry of the Cupola is incompatible with *circular* hooping. Viviani seems to have realized this, since he sketched a plan for a twenty-four-sided iron chain, possibly slightly curved and laid out in a way not dissimilar to that of the wooden chain. It should be pointed out that the installation of such a chain would have required extensive modification to the existing masonry. The *active* octagonal hooping would avoid this difficulty, in that the thrusters placed at the corners of the octagon would allow the cables to be laid out in straight lines along the eight sides, and still exert radial forces on the inner shell.

The total cable tensioning to be applied along each side could be limited, according to preliminary evaluations, to just a few hundred metric tons; therefore, the high-strength steel cables would only need to be a few dozen centimetres in diameter. The application of this system of

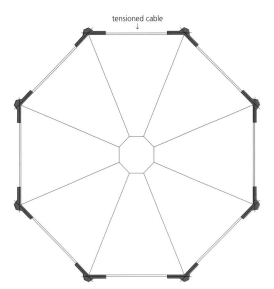

tensioned cable
↓

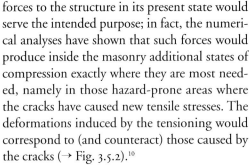

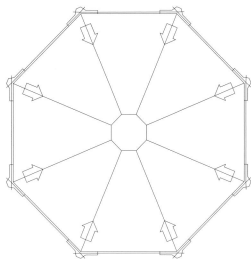

3.5.1a. Diagram illustrating the proposed scheme to increase the structural strength of the Cupola with eight tensioned steel cables installed at the springing line.

3.5.1b. Radial forces produced by the tensioning of the eight steel cables.

forces to the structure in its present state would serve the intended purpose; in fact, the numerical analyses have shown that such forces would produce inside the masonry additional states of compression exactly where they are most needed, namely in those hazard-prone areas where the cracks have caused new tensile stresses. The deformations induced by the tensioning would correspond to (and counteract) those caused by the cracks (→ Fig. 3.5.2).[10]

The whole system of cables would have the further advantage of being totally *invisible* from both outside and inside the Cathedral. Their tensioning could also be effected very gradually, in order to enable careful monitoring of its effects on the Cupola and to fine-tune the procedure. Furthermore, this measure would be fully *reversible*, should other options become available in the course of time.

Finally, this measure would be respectful of the original design of the Cupola, inasmuch as it would simply make up for a deficiency in the tensile strength of the masonry which could not possibly have been foreseen by Brunelleschi and was not therefore worked into his design, even

though the architect might subconsciously have been aware of it.

Any other proposals to strengthen the Cupola (although it is difficult at present to imagine what other solutions there could be) should of course be carefully evaluated, in order to be quite sure that the best available option is chosen. One thing, however, is clear: the worst possible course of action would be to ignore the concrete risk that extraordinary events might irreparably undermine the delicate equilibrium of the Cupola (see the comments on preliminary dynamic simulations: § 3.6, Table II).

The most suitable initiative would be to hold an international competition as soon as possible, inviting architects and engineers to submit design solutions, as has already been done in the case of the Leaning Tower of Pisa. This would be the most fitting way to revive the ancient tradition of involving the best minds of the age in a collective endeavour (a tradition to which we owe the building of the Cupola itself), and at the same time would be a reminder that this unique monument is part of the heritage not only of Florence, but of all mankind.

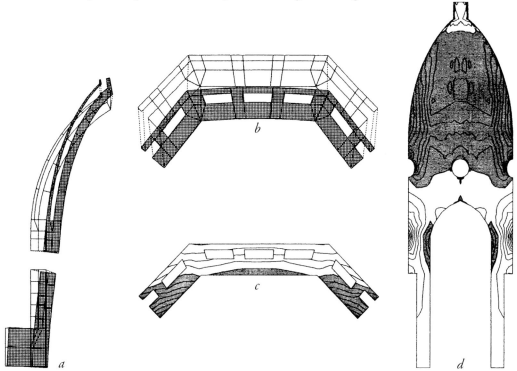

3.5.2a–d. Deformation and stress distribution induced by the hooping action of the eight tensioned steel cables (→ Fig. 3.5.1).

3.6. The Need for Further Studies

The analyses that have been carried out to date using Finite Element or more elementary mathematical models have provided a fairly accurate outline of the static behaviour of the Cupola, both in the undamaged and the cracked state. Of course such models have entailed a significant degree of schematisation, including for instance: their assumed symmetry; the approximate representation of the constraints provided by the surrounding structures (most notably the nave); the linear elastic constitutive law employed in the analysis of the data; the incomplete representation of thermal loads; and the lack of attention given to the rheological properties of the materials due to insufficient knowledge. Nevertheless, the close match between the results of the models and the evidence yielded by *in situ* investigations have demonstrated that the models are both reliable and representative.

The Finite Element models also made it possible to commence investigation of the dynamic properties of the structure in both the undamaged and the cracked state by providing a means of calculating the modes and frequencies of vibration in the Cupola (→ Inset 10).

The mathematical models have yielded about as much information as they are capable of given their current degree of refinement. What is required now is a closer analysis of the objective evidence, which has been greatly increased by the mass of observational data made available following the installation of the monitoring and data-acquisition system in recent years. Careful interpretation of this evidence would provide fresh input enabling further calibration of the models, which in turn would yield results of an even higher quality.

Unfortunately, only limited human and financial resources have thus far been devoted to the task. Several possibilities that could usefully be pursued will be described in the next section.

*   *   *

As far as the *static analysis* of the Cupola is concerned, the acquisition and processing of data relating to the absolute and relative movements of its different parts over the course of the seasons and at different times of the day, combined with thermometric readings of the masonry and a thermographic study of the external surfaces, would provide a much better understanding of the periodic component in the structure's static behaviour, as well as a clearer picture of asymmetries in the thermal loads, which are undoubtedly important for the outer shell (if not for the inner one) and have so far been completely neglected.

The main objectives of such in-depth thermal investigation would be the following:

- to obtain from the mathematical model a quantitatively reliable forecast of the *thermal component* in the absolute and relative *displacement field*—first and foremost the variations in the width of the cracks; comparison with the objective measurements would allow validation of the model, identification of the thermal constants and also, in the long run, of the irreversible component (*drift*), if any, in crack width variation as opposed to the reversible (seasonal) component;

- to obtain from the mathematical model, once the value of the Young's modulus of the materials has been determined, a quantitatively reliable evaluation of the *thermal component* in the *stress field* in both the undamaged and the cracked state; this would provide a fuller diagnosis of the cause of the cracking and help to interpret its development over time (the basic diagnosis is already convincing, but the secondary role of the thermal factor in the development of the cracks has not yet been sufficiently clarified; while it is likely that thermal variations may have played a secondary role in the propagation of the cracks, favouring their extension over time, this is still only a working hypothesis, and more specific investigations such as the ones described above are required if this is to be definitively proved one way or another).

In order to obtain a closer match between the observed data and the results of the mathematical model (especially in order to achieve a more effective modelling of the cracks), it would be advisable to extend the model so as to include the nave. It will be recalled that in the current model it is assumed that the structure is symmetrical with respect to the north–south and east–west planes, and as a result the nave is replaced by a fourth apse. The stiffness of this hypothetical apse as a lateral constraint against the thrust of the Cupola and the drum is clearly much less than that of the nave. It would also be appropriate to add the foundation layers and their geotechnical properties into the model; these would of course have to be determined by specific investigations. It should be noted that the assumed fourfold symmetry meant that the current model could be limited to one quarter of the structure. On the other hand, a more realistic version of the model that included the nave would have to reproduce at least one half of the structure, symmetrical to the other half with respect to the east–west plane. Obviously there would be a huge increase in the number of degrees of freedom (the unknowns) in the model, and a corresponding increase in cost. However, this refined version of the model would also offer a means of more realistically determining the modes and frequencies of vibration in the structure (see further on).

As briefly mentioned above, the use of tried and tested identification techniques when effecting comparisons between objective measurements and numerical projections will yield reliable estimates of the mechanical and thermal properties of the materials. The value of the Young's modulus, however, cannot be calculated merely on the basis of static observations, in that the static loads acting on the structure (essentially the dead weight) do not vary with time and therefore do not produce those variations in the observable effects that are necessary to apply the identification techniques. Nor can the variable displacements produced by thermal variations be used to this end, because—as is well known—they are independent from the value of the Young's modulus. On the other hand, *in situ* dynamic tests (see further on) would permit reliable calculation of the value of the Young's modulus in terms of the structure's short-term behaviour. Some *local* direct measurements, albeit limited in number and affected by a large scatter, have already been carried out in different points of the masonry using the flat-jack testing technique (→ § 3.3).

For the above-mentioned purposes the extended model envisaged here could still be limited to a linear elastic constitutive law. If at some point the model were to be extended even further, which given the complexity and cost involved seems unlikely at present, a more accurate representation of the rheological properties of the materials (anisotropic properties of the masonry, creep effects) could also be included, and concepts derived from Fracture Mechanics could usefully be applied, which may well enable a more accurate interpretation of the propagation of the cracks over time.

*   *   *

The contribution of observational data appears crucial also with respect to *dynamic analyses*.

In situ dynamic observations have so far been extremely limited: measurement of the vibrations induced in the Cupola by environmental factors such as wind or traffic has enabled only the frequency of the structure's first mode to be ascertained with an adequate degree of reliability. This value, estimated at about 1.8 Hz, tallies with the frequency yielded by the mathematical model of the cracked structure for the first symmetric mode, while the lowest frequency, according to the model, should correspond to the first anti-symmetric mode, estimated at about 0.9 Hz (→ Table II).

The considerable drop in nearly all the frequencies when passing from the undamaged to the cracked state (see second and third columns of Table II) is an indication of the considerable

loss of stiffness caused by the cracks (see last column of the Table). This indirectly reflects the greater vulnerability—or rather the reduced margin of safety with respect to dynamic excitations—of the cracked structure in comparison with the undamaged one.

Examination of the structure's modes of vibration and relative dynamic motions (interesting computer animations have been realised by CRIS–ENEL) clearly shows that in the case of many of these modes the cracks would tend to cyclically increase and decrease in width. This would lead to propagation of the cracks themselves, and to further weakening of the Cupola. Given the low frequencies of the modes in question, the latter would certainly be excited by seismic activity. All these considerations point to the plausible conclusion that earthquakes may be one of the secondary factors involved in exacerbating the damage, as has already been mentioned elsewhere.

It would be worth carrying out *in situ* vibration tests by means of artificial excitation. This technique has been widely tested on many different structures, monumental and otherwise, and involves the use of small vibration-inducing shakers that can be regulated both in frequency and intensity; clearly the level of excitation is so minimal that the structure is not endangered in any way. This procedure would not only enable further validation of the numerical model, but would also yield a *global* estimate of the Young's modulus which, as we have seen, cannot be obtained from static behaviour measurements.

The tests in question should be carefully designed and planned; although still to be validated and calibrated in this respect, the current model would provide valuable help at this stage in estimating a priori the magnitude of the frequencies and the vibration amplitudes (as well as the levels of stress) produced by excitation of a given intensity. It would thus be possible to establish in advance whether a programme of *in situ* dynamic testing can be successfully carried out with the small, low-powered shakers that are commonly used. The model could also help to pinpoint the most appropriate position for installing the shakers.

A thorough and well-documented survey of the spatial amplitude distributions of the different modes would not only permit comprehensive validation and calibration of the numerical model, but would also establish a reliable baseline against which any variations emerging from later surveys could be assessed.[11] Such surveys would be the only means of ascertaining the values of the *damping coefficients* required for developing a reliable forecast of the structure's response to earthquakes.[12] It would also seem sensible to extend the scope of the monitoring and data-acquisition system now in place so as to include recording of the Cupola's response to micro- and macroseismic events. Once the relevant data have been acquired and the model has been updated accordingly, the delicate issue of forecasting the *reaction of the structure to seismic activity* could be tackled. It goes without saying that in order to produce a realistic assessment of the seismic hazard and take any strengthening measures that may be required, it is indispensable to draw on the expertise of seismologists to build up a picture of the various earthquake scenarios that are compatible with local geological and seismotectonic features.

From a more general point of view, it would seem wise to organise the vast body of data being obtained by both the numerical models and the *in situ* investigations in a systematic fashion. Above all else, this would involve setting up a user-friendly database that is easy to update and modify. The database would need to be fully interactive, using state-of-the-art software for on-line data processing and visualisation.

It cannot be sufficiently emphasised that the ultimate goal of the proposed tests is to provide a solid basis for the designing of possible reinforcement measures to reduce the risk of damage that might be caused by natural hazards such as earthquakes. This is a real priority, and one that needs to be addressed urgently in order to place the powers that be in a position to take a responsible, clear-cut decision regarding the strategy to be adopted.

In this regard, it is worth recalling here what was discussed in detail in the previous section, namely that it is entirely possible to devise measures in keeping with Brunelleschi's original approach (he had envisaged using chains in the Cupola, inadequate though they were) and with the spirit of subsequent proposals by the likes of Viviani and Poleni. Tensioned steel cables installed in the space between the two shells, laid out in an octagonal pattern and anchored to thrusters at the corners would provide the necessary radial thrust to the corner spurs. Preliminary evaluations suggest that a tensioning of a few hundred metric tons on each side would be sufficient to give to the Cupola the circumferential containment that the masonry and surrounding structures have failed to provide. The structure would thus regain the solidity it was intended to have—and would undoubtedly have had if only the materials had been endowed with sufficient tensile strength. This solution would not impinge upon the aesthetics of the Cupola in any way whatsoever, and could be carried out in complete safety and in a step-by-step, carefully monitored manner.

Meanwhile, of course, other options could and should be elicited and assessed by experts of international repute.

10. Modes and Frequencies of Vibration

Any given structure can vibrate at different frequencies and with different spatial distributions of the amplitudes depending on how it is dynamically excited by external forces. There are, however, particularly well-defined frequencies, each with its relative amplitude distribution, at which the structure, once excited into vibration, would in theory continue to vibrate indefinitely, were it not for the energy dissipation (damping) that causes the amplitudes to decrease exponentially over time. The potentially perpetual nature of specific combinations of frequencies and amplitudes is due to the fact that in those circumstances there is an exact equilibrium between the internal forces arising from the deformation of the structure and the inertial forces. These frequencies and amplitude distributions (which form a discrete but infinite succession for a spatially extended structure) are called respectively the *eigenfrequencies* and *eigenmodes* of the structure, and can be determined (for instance by means of Finite Element numerical models) once the geometrical shape, mechanical properties, mass distribution and constraints are known. Eigenfrequencies are measured in Hertz (Hz), 1 Hz corresponding to one cycle of vibration per second; the eigenmodes are determined with an arbitrary multiplicative constant. Suitable instruments and techniques are available for exciting a real structure into vibration so that its eigenfrequencies and eigenmodes can be measured. Once these characteristics (and the respective damping coefficients) are known, it is possible to calculate the dynamic response of the structure to any kind of external excitation (for instance, a seismic event); knowledge of the eigenfrequencies, eigenmodes and damping coefficients of a given structure thus provides the key to its dynamic properties.

It can be shown that, given a geometrically and physically symmetrical structure (as is the case with the numerical models of the Cupola generated thus far), the only possible eigenmodes are either symmetric or anti-symmetric (→ Table II).

Assuming that eigenfrequencies and eigenmodes have been calculated for both the undamaged and the cracked structure, comparing the respective eigenfrequencies corresponding to similar eigenmodes makes it possible to estimate the loss of stiffness induced by the cracks (→ last column of Table II).

vibration mode	undamaged Cupola	cracked Cupola	residual stiffness
symmetric modes	2.14	1.86	76%
	4.08	1.95	23%
anti-symmetric modes	1.03	0.89	75%
	3.03	2.25	55%
torsional modes	1.65	1.60	94%
	2.70	2.16	64%

Table II. Frequency values (Hz) of the first vibration modes yielded by the CRIS–ENEL mathematical model.

Notes (Part One)

Chapter 1

1 M. Haines, "Brunelleschi and Bureaucracy: The Tradition of Public Patronage at the Florentine Cathedral", *I Tatti Studies: Essays in the Renaissance* 3 (1989), 92–3.

2 For a discussion of how the Cathedral building programme was funded, see M. Haines, "Firenze e il finanziamento della Cattedrale e del Campanile", in T. Verdon (ed.), *Alla riscoperta di Piazza del Duomo in Firenze*, vol. 3, *Il Campanile di Santa Maria del Fiore* (Florence: Centro Di, 1994), 71–83. In 1392 a law was passed introducing a tax on wills, the revenue from which went to the Opera. The introduction of the tax yielded a relatively modest sum; still, it is a significant sign of the involvement of the whole community: see L. Ippolito and C. Peroni, *La cupola di Santa Maria del Fiore* (Florence: La Nuova Italia, 1997), 25 n. 38.

3 Since 1294 officials known as *operai* had been appointed by the city government to administer the funds for the restoration of the old cathedral of Santa Reparata.

4 For instance, Niccolò di Donato Barbadori, *capitano* of the Parte Guelfa (the institution which commissioned Brunelleschi to redesign its offices), held the post of *camarlingo* of the Opera di Santa Maria del Fiore once, and that of *operaio* on a number of occasions. He was a consul of the Arte della Lana in 1404 and again in 1417. Together with his brother Giovanni, Niccolò completed the family chapel in Santa Felicita and built the *palazzo* in Borgo San Jacopo, both to designs by Brunelleschi: see D. Finiello Zervas, *The Parte Guelfa, Brunelleschi & Donatello* (Locust Valley, N.Y.: J.J. Augustin, 1988) and Ippolito–Peroni, *La cupola*, 12.

5 C. Guasti, *Santa Maria del Fiore. La costruzione della chiesa e del campanile…*, photographic reprint of the original edition, Florence 1887 (Bologna: Forni, 1974), 95.

6 For a review of this question, see C. Bozzoni, "Le cattedrali del Due-Trecento in Umbria e in Toscana", in *Il Duomo di Orvieto e le grandi cattedrali gotiche*, proceedings of the conference: Orvieto, 12–14 November 1990 (Turin: Nuova ERI, 1995), 223–31.

7 See H. Saalman, "Santa Maria del Fiore: 1294–1418", *Art Bulletin* 46 (1964), 491.

8 Andrea appears to have painted buttresses reaching as high as the entablature at the base of the dome, and then to have had second thoughts and removed them. This may be taken as an indicator of contemporary debate on the issue.

9 Guasti, *Santa Maria del Fiore*, 299–300 (doc. 425).

10 G. Vasari, *Lives of the Artists*, 2 vols., a selection translated by G. Bull (Harmondsworth: Penguin, 1987), I.141.

11 C. Guasti, *La Cupola di Santa Maria del Fiore, illustrata con i documenti dell'Archivio dell'Opera secolare* (Florence: Barbera Bianchi e Comp., 1857), 17 (doc. 16).

12 Ibid., 19 (doc. 21).

13 This hypothesis was advanced by Howard Saalman in *Filippo Brunelleschi. The Cupola of Santa Maria del Fiore* (London: Zwemmer, 1980), 60. It is indirectly supported by the fact that Brunelleschi and Manno must have known each other well, since Brunelleschi worked for Manno's father, the goldsmith Benincasa Lotti, around 1399.

14 Guasti, *La Cupola*, 19 (doc. 23); see also Saalman, *Filippo Brunelleschi. The Cupola*, 58.

15 Guasti, *La Cupola*, 15 (doc. 11).

16 Ibid., 21 (doc. 30).

17 Ippolito–Peroni, *La cupola*, 10 and 44; but see also Saalman, *Filippo Brunelleschi. The Cupola*, 253 (doc. 100, dated 1 April 1420).

18 Saalman, *Filippo Brunelleschi. The Cupola*, 62.

19 Guasti, *La Cupola*, 17 (doc. 17) and 18 (doc. 19).

20 A. Manetti, *Vita di Filippo Brunelleschi*, edited by C. Perrone (Rome: Salerno, 1992), 83–5. All references are to this edition; for an English translation, see *The Life of Brunelleschi, by Antonio di Tuccio Manetti*, introduction, notes, and critical text edited by H. Saalman, English translation by C. Enggass (University Park, Penn.: Pennsylvania State University Press, 1970). Manetti mentions that Brunelleschi's ideas for building without centring began to be viewed with greater favour only after he had successfully completed the small dome of the Ridolfi chapel in San Jacopo Sopr'Arno in this way. However the exact date of construction of this chapel (destroyed in 1709) is not known.

21 Guasti, *La Cupola*, 27 (doc. 48).

22 Ibid., 27 (docs. 48 and 49). The document has been variously interpreted. Some scholars have taken it as evidence of the collaboration between the two masters in producing a new model, whereas Saalman (*Filippo Brunelleschi. The Cupola*, 63–5) believes that the materials (wood, glue, wire, nails) were used to make a model of the drum alone, to be attached to the model of the dome that Brunelleschi had made two years earlier.

23 Guasti, *La Cupola*, 36 (doc. 71).

24 Ippolito–Peroni, *La cupola*, 17.

25 See C. von Fabriczy, "Brunelleschiana", *Jahrbuch der königlich preuszischen Kunstsammlungen* 28 (1907) Beiheft (Supplement), 15.

26 Ippolito–Peroni, *La cupola*, 51.

27 There is no proof that Brunelleschi derived the spiral herringbone pattern from earlier Tuscan buildings or from ancient Roman architecture. It is conceivable that he knew of the vaults or domes with herringbone brickwork that had begun to be built in the 12th century in the Middle East, in some cases with complex geometrical designs on the bare

surface of the intrados. As previously mentioned, Brunelleschi had already built a dome with herringbone brickwork and without using scaffold-supported centring for Schiatta Ridolfi's family chapel in the church of San Jacopo Sopr'Arno. By the early 16th century, use of the herringbone technique appears to have become widespread in Tuscany, as suggested by a comment scrawled on a drawing by Antonio da Sangallo the Younger (Florence, GDSU, A 900v; → Fig. 33)—the drawing illustrates how the rows of offset bricks assume a distinctive spiral course as they converge towards the oculus.

Chapter 2

1   See R.A. Goldthwaite, *The building of Renaissance Florence: an economic and social history* (Baltimore: Johns Hopkins University Press, 1980).

2   Haines, "Firenze e il finanziamento", 74.

3   In 1435 the noise of the stonecutters' hammers so disturbed preaching during Lent that it was decided not to count the hours of work they did during religious services: see Guasti, *La Cupola*, 84 (doc. 235).

4   Saalman, *Filippo Brunelleschi. The Cupola*, 191–3.

5   Ibid., 248 (doc. 36).

6   Manetti, *Vita*, 98.

7   See Ippolito–Peroni, *La cupola*, 92–4.

8   Guasti, *La Cupola*, 80–1 (doc. 219).

9   Ibid., 82 (doc. 226). A similar measure was adopted at Orvieto Cathedral: see L. Riccetti, *Il Duomo di Orvieto* (Rome-Bari: Laterza, 1988), 139–215.

10   Guasti, *La Cupola*, 80 (doc. 217).

11   Manetti, *Vita*, 103.

12   Guasti, *La Cupola*, 83 (doc. 232).

13   Manetti, *Vita*, 104.

14   Saalman, *Filippo Brunelleschi. The Cupola*, 254 (doc. 123) and 259 (doc. 162).

15   There are interesting parallels with the building of Orvieto Cathedral, as regards the presence of secondary worksites and of a furnace in the immediate vicinity of the cathedral, and the organisation of work in the quarries: see Ippolito–Peroni, *La cupola*, 99 n. 12.

16   Saalman, *Filippo Brunelleschi. The Cupola*, 197.

17   See P. Galluzzi (ed.), *Prima di Leonardo. Cultura e macchine a Siena nel Rinascimento*, exhibition catalogue: Siena, Magazzini del Sale, 9 June–30 September 1991 (Milan: Electa, 1991), 187.

18   Saalman, *Filippo Brunelleschi. The Cupola*, 199.

19   For the same reasons similar precautions are recommended, but not always adopted, for laying concrete today.

20   See P. Sanpaolesi, *Brunelleschi* (Milan: Club del Libro, 1962).

21   According to Paolo Galluzzi, the figure was over four million: see id., *Mechanical Marvels. Invention in the Age of Leonardo*, exhibition catalogue: New York, World Financial Center, Liberty Street Gallery, 24 October 1997–1 March 1998 (Florence: Giunti, 1997), 94.

Chapter 3

1   Saalman, *Filippo Brunelleschi. The Cupola*, 253 (doc. 109).

2   Ibid., 254 (doc. 123).

3   G.B. Gelli, *Vite d'artisti*, published by G. Mancini, *Archivio storico italiano*, s. V, 17 (1896), 1:54.

4   Guasti, *La Cupola*, 38–41 (doc. 75).

5   Saalman, *Filippo Brunelleschi. The Cupola*, 108.

6   "We still do not recommend centring: not that the fabric would not be stronger, and more beautiful; but not having begun it, it would seem that centring it now would make the new fabric different from that which has been built, and of different shape: also, it would be difficult to have centring without fixed scaffolding; and it was decided from the beginning not to have centring so as not to have to build fixed scaffolding": Guasti, *La Cupola*, 40 (doc. 75).

7   Saalman, *Filippo Brunelleschi. The Cupola*, 275 (doc. 284).

8   Ibid., 275 (doc. 286).

9   Guasti, *La Cupola*, 86 (doc. 248).

10   Ibid., 87 (doc. 250).

11   Ibid., 87 (doc. 251).

12   Ibid., 93–4 (doc. 273).

13   Ibid., 113 (doc. 332).

14   Vasari, *Lives*, 1.158.

15   Guasti, *La Cupola*, 123–4 (doc. 343).

16   A. Parronchi, "Le illustrazioni del Botticelli per la Commedia e il progetto di un «Pantheon» fiorentino", in C. Gizzi (ed.), *Botticelli e Dante*, exhibition catalogue: Torre de' Passeri, Pescara, Casa di Dante in Abruzzo (Milan: Electa, 1990), 77.

17   When the frescoes were finally unveiled, Agostino Lapini noted in his journal: "some people said one thing, some said another: the Dome looks lower; it was more beautiful without the frescoes, and it seemed higher and bigger; and some people contradicted themselves, and everyone had his own opinion". See A. Lapini, *Diario fiorentino ... dal 252 al 1596* [c. 1587–96], edited by G.O. Corazzini (Florence: Sansoni, 1900).

18   Parronchi, "Le illustrazioni del Botticelli", 77–80.

Chapter 4

1   Manetti, *Vita*, 122.

2   G. Marchini, in G. Marchini et al. (eds.), *Disegni di fabbriche brunelleschiane* (Florence: Olschki, 1977), 6.

3   There are many documentary references to lightning striking the dome: e.g. 5 April 1492; June 1498; 4 November 1511; 1536; 22 December 1542; 5 November 1570; 11 October 1577; 3 November 1578; 28 August 1586 (see also Part Two, Chapter 2, n. 18).

4 "It [the bolt of lightning] struck at the fifth hour of the night, with a tremendous crash and great damage: the ball, the cross and a great quantity of marble hit the ground with such violence and force that they rolled half way up Via dei Servi": F.L. Del Migliore, *Firenze città nobilissima illustrata* (Florence: Stamp. della Stella, 1684).

5 See Saalman, *Filippo Brunelleschi. The Cupola*, 146–7.

6 As Leon Battista Alberti remarks in *De re aedificatoria* (1485), book VII, chapter XII: "the sense of awe aroused by darkness makes the mind susceptible to veneration".

7 L. Benevolo, *Storia dell'architettura del Rinascimento* (Rome–Bari: Laterza, 1968), 1.57–8.

8 L.B. Alberti, *De pictura* [1435–6], edited by C. Grayson (Rome–Bari: Laterza, 1980).

9 C.L. Ragghianti, "Letture di Wright", *Critica d'arte* (1954) 4, 372.

Chapter 5

1 Manetti, *Vita*, 45.

2 Lamberto Ippolito points out the similarities between this text and the funerary inscription of the architect of Pisa Cathedral, Buscheto, who was famous for his ingenious methods of raising great weights: Ippolito–Peroni, *La cupola*, 102 n. 58.

3 Quoted in Saalman, *Filippo Brunelleschi. The Cupola*, 12.

4 Giuliano Tanturli dates it to 1471—see A. Manetti, *Vita di Filippo Brunelleschi*, edited by D. De Robertis and G. Tanturli (Milan: Il Polifilo, 1966); in the introduction to her edition of Manetti's *Vita*, Carlachiara Perrone dates it to between 1482 and 1489—see "Introduzione", 28 in Manetti, *Vita*. As has been observed by Sanpaolesi, Manetti's unpublished manuscript was drawn upon extensively by Vasari.

5 See "Introduzione", 8 in Manetti, *Vita*.

6 Vasari, *Lives*, 1.133 and 160.

7 Marchini, *Disegni di fabbriche brunelleschiane*, 25–7.

8 F. Baldinucci, *Notizie de' Professori del disegno da Cimabue in qua, per le quali si dimostra come, e per chi le Belle Arti di Pittura, Scultura e Architettura, lasciata la rozzezza delle maniere Greca e Gottica, si siano in questi secoli ridotte all'antica loro perfezione*, 6 vols. (Florence 1681–1728), IV.

9 C.M. von Stegmann and H.A. von Geymüller, *Die Architektur der Renaissance in Toscana* (Munich: Bruckmann, 1885–1908).

10 Opera di Santa Maria del Fiore, *Rilievi e studi sulla Cupola del Brunelleschi* (Florence, 1939).

11 See W. Ferri, M. Fondelli, P. Franchi and F. Greco, "Il rilevamento fotogrammetrico della Cupola di S. Maria del Fiore in Firenze", *Bollettino di Geodesia e Scienze Affini* 30 (1971), 158–84.

Chapter 6

1 Zocchi's etchings were published in 1744 by the Florentine printer Giuseppe Allegrini with the title *Scelta di XXIV vedute delle principali Contrade, Piazze, Chiese e Palazzi della Città di Firenze*.

2 See G. Fanelli, *Anton Hautmann. Firenze in stereoscopia* (Florence: Octavo, 1999).

3 Vasari, *Lives*, 1.160 and 142–3.

4 G. Targioni Tozzetti, *Prodromo della corografia e della topografia fisica della Toscana* (Florence: nella Stamperia Imperiale, 1754), 177.

5 Gibbon's manuscript was published in 1961 with the title *Gibbon's Journey from Geneva to Rome. His Journal from 20 April to 2 October 1764*, edited by G.A. Bonnard (London–New York: Nelson, 1961).

6 First edition: H. Taine, *Voyage en Italie* (Paris: Hachette, 1866).

7 G. Papini, *Città Felicità. Firenze*, edited by V. Paszkowski Papini (Florence: Vallecchi, 1960).

8 Quoted in G. Gobbi et al. (eds.), *Le Corbusier. Il viaggio in Toscana (1907)*, exhibition catalogue: Florence, Pitti Palace, 1987 (Venice: Marsilio, 1987), 125 and 136.

9 C.L. Ragghianti, *Filippo Brunelleschi. Un uomo, un universo* (Florence: Vallecchi, 1977), 233–4.

10 *Rome, Naples et Florence, en 1817* was published in Paris by Delaunay in 1817; the date was dropped from the title of the definitive edition, published in 1826.

11 The letters of Felix Mendelssohn-Bartholdy (*Reisebriefe von Felix Mendelssohn-Bartholdy aus den Jahren 1830 bis 1832*) were first published in Leipzig in 1861.

12 First edition: W. Somerset Maugham, *Then and Now* (Garden City, N.Y.: Doubleday, 1946).

13 Quoted in *Le voyage d'Italie d'Eugène Viollet-le-Duc 1836–1837*, exhibition catalogue: École nationale supérieure des beaux-arts, 1979, edited by G. Viollet-le-Duc (Paris–Florence: Aillagon, 1980), 186.

14 First edition: Ch. Dickens, *Pictures from Italy* (London: Bradbury & Evans, 1846).

15 Mark Twain's autobiography first appeared in *The North American Review* between September 1906 and December 1907.

Notes (Part Two)

Chapter 1

1 This measure is extrapolated from the geometry of the intrados of the inner shell.

2 See P. Sanpaolesi, *La cupola di Santa Maria del Fiore: il progetto, la costruzione*, photographic reprint of the original edition, Rome 1941, with a new preface by the author (Florence: Edam, 1977).

3 Andrea Chiarugi and Demore Quilghini have shown that the distinctive skew course of the brick rows on the surface of any given segment can approximately be defined in terms of the intersection of a parabolic-section cylinder with this surface: in fact, the two straight lines tangent to the brick rows at their ends (i.e. at the edges of the segment) meet at an elevation that is two times lower than the apex of the above-mentioned curve with respect to the horizontal line passing through those ends (→ Fig. 1.5.1a–b). If we assume the bricklaying surfaces to be lying on conical surfaces that are co-axial with the Cupola, the skew course in question resembles respectively a parabolic curve at an elevation corresponding to a 45° inclination of the mortar beds towards the centre, a hyperbolic curve below this elevation, and an elliptic curve above it. See A. Chiarugi, "La Cupola del Brunelleschi: problemi di tracciamento e costruzione; il modello dell'ACMAR", *Inarcos. Ingegneri Architetti Costruttori* (June–September 1984); D. Quilghini, "La Cupola del Brunelleschi: la geometria", ibid.

4 However, recent investigations conducted on limited portions of the masonry texture on the intrados of the inner shell during restoration of the frescoes have raised doubts as to whether this solution was actually adopted at the intersection between two adjacent segments: see C. Acidini Luchinat and R. Dalla Negra (eds.), *La Cupola di Santa Maria del Fiore. Il cantiere di restauro, 1980–1995* (Rome: Istituto Poligrafico e Zecca dello Stato, 1995).

5 The 'slack-line' arrangement of the brickwork was duplicated and verified by Andrea Chiarugi in 1984 in the course of an experiment involving the construction of part of a brick-and-mortar octagonal dome by a team of expert masons (ACMAR, Ravenna): see Chiarugi, "La Cupola del Brunelleschi".

6 R.J. Mainstone, "Brunelleschi's Dome", *The Architectural Review* 162 (1977).

7 More detailed consideration and conjecture regarding the possible tracing methods employed can be found in the above-mentioned studies by Chiarugi and Quilghini.

8 See F.D. Prager and G. Scaglia, *Brunelleschi. Studies of his Technology and Inventions* (Cambridge, Mass.–London: MIT Press, 1970).

9 Saalman, *Filippo Brunelleschi. The Cupola*.

10 According to Saalman, Brunelleschi's model of the Cupola, which was kept until building work had been completed, might also have been used to study interior lighting conditions following the 1425–6 controversy between Giovanni di Gherardo da Prato and Brunelleschi. Beside the question of segment tracing, the controversy also concerned alleged insufficient lighting inside the Cupola; Giovanni di Gherardo da Prato was in favour of inserting large windows at the base of the Cupola.

11 See, amongst others, the *Zibaldone* by Bonaccorso Ghiberti (1451–516), grandson of Lorenzo Ghiberti. The manuscript is housed in the Biblioteca Nazionale Centrale, Florence (MS BR 228).

12 Galluzzi, *Mechanical Marvels*, 104.

13 A detailed treatment of the different kinds of cranes and other building machines, and how they were used in the various stages of construction of the Cupola and lantern (including repair of the latter following lightning damage in 1601), can be found in Saalman, *Filippo Brunelleschi. The Cupola*.

Chapter 2

1 See Galileo Galilei, *Le meccaniche* [1634] and *Discorsi e dimostrazioni matematiche intorno a due nuove scienze attenenti alla mecanica e i movimenti locali* [1638].

2 E. Benvenuto, *La Scienza delle Costruzioni e il suo sviluppo storico* (Florence: Sansoni, 1981), 105 ff.

3 The first systematic treatment of this subject can be found in E. Buckingham, "On physically similar systems: illustration of the use of dimensional equations", *Physical Review* 4 (1914), 345–76.

4 A more sophisticated, albeit still approximate, procedure entails subjecting a small-size model to an acceleration field created by centrifugation: the model is placed in a container attached to the end of a horizontal arm rotating at great speed around a vertical shaft. This procedure is widely used in geotechnics and fracture mechanics.

5 Manetti, *Vita*, 85.

6 To use Robert Hooke's celebrated expression, *ut tensio sic vis*, "as the extension, so the force": see id., *Lectures 'de potentia restitutiva', or, Of spring explaining the power of springing bodies...* (London: Martyn, 1678).

7 It is interesting to note that the Theory of Elasticity does not explicitly deal with the conditions of *global equilibrium*, but instead expresses, through a system of differential equations, the conditions of *local equilibrium, material continuity* (no local separation or overlapping of particles, which might affect displacement) and *constitutive laws*. Assuming the mathematical difficulties can be overcome, these

differential equations can be integrated (solved) by taking into account the boundary conditions describing external forces and constraints. Although *global* equilibrium is not explicitly expressed by the equations, it results necessarily from satisfaction of *local* equilibrium conditions at all points (provided of course that the equations have a finite solution). All this makes for a powerful mathematical tool capable, in principle, of solving any structural problem; if applied in too rigid a fashion, however, there is a risk of losing clear sight of the global picture. In particular, there is a risk of giving inadequate attention to an important characteristic of redundant structures. Even though the differential equations may have theoretical solutions, material continuity conditions sometimes give rise—at certain points or in localised areas of the continuum—to local strains and stresses that are incompatible with the strength of the material. This causes local discontinuities in the actual structure, thereby initiating a reconfiguration of the constraints so that strains and stresses may be brought within admissible limits. The change in internal connections, which also affects boundary surfaces and conditions, has one of two outcomes: either the structure achieves a new equilibrium that is compatible with the strength of the material, whereby the discontinuities stabilise, acting as natural 'joints' and becoming an integral part of the new equilibrium; or the new configuration of internal constraints produces no such equilibrium, ultimately leading the structure to collapse.

8 It is worth pointing out that classical Fracture Mechanics applies to homogeneous materials such as metals; its application to heterogeneous and composite materials, such as concrete or masonry, requires specific mathematical models that are still being developed and perfected.

9 Opera di Santa Maria del Fiore, *Rilievi e studi sulla Cupola del Brunelleschi*, edited by M. Nobili et al. (Florence, 1939).

10 This model is not dissimilar to the notion of 'active vaults' introduced in 1919 by Jean Résal in id., "Formes et dimensions des grands barrages en maçonnerie", *Annales des Ponts et Chaussées* (1919), 2 and developed by Malterre in id., "Calcul des grands barrages réservoirs en forme de voûtes", ibid. (1922), 6.

11 It is remarkable that in the thinking and practice of those times this intuitive model should have coexisted, in an almost 'dualistic' way, with the notion that "the arch will not collapse, if the chord of the outer arches does not touch the inner arch" (Leonardo da Vinci), namely the conviction that the solidity of an arch is guaranteed if it is possible to inscribe in its thickness a line composed of two straight segments without that line touching either the extrados or the intrados (→ Figure).

12 For the sake of simplicity, a perfectly symmetrical single octagonal shell is considered here, and any disturbance caused by boundary conditions at the base and summit is disregarded, similar to what is the case with rotationally symmetric membranes.

13 The analysis is quite simple once the *geometry* of the segment has been expressed in mathematical terms.

14 Mentioned in Sanpaolesi, *La cupola di Santa Maria del Fiore*, 62 (see also Plate 37).

15 See also P.A. Rossi, *Le cupole del Brunelleschi* (Bologna: Calderini, 1982). It should also be noted that the symmetry conditions described are such that each of the eight flat arches that make up the ring have fixed ends (*provided that there are no breaks in the extrados at the corners*: this condition underlines the importance of the strength and continuity of the masonry texture in the corner spurs, an aspect to which Brunelleschi devoted great attention). Such a condition of constraint is practically impossible to achieve in the case of a single flat arch as normally found in a plane structure. It can also be noted that the tensile stresses caused by the bending moments acting on the ring sides are effectively counterbalanced by compression in the upper parts of the Cupola. On the other hand, in the lower parts of the Cupola, where the ring sides are subjected to combined tension and bending, the flat-arch concept does not apply. It is of course doubtful that Brunelleschi could have been fully aware of this. But the fact that he deemed it necessary to insert stone chains in the brick masonry suggests that he had at least an intuitive grasp of the forces involved; and he was certainly acquainted with the outward thrusts of domes, a necessary consequence of the regime of tensile stresses at the level of the lower parallels.

16 Strictly speaking the axial forces must drop to zero at the cracks, but may increase weakly towards the centre of the undamaged segments. For the sake of simplicity, this secondary effect, caused by the meridian gradients of the shear forces acting along the ring sides, is not considered here.

17 As previously said, the simplified analysis of the undamaged structure assumes the existence of two eightfold mirror symmetries: the first one with respect to each of the eight vertical planes passing through the central axis and the midlines of the segments, and the second one with respect to

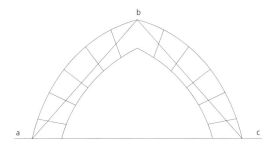

Diagram illustrating Leonardo da Vinci's criterion for judging the stability of an arch.

each of the eight vertical planes passing through the central axis and the edges between the segments. For the analysis to be completely valid, these symmetries should hold good not only in geometrical terms, but also with regard to static conditions, especially the constraint conditions at the base of the segments. In actual fact, there are only two twofold mirror symmetries with regard to the latter: the first one with respect to each of the two vertical planes passing through the central axis and the midlines of the segments directly above the four piers and the second one with respect to each of the two vertical planes passing through the central axis and the midlines of the segments directly above the four pointed arches (neglecting the fact that the two piers adjacent to the nave are not symmetrical to the other two, and that the constraint provided by the nave is not the same as that provided by the apses). As we shall see, it is no coincidence that the family comprising the four main cracks and also a clearly identifiable family of secondary cracks are fairly consistent with the twofold rather than the eightfold symmetry.

18   From 1430 to 1580 there were between five and ten earthquakes of appreciable magnitude in the Florence area; a series of generally less serious seismic events followed between 1580 and 1690. With its copper ball and bronze cross, the lantern was of course a particularly vulnerable target during storms and was frequently struck by lightning that caused varying degrees of damage. The structure had to be repaired several times, and on two occasions (1492, 1601) it was virtually rebuilt following partial destruction (→ Fig. 1.8.11). Florentine chronicles record significant lightning strikes in *1492*, 1494, 1495, 1498, 1511, 1536, 1542, 1570, 1577, 1578, 1586, *1601, 1661*, 1699 etc. (in the years indicated in italics the damage was particularly severe). A lightning conductor was not installed until the second half of the 19th century.

19   The writings of Nelli and Vanni can be found in the MS Riccardiano 2141 (see Saalman, *Filippo Brunelleschi. The Cupola*, 216).

20   See M. Fondelli, W. Ferri, P. Franchi and F. Greco, "Il rilevamento fotogrammetrico della Cupola di S. Maria del Fiore in Firenze", *Bollettino di Geodesia e Scienze Affini* 30 (1971), 158–84.

21   Investigations have also been conducted into the role of *daily thermal variations*. As these are determined, amongst other things, by sunlight exposure (which clearly varies in the course of the day), one might have expected that there would be a marked lack of symmetry in their effects on the Cupola. Temperature readings taken in the space between the two shells and inside the masonry of the inner shell revealed however that thermal conditions in the latter are virtually uniform along the entire perimeter, thanks to the protection provided by the outer shell and good air circulation between the two shells. The overall shielding effect of the outer shell, so acutely envisaged by Brunelleschi, has thus been proved beyond doubt. What still remains unclear is

what role daily thermal variations play in relation to the static regime of the outer shell. It would be extremely interesting, for instance, to conduct an infrared thermographic survey of the external surfaces of the Cupola, on all eight segments, at various times of the day and year. Clearly the outer shell is subject to an asymmetric thermal regime that varies cyclically in the course of the day, and it can be surmised that such a regime would tend to cause dilation and contraction, accompanied by ovalling, of the horizontal sections. This deformation is counteracted by the constraint provided by the spurs—particularly the eight huge corner spurs—that connect the outer shell to the inner one, which is stiffer and, as we have seen, basically unaffected by thermal dissymmetries. Apart from any other function Brunelleschi may have ascribed to them, *the real function of the 144 horizontal arches situated where the outer shell adjoins with the corner spurs could then be that of providing an adequate resisting section to absorb the fixed-end bending moments arising from the constraint in question*; without the increase in the resisting section provided by the horizontal arches, it is probable that these fixed-end moments would induce local fractures, tending to disconnect the segments from the corner spurs.

Chapter 3

1   It should be noted that the crack in segment 2 (the south-west segment), which has the appearance of a series of somewhat irregular dislocations in the masonry texture, is much less pronounced than the other three main cracks, and indeed relatively recently Mainstone included only three cracks in this family. This may be the result of a lack of symmetry in the behaviour of the Cupola, which could have caused shear stresses in addition to tensile ones along the midline of the segment. This lack of symmetry is as yet unaccounted for, and it has therefore not been possible to represent it in the current mathematical models. One hypothesis is that the south-west pier underlying segment 2 settled differently with respect to the other three; combined with the slight inclination of the structure observed by Leonardo Ximenes, this slight differential settling may have caused the vertical reaction of this pier to be inferior to that of the other three, and the corresponding fixed-end moment at the summit of the drum also to be inferior to those of the other even-numbered segments. It may be, then, that in segment 2 the average tensile strength of the masonry was exceeded to only a small extent and that therefore those areas of the masonry which happened to be stronger prevented the formation of a continuous crack. Even if this working hypothesis were to be confirmed by further study, however, the interpretation of the *origin* of all four cracks in this family would still be closely bound up with the effect of dead weight, and any differential settling of the south-west pier would only be responsible for the different *development* of the corresponding crack.

2 The tile covering has not made it possible to visually verify whether there is in fact horizontal cracking on the extrados of the outer shell where the analyses indicate the presence of vertical tensile stresses. This is a missing element in the generally close match between numerical analysis and visual observation; indirect confirmation of the findings of the mathematical model may however be found in the fact that *in situ* observations conducted with the flat-jack testing technique have revealed unstressed areas on the intrados of the outer shell, which is what one would expect in the presence of cracking (→ § 3.3).

3 It should also be emphasised that the numerical analyses of thermal effects conducted so far have assumed symmetrical temperature variations, whereas at least for the outer shell these are certainly asymmetrical, being the result of varying degrees of sunlight exposure during the day. (An analysis that considered this factor would also help to clarify the function of the 144 horizontal arches connecting the outer shell and the corner spurs: → § 2.3.) In order to accurately determine the value and distribution of such asymmetrical variations, detailed *in situ* thermometric and thermographic readings would be required, but are not currently available.

4 It should be noted that, although the model and the *in situ* observations match in many respects, they diverge as regards the value of the opening width of the main cracks. According to the model, these are a few millimetres wide, while the real value, as has been noted on a number of occasions, is up to several centimetres. However, there are reasons that can explain this discrepancy, at least in qualitative terms. The numerical analyses conducted to date assume a linear elastic constitutive law (and the decidedly excessive value of 50,000 kgf/cm² has been attributed to the Young's modulus), while there is no doubt that significant non-elastic deformation (creep phenomena, etc.) must have occurred over the centuries. These non-elastic components have not yet been integrated into the mathematical model, but on an initial approximation they yield a significantly lower value of the Young's modulus, which would produce an inversely proportional increase in the value of all displacements, including the opening width of the cracks. Besides, the relaxing of internal constraints was simulated in the model only with regard to the four main full-thickness cracks; to achieve a more faithful simulation, it would be necessary to do the same for the other families of systematic cracks, corresponding to areas of appreciable tensile stress, and this would lead to a significant increase in the estimated value of the opening width of the cracks. Finally, the *current* stiffness of the constraint provided by the structures surrounding the Cupola is in all probability greatly overestimated in the mathematical model (which moreover assumes these structures to be undamaged when in fact they are cracked). For confirmation of this, see § 3.4, in which there is an analysis

of a simplified model that totally disregards this constraint. This model hypothesises a slightly greater crack extension than is actually the case and yields values for the maximum opening width of the cracks that are slightly lower than those observed in the structure. It can therefore be argued—pending further analyses—that the weakening of the lateral constraints, together with long-term creep effects, may explain the discrepancy between theoretical and observed data. It will of course be necessary to interpret in a quantitative way why the stiffness of the lateral constraint provided by the surrounding structures is so much lower than the theoretical value, taking into account both the lesions at the junction between the Cupola and the drum and other non-elastic effects. The discrepancy in question does however suggest that a comprehensive understanding of the phenomena affecting the Cupola requires not only further investigation, but also introduction into the mathematical models of much more sophisticated constitutive laws than the simple linear elastic one assumed thus far. A further observation is in order here: in almost all the Finite Element analyses conducted to date, only the effect of dead weight on the *completed* structure has been considered, as if the material had possessed stiffness but no weight during the building process, with the gravity field being 'switched on' only after completion. However, comparative calculations carried out on vaulted structures (including the Cupola itself) justify the belief that the results of the simplified analysis are not significantly different to those obtained by simulating the various stages of raising, which would require assigning weight to each successive layer and stiffness to the ones that have already set. It might nevertheless be advisable to include an accurate modelling of the various stages of construction in future analyses (→ § 3.6). In this context it is also worth mentioning that a certain degree of precompression arises in every ring of the Cupola as it is constructed, which becomes all the more pronounced as the inclination of the mortar beds towards the centre increases. The closer the ring is to the base of the Cupola, the weaker the precompression: this is unfortunate, because this is precisely where precompression would be most useful in counteracting the tensile stresses that increase gradually as the construction nears completion.

5 Following heated dispute that arose when the putlog holes were filled in to anchor the flying scaffolding used to restore the frescoes (→ § 2.3), between 1986 and 1987 forty-eight displacement transducers were installed immediately above the holes themselves. Readings are taken manually once a fortnight.

6 In addition to the equipment already in place, in 1989–90 the Istituto Geografico Militare (IGM) installed a further network of levelling instruments: this is based on benchmarks arranged at the vertices of a closed polygon outside the Cathedral and of three more polygons (at different elevations) inside it.

7 See R. Dalla Negra, "La Cupola del Brunelleschi: il cantiere, le indagini, i rilievi", in Acidini Luchinat–Dalla Negra (eds.), *La Cupola di Santa Maria del Fiore*, 31–66.

8 Reference is made here to an unpublished paper by the writer reporting the findings of a study carried out between December 1984 and February 1985: *Un possibile stato-limite della Cupola del Brunelleschi: prima valutazione approssimata della stabilità della struttura e dell'apertura massima delle fessure principali*, CRIS–ENEL internal report no. 3268.

9 It should be noted that the shape of the support structures through which the loads of the four cantilevers are transmitted to the ground is not the same. The support structure is only symmetrical with respect to the plane of the cantilever's undamaged segment in the case of the apsidal cantilever (the one facing east) and of the opposite one (the one facing west); the north- and south-facing cantilevers, on the other hand, rest on two half-piers that are markedly asymmetric with respect to the symmetry plane of the respective undamaged segments. For the sake of simplicity, we shall, unless otherwise stated, assume the four cantilevers to be identical and symmetrical with respect to the midline of the corresponding undamaged segments.

10 One delicate aspect of the proposed measure would be the design and building of the thrusters for transmitting the radial resultant of the forces produced by tensioning the cables on two adjacent sides to the extrados of the inner shell. The radial force would need to be distributed as evenly as possible over an extensive surface in order to avoid potentially damaging local stress concentrations. Even this problem, however, does not pose insurmountable difficulties, since the materials and technologies now available offer a variety of options. Another aspect requiring careful investigation is the partial closing up of the cracks that would result from the tensioning of the cables; this effect might cause problems if there is detritus in the cracks. The time of year would also need to be carefully considered and simulated, so as to ensure that subsequent variations in the thermal regime do not cause undesired stress states.

11 Variations in the modes and frequencies can provide valuable information regarding structural alterations with a bearing on safety.

12 The current model would have to be modified for this type of investigation as well, so as to include the additional stiffness and inertia provided by the nave.

Glossary

anisotropy   (of an object or substance) the quality of being anisotropic, i.e. of having a physical property (e.g. stress resistance) which has a different value when measured in different directions.
→ also **isotropy**

apsidiole   (It. *tribuna morta*) each of the four circular-plan and conical-dome aedicules that crown the piers supporting the Cupola and serve as transitional elements between the three large apses. The origin of their Italian designation, found in documents since the 1440s and loosely rendered by Saalman as 'false arm', is uncertain: it probably refers to the fact that the apsidioles are not accessible from the inside and do not have any ceremonial function.

beam   a (usually horizontal) structural member, the height and thickness of which are negligible with respect to its length; it carries the load by bending.
→ also **deep beam**

benchmark   a point of reference that serves as a basis for future evaluation or comparison; more specifically, a mark (e.g. a metallic knob) attached to a structure at a certain elevation, used in topographic surveys to monitor relative displacements by means of procedures such as triangulation, levelling, etc.

bending   the deformation behaviour of a beam subjected to a bending moment—the axis bends without either dilating or contracting; this may occur in the same plane as the bending moment (→ **straight bending**) or in a different plane (→ **skew bending**).

bending moment   the sum of the moments acting on the cross-section of a beam or plate, causing it to bend.

boundary conditions   the conditions that are required to be satisfied at all or part of the boundary of a region in which a set of differential equations is to be solved; in a structure or model, the relationships between the unknown quantities and the actions or constraints acting on its external surfaces, which need to be established in order to solve the differential equations expressing a static or dynamic problem.

braccio   (pl. *braccia*; lit. 'arm') a unit of linear measure used in Florence until the 19th century, equal to 0.584 m (approx. 23 inches).

calibration   the procedure by which one identifies the most plausible values to be assigned to the parameters of a mathematical model, so that it may reproduce the behaviour of the actual structure.

camera obscura   a darkened box with a convex lens or aperture for projecting the image of an external object on to a screen inside, whereon an upside-down mirror image of the object is displayed.

catenary   a curve formed by a wire, rope or chain hanging freely from two points that are on the same horizontal level.

centring   framing used to support an arch or dome while it is under construction.

centroid   the centre of mass of an object of uniform density.

chain   a structural member composed of a series of wooden, stone or iron elements connected to one another end to end, used to strengthen the masonry with respect to tensile stresses, or an arch, vault or dome against splaying.

combined compression and bending   a stress state whereby a beam or plate is simultaneously subjected to a bending moment and to axial compression—the axis bends and shortens.

combined tension and bending   a stress state whereby a beam or plate is simultaneously subjected to a bending moment and to axial tensile stress—the axis bends and lengthens.

compatibility   the condition that is required to be satisfied at the junction of two connected parts of a solid, whereby the material points of each part undergo the same displacements when the solid is deformed under the action of a system of forces.

compressive stress → normal (or axial) stress

conjugate diameter The bending behaviour of a beam is determined by the Young's modulus, and by the shape and size of its cross-section; once the latter are given, an ellipse ('ellipse of inertia') can be determined, which describes how this behaviour varies according to the plane in which the bending occurs. If one draws the two tangents to the ellipse perpendicularly to the bending plane, the diameter of the ellipse joining the two points of tangency is the conjugate diameter with respect to the intersection of the cross-section plane with the bending plane; this diameter is parallel to the plane where the bending occurs (→ Figure).

constraint in a structure, any connection to the exterior (e.g. foundations) or to other structures that restricts the free displacement of the parts constrained. Constraints may prevent displacement altogether (a theoretical condition which never occurs in practice) or counter it with a finite force, elastic or otherwise (when the constraint is elastic, the force is proportional to the displacement).

creep the gradual deformation of a plastic solid under stress; a pier under constant load, for instance, will slowly shorten over time.

damping a decrease in the amplitude of a free oscillation as a result of energy being drained from the system to overcome frictional or other resistive forces; measurement of the speed at which such decrease occurs yields a value called the damping coefficient.

deep beam a beam the cross-section of which has a depth that is not negligible with respect to its length, i.e. the beam has an appreciable span-to-depth ratio.

deformation, strain the action or process of changing in shape, or the result thereof, at a point of a solid body under the action of applied forces.

degrees of freedom each of a number of independently variable factors affecting the range of states in which a system may exist; in structural terms, they enable definition of the deformation state of a structure (in an extended structure their number is infinite, but they can be reduced in mathematical models using Finite Element discretisation).

derivative, differential coefficient an expression representing the rate of change of a function (a relation or expression involving one or more variables) with respect to an independent variable.
→ also **gradient**

differential equation an equation involving derivatives of a function or functions, namely expressing a mathematical relationship between the derivatives of particular quantities; in Structural Analysis, differential equations express the laws of local variation of the quantities relevant to structural equilibrium (stresses, strains, etc.).

dihedral angle an angle formed by two plane faces.

dilatation local increase in the length of a material segment of unit length under the action of a system of forces; a positive value (the segment lengthens) corresponds to a tensile state, a negative value (the segment shortens) to a compressive state.

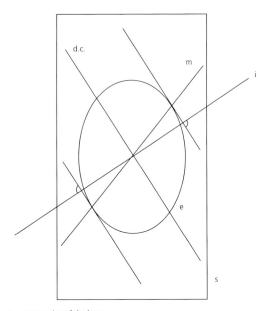

s = cross-section of the beam
m = intersection of the bending plane with the plane of the cross-section
e = ellipse of inertia of the cross-section
d.c. = diameter of the ellipse conjugated with respect to m
i = bending plane of the beam under the action of the bending moment acting in the plane m

Diagram showing the ellipse of inertia (e) of the cross-section of a beam, of the diameter (d.c.) conjugated with respect to the plane (m) of the bending moment and of the bending plane (i) of the axis of the beam.

displacement transducer an instrument for measuring the relative displacement between two points of a structure, for instance variations in the distance between two points on opposite sides of a crack.

drift in a structure that is assumed to behave elastically, the systematic increase over time of a displacement component that cannot be explained in terms of the action of external forces; also a delayed-response displacement component occurring over time, even under the action of constant forces ($\rightarrow$ **creep**).

drum the circular or polygonal wall supporting a dome; here, the part of the structure between the summit of the piers and the springing of the Cupola.

eccentricity the effect of combined compression and bending on the cross-section of a beam is equivalent to that of an axial stress acting on a point distinct from the section's centroid: the distance of this point from the centroid yields the value of eccentricity.

eigenfrequency (*eigen-*, proper, characteristic; from the German *eigen*, 'own') one of the natural resonant frequencies (i.e. number of vibrations per second) at which, in the absence of energy dissipation ($\rightarrow$ **damping**), a structure would vibrate indefinitely without external excitation; the number of a structure's eigenfrequencies is equal to the number of its degrees of freedom ($\rightarrow$ **degrees of freedom**).

eigenmode one of the natural spatial distributions of vibration amplitudes in a structure vibrating at one of its eigenfrequencies; to each eigenfrequency there corresponds a different eigenmode.

elastica the course followed by an ideal line traced in the structure after deformation caused by loads.

elasticity the property of an object or a material to resume its normal shape spontaneously after deformation (the deformation is reversible in that it disappears when its cause, e.g. a load, is removed); elasticity is called 'linear' when the deformation is proportional to the load, 'non-linear' when the relation is more complex.

extrados the upper or outer surface of a structure; esp., the outer face or curve of an arch or vault.

finite elements small (if compared to the whole structure) polyhedra which, when joined together, reproduce the geometry of the structure; local mechanical properties (stress-strain relationship) are assigned to each element, and the forces acting on the structure are replaced with equivalent forces acting on the vertices of the elements: the equations expressing the equilibrium conditions between such forces and the elements' reactions to deformation (constraints being also taken into account) will then constitute a valid approximation of the behaviour of the structure.

fixed-end constraint a constraint, usually at one or both ends of a beam, that prevents (or restricts) end-displacement and rotation.
$\rightarrow$ also **constraint**

flat arch (also known as straight arch) an arch that has a straight horizontal extrados and intrados, composed of mutually supporting wedge-shaped stones that lock together, generating compression; it differs from the architrave and the arch (subject to bending and axial stress respectively) in that it is subjected to combined compression and bending.

formwork wood in planks or strips used as a temporary structure for fencing to contain setting masonry.

gallery a balcony, platform or upper floor projecting from the back or side wall of a church or hall. On the inside of the drum of Florence Cathedral there are three full-perimeter galleries at different elevations; the level of the third gallery coincides with the springing line of the Cupola. An exterior gallery on two levels had been planned around the drum at this elevation, but only the section at the base of the south-east segment was actually built.

gradient the change in the value of a quantity (e.g. temperature, pressure, etc.) with the change in a given variable, especially per unit distance in a specified direction; also, the rate of such a change.
$\rightarrow$ also **derivative**

gualandrino con tre corde curvature-control system requiring the use of three strings (*corde*) for the radial disposition of the various building elements and their inclination toward their respective pointed-fifth centre of curvature.

herringbone (It. *spinapesce*) an arrangement consisting of columns of short parallel lines, with all the lines in one column sloping one way and all the lines in the next column sloping the other way so as to resemble the bones in a fish; with regard to the placing of bricks, the term is used to describe a masonry texture in which spiralling rows of vertically laid, offset bricks enclose sections of bricks laid horizontally, counteracting the inclination of the mortar beds that would cause the latter to slide inwards.

hydrostatic levelling the procedure by which variation in the relative elevation of two material points can be detected by means of the principle of communicating vessels. Two vessels, attached to the points in question and connected by a pipe, are filled with a liquid (usually water); if one point moves up or down with respect to the other one, the level of the liquid in the vessel will respectively sink or rise by a corresponding quantity on a graded scale.

identification the mathematical procedure that allows one to determine some constants (mechanical, thermal or otherwise) of a structure by gathering data on its behaviour through observation and interpreting them with the help of numerical models.

integral the integral is a function of which a given function is the derivative, i.e. which yields that function when differentiated; the procedure by which one can find an unknown function from its derivative (for instance, a differential equation and relative boundary conditions) is called integration.

intrados the lower or inner surface of a structure; esp., the inner face or curve of an arch or vault.

isolines lines on a map or diagram (typically meteorological charts) along which a given property or feature has a constant value.

isostatic lines lines that are everywhere tangent to the principal directions of the stresses; they form a lattice of orthogonal curves.
→ also **principal directions**

isotropy (of an object or substance) the quality of being isotropic, i.e. of having a physical property which has the same value when measured in different directions; thus, for instance, the mechanical or thermal properties of an isotropic solid are independent of the direction in which the corresponding phenomenon (deformation, heat flow) occurs.
→ also **anisotropy**

lattice an interlaced structure consisting of beams crossed and possibly fastened together, with square or diamond-shaped spaces left in between.

levelling → **hydrostatic levelling**

linearity the structural property by which strains are proportional to stresses; in practice it holds good only when the stresses are well within failure values.

macigno a variety of calcareous sandstone found in the Northern Apennines, composed of sedimentary layers of different colour and petrographic features, and characterised by good mechanical strength; it was used in various parts of the Cupola (for instance, the three stone chains).

membrane a three-dimensional structure having the shape of a thin shell—its shape is defined by a generally curved middle surface and its thickness is negligible with respect to the other dimensions (e.g. an eggshell); it is considered to have no bending stiffness.

moment (couple) a couple is a pair of equal and parallel forces acting in opposite directions and tending to cause rotation (or bending or torsion) about an axis perpendicular to the plane containing them; the couple's moment is the product of its force and the distance between the two forces' line of action.
→ also **bending moment, torque, torsional moment**

moment of inertia a measure of the resistance of a body to angular acceleration about a given axis, used in the study of the bending and torsional behaviour of beams; it varies with direction, such variation being described by the ellipse of inertia.

normal (or axial) stress the stress state whereby the centroid of a beam is subjected to a force normal (perpendicular) to the beam's cross-section (namely directed along the axis of the beam); it can be either compressive or tensile—the axis respectively shortens or lengthens without bending.

occhi con rampo slender iron bars with an eyelet at one end, used to support cantilevered structures, either fixed or provisional.

oculus ring (It. *serraglio*) a structure shaped like a truncated pyramid with the (missing) vertex facing downwards: located at the summit of the Cupola proper, it provides the junction between the two shells (and the spurs) and supports the lantern.

pergamena the cone-shaped marble element with a mixtilinear perimeter that crowns the lantern and supports the ball.

pier a vertical member, circular or polygonal in plan, that supports the end of an arch or lintel.

pietra forte a fine-grained, yellow-brown sandstone of considerable resilience, widely employed in Florentine architecture (including, for instance, Palazzo Vecchio, Orsanmichele, Santa Croce, Santa Maria Novella and Palazzo Pitti).

pietra serena a variety of *macigno*, silvery grey with bluish undertones, much favoured by Brunelleschi, who employed it in a number of projects.

piezometer an instrument for measuring the pressure of a liquid or gas; often used to monitor the pressure or depth of groundwater.

pointed fifth the curvature of a half-arch the radius of which is four fifths of the springing span.

principal directions In any given point of a structure subject to the action of a system of forces one will find a series of stresses that vary depending on the orientation of the surface element on which they act. In general there will be both normal stresses (perpendicular to the surface element) and shear stresses (tangent or parallel to the surface element). At any point, however, it is possible to define three orthogonal directions such that the surface elements oriented along them are subject only to normal stresses (either of a tensile or compressive nature), to the exclusion of any shear component: these directions are called 'principal directions', and the relative normal stresses are the 'principal stresses'.
→ also **principal stresses**

principal stresses In a structure subject to the action of a system of forces, the stresses acting on the surface elements vary with the orientation of the elements and generally have a component normal to the surface and a component tangent to it. At any point, however, it is possible to define three orthogonal directions (the 'principal directions') such that the surface elements oriented along them are subject only to normal stress (without shear): these three stresses are called the 'principal stresses'.
→ also **principal directions**

putlog holes (It. *buche pontaie*) the parallelepiped-shaped cavities left in the masonry where horizontal poles are inserted in order to support the scaffold floorboards of work platforms.

ratta marble cornice and gutter supported by consoles at the springing line of the outer shell, shaped to collect the rainwater running off the segments and to channel it into the gutter-spouts at the corners of the drum.

resultant a force or other vector quantity which is equivalent in its effect (particularly with respect to global equilibrium) to the combined effect of two or more component vectors acting at the same point.

rheology the branch of physics that deals with the deformation and flow of matter, especially the non-Newtonian flow of liquids and the plastic flow of solids.

shaker an instrument capable of generating oscillating forces of variable frequency and intensity, used to artificially excite a structure so that its eigenfrequencies and eigenmodes may be determined.

shear a deformation whereby an object or material changes its shape (the angle formed by two perpendicular lines is no longer a right angle after deformation) but not its volume: the layers or fibres of the material are laterally shifted in relation to each other along the direction of the stress.

shear stress the stress state whereby the centroid of a beam is subjected to a force parallel to the beam's cross-section (namely, directed perpendicularly to the axis of the beam).

skew bending a bending such that the conjugate diameter does not coincide with the plane of the bending moment—the bending moment does not act along either of the two axes of the ellipse of inertia.
→ also **bending, conjugate diameter**

'slack line' (It. *corda blanda*) the upward-concave course of the bricklaying beds that can be observed on the extrados and intrados surfaces of the eight segments of the Cupola; the degree of curvature is such that at any given elevation the mortar beds belong very nearly to common conical surfaces (the cone's vertical axis coinciding with the axis of the Cupola and its vertex pointing downwards).

spur a reinforcing radial buttress of masonry; in the Cupola, the corner and intermediate spurs connect the two shells, binding them together.

stiffness a quantitative measure of the inherent ability of a material to resist deformation when subjected to a given kind of stress; thus one may speak of 'bending' stiffness, 'axial' stiffness, 'torsional' stiffness, etc.

straight bending a bending such that the conjugate diameter coincides with the plane of the bending moment—the bending moment acts along one of the two axes of the ellipse of inertia.
→ also **bending, conjugate diameter**

strain → **deformation**

stress the pressure or tension exerted on a material object and resulting in strain; also, the degree of this measured in units of force per unit area. Considering the ratio between the force acting on a given surface element and the area of this element, the value of such a ratio when the area tends to zero is the value of the stress with respect to the orientation of the element.

telecoordinometer an instrument for measuring the displacement of a point of a structure in one or more directions.

template a shaped piece of metal, wood or other material used as a model for processes such as cutting out, shaping or drilling; also, a shaped piece used during construction to guide the tracing of the structure being built (curvature-control template).

tensile stress → **normal (or axial) stress**

torque a force that tends to cause rotation.

torsional (twisting) moment torque acting in a plane parallel to the cross-section of a beam or plate and tending to cause torsion, i.e. to twist its successive sections (each in its own plane) relative to the others.

tracing control of the geometrical shape and profile of a structure during construction using absolute and relative (local) reference points.

tribuna morta → **apsidiole**

validation the procedure by which one ensures that a mathematical model accurately reproduces the behaviour of the modelled structure: it involves comparing the results yielded by the model with observational data.

walkway full-perimeter passage in the space between the inner and the outer shell; there are three walkways at various elevations in the Cupola, and a fourth one inside the oculus ring.

water table the level below which the ground is saturated with water; variations in this level may cause settling of the foundations (and serious downward displacements if the variation is prolonged).

Young's modulus a measure of elasticity, equal to the ratio of the stress acting on a substance to the strain produced (in a regime of purely axial stress); is named after Thomas Young (1773–1829), English physicist, physician and Egyptologist.
→ also **elasticity**

BIBLIOGRAPHY

A. Manetti, *Vita di Filippo Brunelleschi*, [*c.* 1480], edited by C. Perrone (Rome: Salerno, 1992)—but see also the edition by D. De Robertis and G. Tanturli (Milan: Il Polifilo, 1966); for an English translation, see *The Life of Brunelleschi, by Antonio di Tuccio Manetti*, introduction, notes, and critical text edited by H. Saalman, English translation by C. Enggass (University Park: Pennsylvania State University Press, 1970).

G. Vasari, "Filippo Brunelleschi, Scultore et Architetto", in id., *Le Vite de' più eccellenti architetti, pittori, et scultori italiani, da Cimabue, insino a' tempi nostri*, in the 1550 edition published in Florence by Lorenzo Torrentino, edited by L. Bellosi and A. Rossi, 2 vols. (Turin: Einaudi, 1991²), I.275–309—but see also the 1568 edition of this work edited by G. Milanesi (Florence: Sansoni, 1878–85) and *Le vite … nelle redazioni del 1550 e 1568*, edited by R. Bettarini, with a commentary by P. Barocchi (Florence: Sansoni [later SPES], 1966–88); for an English translation, see G. Vasari, *Lives of the Artists*, 2 vols., a selection translated by G. Bull (Harmondsworth: Penguin, 1987).

F. Baldinucci, *Vita di Filippo di Ser Brunellesco architetto fiorentino …* [17th century], *ora per la prima volta pubblicata con altra più antica inedita di anonimo contemporaneo scrittore* [for its attribution to Manetti, see Gaetano Milanesi's preface to *Operette istoriche edite e inedite di Antonio Manetti…*, edited by G. Milanesi (Florence: Le Monnier, 1887)], edited by D. Moreni (Florence: presso Niccolò Carli, 1812).

      *   *   *

[G.B. Nelli and B.S. Sgrilli], *Descrizione e studi dell'insigne Fabbrica di S. Maria del Fiore, Metropolitana Fiorentina…* (Florence: per Bernardo Paperini, 1733).

G.B. Nelli, "Ragionamento sopra la maniera di voltar le cupole senza adoperarvi le centine", in *Discorsi di architettura del Senatore Giovan Batista Nelli … e due Ragionamenti sopra le Cupole di Alessandro Cecchini* (Florence: per gli Eredi Paperini, 1753).

L. Ximenes, *Del vecchio e nuovo gnomone Fiorentino e delle osservazioni astronomiche, fisiche e architettoniche fatte nel verificare la costruzione* (Florence: Stamperia Imperiale, 1757).

C. Guasti, *La Cupola di Santa Maria del Fiore, illustrata con i documenti dell'Archivio dell'Opera secolare*, photographic reprint of the original edition, Florence 1857 (Bologna: Forni, 1974).

—, "Un disegno di Giovanni di Gherardo da Prato Poeta e Architetto", in id., *Belle Arti. Opuscoli descrittivi e biografici* (Florence: Sansoni, 1874).

A. Nardini Despotti Mospignotti, *Filippo di Ser Brunellesco e la Cupola del Duomo di Firenze* (Livorno: Tipografia Giuseppe Meucci, 1885).

J. Durm, "Die Domkuppel in Florenz und die Kuppel der Peterskirche in Rom: zwei Grossconstructionen der italienische Renaissance", *Zeitschrift für Bauwesen* 37 (1887), 353–74 and 481–500.

C. Guasti, *Santa Maria del Fiore. La costruzione della chiesa e del campanile secondo i documenti tratti dall'Archivio dell'Opera secolare e da quello di Stato*, photographic reprint of the original edition, Florence 1887 (Bologna: Forni, 1974).

C. von Fabriczy, *Filippo Brunelleschi. Sein Leben und seine Werke* (Stuttgart: Cotta, 1892).

A. Doren, "Zum Bau der Florentiner Domkuppel", *Repertorium für Kunstwissenschaft* 21 (1898) 4, 249–62.

Opera di Santa Maria del Fiore, *Rilievi e studi sulla Cupola del Brunelleschi…*, edited by M. Nobili, R. Sabatini, G. Alfani, P.L. Nervi and G. Padelli (Florence: Tipografia Ettore Rinaldi, 1939).

P. Sanpaolesi, *La cupola di Santa Maria del Fiore: il progetto, la costruzione*, photographic reprint of the original edition, Rome 1941, with a new preface by the author (Florence: Edam, 1977).

—, "Ipotesi sulle conoscenze matematiche, statiche e meccaniche del Brunelleschi", *Belle Arti* 2 (1951), 25–54.

G.C. Argan, *Brunelleschi* (Milan: Mondadori, 1955).

H. Saalman, "Giovanni di Gherardo da Prato's designs concerning the Cupola of Santa Maria del Fiore in Florence", *Journal of the Society of Architectural Historians* 18 (1959), 11–20.

P. Sanpaolesi, *Brunelleschi* (Milan: Edizioni per il Club del Libro, 1962).

E. Luporini, *Brunelleschi: forma e ragione* (Milan: Edizioni di Comunità, 1964).

W. Braunfels, "Drei Bemerkungen zur Geschichte und Konstruktion der Florentiner Domkuppel", *Mitteilungen des Kunsthistorischen Institutes in Florenz* 11 (1965), 203–26.

F.D. Prager and G. Scaglia, *Brunelleschi. Studies of his Technology and Inventions* (Cambridge, Mass.–London: MIT Press, 1970).

W. Ferri, M. Fondelli, P. Franchi and F. Greco, "Il rilevamento fotogrammetrico della cupola di Santa Maria del Fiore", *Bollettino di Geodesia e Scienze Affini* 30 (1971), 158–84.

G. Fanelli, *Firenze, architettura e città*, photographic reprint of the original edition, Florence 1973 (Florence: Mandragora, 2002).

E. Battisti, *Filippo Brunelleschi* (Milan: Electa, 1976).

S. Di Pasquale, "Una ipotesi sulla struttura della cupola di Santa Maria del Fiore", *Restauro. Quaderni di restauro dei monumenti e di urbanistica dei centri antichi* 5 (1976) 28, 1–77.

Ch. de Tolnay (ed.), *Brunelleschi e Michelangelo*, exhibition catalogue: Florence, Casa Buonarroti, 15 October–14 November 1977 (Florence: Centro Di, 1977).

S. Di Pasquale, *Primo rapporto sulla cupola di S. Maria del Fiore* (Florence: Clusf, 1977).

S. Di Pasquale, P.L. Bandini and G. Tempesta, *Rappresentazione analitica e grafica della cupola di Santa Maria del Fiore* (Florence: Clusf, 1977).

G. Fanelli, *Brunelleschi* (Florence: Becocci–Scala, 1977).

Gabinetto Disegni e Stampe degli Uffizi, *Disegni di fabbriche brunelleschiane*, with introductions by Anna Forlani Tempesti et al., catalogue edited by G. Marchini et al. (Florence: Olschki, 1977).

P. Galluzzi, "Le colonne fesse degli Uffizi e gli screpoli della cupola: il contributo di Vincenzo Viviani al dibattito sulla stabilità della cupola del Brunelleschi", *Annali dell'Istituto e Museo di Storia della Scienza di Firenze* 2 (1977), 71–111.

R.J. Mainstone, "Brunelleschi's Dome", *The Architectural Review* 162 (1977), 156–66.

G. Marchini, "Fulmini sulla Cupola", *Antichità Viva* 16 (1977) 4, 22–5.

P.A. Rossi, *Brunelleschi. Vera Cupola* (Florence: Eurocopia, 1977).

C.L. Ragghianti, *Filippo Brunelleschi. Un uomo, un universo* (Florence: Vallecchi, 1977).

C. Bozzoni and G. Carbonara, *Filippo Brunelleschi. Saggio di bibliografia*, 2 vols. (Rome: Istituto di Fondamenti dell'Architettura, 1977–8).

P.A. Rossi, "Principi costruttivi nella Cupola di Santa Maria del Fiore", *Critica d'Arte* 43 (1978), 85–118.

Filippo Brunelleschi: la sua opera e il suo tempo, proceedings of the international symposium: Florence, 16–22 October 1977, 2 vols. (Florence: Centro Di, 1980).

H. Saalman, *Filippo Brunelleschi. The Cupola of Santa Maria del Fiore* (London: Zwemmer, 1980).

P.A. Rossi, *Le cupole del Brunelleschi: capire per conservare* (Bologna: Calderini, 1982).

A. Chiarugi, M. Fanelli and G. Giuseppetti, "Analysis of Brunelleschi-type dome including thermal loads", CRIS–ENEL internal report no. 3106 (Milan, March 1983), in *Strengthening of Building Structures, Diagnosis and Therapy*, IABSE Symposium (Venice, September 1983), *IABSE Reports* 45–6.

—, "Sulla statica di cupole tipo S. Maria del Fiore in Firenze", CRIS–ENEL internal report no. 3162 (Milan, December 1983).

C. Blasi and A. Ceccotti, "La Cupola del Brunelleschi: indagine sullo stato di fessurazione", *Inarcos. Ingegneri architetti costruttori* (June–September 1984), 7–15.

A. Chiarugi, 'La Cupola del Brunelleschi. Problemi di tracciamento e costruzione: il modello dell'ACMAR", *Inarcos. Ingegneri architetti costruttori* (June–September 1984).

M. Fanelli and G. Giuseppetti, "I modelli di comportamento strutturale per la Cupola del Brunelleschi: loro ruolo, prime esperienze e prospettive", CRIS–ENEL internal report no. 3207 (Milan, June 1984), 17–25.

Ministero per i Beni Culturali e Ambientali, *Catalogo dei plessi fessurativi della Cattedrale di Santa Maria del Fiore in Firenze*, edited by G. Petrini (Florence, 1984), 31–7.

D. Quilghini, "La Cupola del Brunelleschi: la geometria", *Inarcos. Ingegneri architetti costruttori* (June–September 1984).

M. Fanelli, "Un possibile stato-limite della Cupola del Brunelleschi: prima valutazione approssimata della stabilità della struttura e dell'apertura massima delle fessure principali", CRIS–ENEL internal report no. 3268 (Milan, February 1985).

M. Haines, "The Builders of Santa Maria del Fiore: an Episode of 1475 and an Essay towards its Context", in A. Morrogh et al. (eds.), *Renaissance Studies in Honor of Craig Hugh Smyth*, 2 vols. (Florence: Giunti Barbera, 1985), 1.89–115.

Rapporto sulla situazione del complesso strutturale Cupola-basamento della Cattedrale di Santa Maria del Fiore in Firenze emesso dalla Commissione di studio … con particolare riguardo a problemi di statica della Cupola (Florence, March 1985).

S. Di Pasquale, "Filippo Brunelleschi dal mito al mistero", in F. Bonilauri (ed.), *Paolo Monti fotografo di Brunelleschi. Le architetture fiorentine*, exhibition catalogue: Florence, Palazzo Strozzi, 19 July–12 August

1986 (Casalecchio di Reno: Grafis, 1986), 9–58.

M. Fanelli, "Indagini dinamiche sui monumenti antichi: alcune riflessioni e qualche risultato", *Costruzioni* 372 (1986), 1343–7.

A. Castoldi, A. Chiarugi, M. Fanelli and G. Giuseppetti, "In-situ dynamic tests on monumental buildings: their role and use", CRIS–ENEL internal report no. 3524 (July 1987), in *Monitoring of Large Structures and Assessment of their Safety*, IABSE Colloquium (Bergamo, October 1987), *IABSE Reports* 56, 131–44.

A. Castoldi, A. Chiarugi, M. Fanelli, G. Giuseppetti and G. Petrini, "Functions and planning of the static monitoring system for the Brunelleschi Dome in Florence", CRIS–ENEL internal report no. 3538 (September 1987), in *Monitoring of Large Structures and Assessment of their Safety*, IABSE Colloquium (Bergamo, October 1987), *IABSE Reports* 56, 17–33.

L. Barbi and F.P. Di Teodoro, "1695–1698: i rilievi di Giovan Battista Nelli per la Cupola di Santa Maria del Fiore", *Rivista d'Arte. Studi documentari per la storia delle arti in Toscana* 41, s. IV, 5 (1989), 57–III.

A. Chiarugi, M. Fanelli, G. Giuseppetti and F. Pari, "L'analisi numerica e la grafica di alta qualità per la salvaguardia dei monumenti", CRIS–ENEL internal report no. 3789 (Milan, July 1989), *Pixel: computer graphics, CAD/CAM, image processing* 10 (1989).

M. Haines, "Brunelleschi and Bureaucracy: The Tradition of Public Patronage at the Florentine Cathedral", *I Tatti Studies: Essays in the Renaissance* 3 (1989), 89–125.

Soprintendenza per i Beni Ambientali e Architettonici di Firenze / Dipartimento di Ingegneria Civile di Firenze, *Interpretazione dei dati provenienti dal sistema di monitoraggio della cupola del Brunelleschi* (Florence 1990 and 1992).

ISMES, *Indagine diagnostica sulle strutture murarie della Cattedrale di Santa Maria del Fiore*, ISMES RAT–DPM–554 report (Bergamo, December 1991).

P. Galluzzi (ed.), *Prima di Leonardo. Cultura delle macchine a Siena nel Rinascimento*, exhibition catalogue: Siena, Magazzini del Sale, 9 June–30 September 1991 (Milan: Electa, 1991).

A. Chiarugi, M. Fanelli and G. Giuseppetti, "Diagnosis and reinforcement hypothesis for the strengthening of the Brunelleschi dome in Florence", CRIS–ENEL internal report no. 4621 (Milan, January 1993), now in *Structural Preservation of the Architectural Heritage*, IABSE Symposium (Rome, September 1993), *IABSE Reports* 70, 441–8.

M. Haines, "Firenze e il finanziamento della Cattedrale e del Campanile", in T. Verdon (ed.), *Alla riscoperta di Piazza del Duomo in Firenze*, vol. 3, *Il Campanile di Santa Maria del Fiore* (Florence: Centro Di, 1994), 71–83.

L. Bartoli, *Il disegno della cupola del Brunelleschi* (Florence: Olschki, 1994).

F. Gurrieri and C. Acidini Luchinat (eds.), *La Cattedrale di Santa Maria del Fiore a Firenze*, 2 vols. (Florence: Giunti–Cassa di Risparmio, 1994–5).

C. Acidini Luchinat and R. Dalla Negra (eds.), *La Cupola di Santa Maria del Fiore. Il cantiere di restauro, 1980-1995* (Rome: Istituto Poligrafico e Zecca dello Stato, 1995).

T. Verdon (ed.), *Alla riscoperta di Piazza del Duomo in Firenze*, vol. 4, *La Cupola di Santa Maria del Fiore* (Florence: Centro Di, 1995).

P. Galluzzi, *Mechanical Marvels. Invention in the Age of Leonardo*, exhibition catalogue: New York, World Financial Center, Liberty Street Gallery, 24 October 1997–1 March 1998 (Florence: Giunti, 1997).

L. Ippolito and C. Peroni, *La cupola di Santa Maria del Fiore* (Rome: NIS, 1997).

M. Haines, "Gli anni della Cupola. Una banca dati testuale della documentazione dell'Opera di Santa Maria del Fiore", in T. Verdon and A. Innocenti (eds.), *Atti del VII centenario del Duomo di Firenze*, vol. 1, *La Cattedrale e la città. Saggi sul Duomo di Firenze* (Florence: Edifir, 2001), 1.2:693–736.

TABLE OF CONTENTS

PART TWO

Printed by Alpilito, Firenze
April 2004